West Ham
and the River Lea

The Nature | History | Society series is devoted to the publication of high-quality scholarship in environmental history and allied fields. Its broad compass is signalled by its title: *nature* because it takes the natural world seriously; *history* because it aims to foster work that has temporal depth; and *society* because its essential concern is with the interface between nature and society, broadly conceived. The series is avowedly interdisciplinary and is open to the work of anthropologists, ecologists, historians, geographers, literary scholars, political scientists, sociologists, and others whose interests resonate with its mandate. It offers a timely outlet for lively, innovative, and well-written work on the interaction of people and nature through time in North America.

General Editor: Graeme Wynn, University of British Columbia

A list of titles in the series appears at the end of the book.

NATURE | HISTORY | SOCIETY
GENERAL EDITOR: GRAEME WYNN

West Ham
and the River Lea

A Social and Environmental History of London's Industrialized Marshland, 1839–1914

JIM CLIFFORD

FOREWORD BY GRAEME WYNN

UBC Press • Vancouver • Toronto

26 25 24 23 22 21 20 19 18 17   5 4 3 2 1

Printed in Canada on FSC-certified ancient-forest-free paper (100% post-consumer recycled) that is processed chlorine- and acid-free.

Library and Archives Canada Cataloguing in Publication

Clifford, Jim, author
    West Ham and the River Lea : a social and environmental history of London's industrialized marshland, 1839-1914 / Jim Clifford ; foreword by Graeme Wynn.

(Nature, history, society)
Includes bibliographical references and index.
Issued in print and electronic formats.
ISBN 978-0-7748-3423-0 (hardcover). – ISBN 978-0-7748-3425-4 (PDF). –
ISBN 978-0-7748-3426-1 (EPUB). – ISBN 978-0-7748-3427-8 (Kindle)

    1. West Ham (London, England) – Social conditions – 19th century. 2. West Ham (London, England) – Social conditions – 20th century. 3. West Ham (London, England) – Environmental conditions – History – 19th century. 4. West Ham (London, England) – Environmental conditions – History – 20th century. I. Title. II. Series: Nature, history, society

HN398.W5C65 2017   942.1'76   C2017-902748-4
                                                        C2017-902749-2

Canadä

UBC Press gratefully acknowledges the financial support for our publishing program of the Government of Canada (through the Canada Book Fund), the Canada Council for the Arts, and the British Columbia Arts Council.

This book has been published with the help of a grant from the Canadian Federation for the Humanities and Social Sciences, through the Awards to Scholarly Publications Program, using funds provided by the Social Sciences and Humanities Research Council of Canada.

Image credit, p. ix: George Cruikshank, *London Going Out of Town – or – The March of Bricks & Mortar!* | World History Archive/Alamy Stock Photo.

UBC Press
The University of British Columbia
2029 West Mall
Vancouver, BC V6T 1Z2
www.ubcpress.ca

Contents

Illustrations

FIGURES

Beyond the March
of Bricks and Mortar

Graeme Wynn

LONDON going out of Town — or — The March of Bricks & Mortar! —

Designed, etched & Published by George Cruikshank — November 1st 1829 —

TWO ENDURING IMAGES come to mind as I read Jim Clifford's careful account of the nineteenth-century transformation of what he calls "London's industrial marshlands" along the lower reaches of the River Lea, on the eastern flank of the rapidly expanding English metropolis.

The first is a remarkable etching, published in 1829 by the notable English caricaturist and book illustrator George Cruikshank, entitled *London Going Out of Town – or – The March of Bricks & Mortar!*

The second is a vivid word-picture, conjured by Friedrich Engels, of a small section of Manchester – "not the worst spot and not one-tenth of the whole Old Town"– as seen from Ducie Bridge on the River Irk in 1845:

> The view from this bridge, mercifully concealed from mortals of small stature by a parapet as high as a man, is characteristic for the whole district. At the bottom flows, or rather stagnates, the Irk, a narrow, coal-black, foul-smelling stream, full of débris and refuse, which it deposits on the shallower right bank. In dry weather, a long string of the most disgusting, blackish-green, slime pools are left standing on this bank, from the depths of which bubbles of miasmatic gas constantly arise and give forth a stench unendurable even on the bridge forty or fifty feet above the surface of the stream. But besides this, the stream itself is checked every few paces by high weirs, behind which slime and refuse accumulate and rot in thick masses. Above the bridge are tanneries, bonemills, and gasworks, from which all drains and refuse find their way into the Irk, which receives further the contents of all the neighbouring sewers and privies. It may be easily imagined, therefore, what sort of residue the stream deposits. Below the bridge you look upon the piles of débris, the refuse, filth, and offal from the courts on the steep left bank; here each house is packed close behind its neighbour and a piece of each is visible, all black, smoky, crumbling, ancient, with broken panes and window-frames. The background is furnished by old barrack-like factory buildings. On the lower right bank stands a long row of houses and mills; the second house being a ruin without a roof, piled with débris; the third stands so low that the lowest floor is uninhabitable, and therefore without windows or doors.[1]

Well known to students of English history, these remarkable vignettes help both to illuminate the processes and consequences of nineteenth-century urbanization and to elucidate Clifford's distinctive contribution to understanding "one of the most cataclysmic phases of demographic, social and economic change to confront mankind."[2] Sometimes referred to by contemporaries as "The Age of Great Cities," the long nineteenth century, and more particularly the reign of Queen Victoria (1837–1901), was marked by unprecedented urban growth. According to the first census of England and Wales, in 1801, about one-third of a population of almost 9 million resided in cities. In 1841, enumerators tabbed 44 percent of the people of England and Wales as town and city dwellers. To the consternation of many, the 1851 census, that counted more than half of some 16 million people as urbanites, bestowed upon England a (dubious) distinction as the world's "first urban nation." By 1911, fully four-fifths of the 36 million people in

England and Wales were urban dwellers. Charted somewhat differently, the reports of a dozen censuses revealed that almost the entire 27 million increase in population between 1801 and 1911 had been absorbed by towns and cities. London had taken the lion's share: its 900,000 residents of 1801 became 2.5 million at mid-century; by 1911, Inner London counted slightly more than 4.5 million people and Greater London topped 7 million. In sum, the urban population of England and Wales increased by a staggering 25.4 million people during the long nineteenth century, and on the eve of the First World War almost 14 million people congregated in forty or so towns with more than 100,000 people – a threshold crossed by London alone in 1801.[3]

Reflecting on this remarkable pattern of urbanization, the prominent historian Asa Briggs once described the cities it produced as "characteristic Victorian achievement[s], impressive in scale but limited in vision, creating new opportunities but also providing massive problems."[4] They offered cause for celebration – and despondency. In Briggs's telling, the provincial city of Leeds presented a case study in civic pride. Its inhabitants' "active industry and enterprising spirit," as well as their appreciation of beauty and "taste for the fine arts," encouraged the construction of a "noble municipal palace," celebrated by the local Madrigal and Motet Society at the laying of the first stone in 1853 as "a trophy to Freedom – to Peace, and to Trade."[5] Manchester, the "symbol of a new age," epitomized Victorian advancement. Statistics charted its rapid rise, marking its growing population (slightly more than 70,000 in 1801 to ten times that in 1911), its escalating output of manufactures, and its rising phalanx of factories that harnessed the power of steam and innovative technologies to produce enormous quantities of cotton textiles shipped around the world. Little more than twenty years after Victoria came to the throne, *Chambers' Edinburgh Journal* opined that neither the dense smoke nor the "ultra-muddy" mud of Manchester could "prevent the image of a great city rising before us as the very symbol of civilization, foremost in the march of improvement, a grand incarnation of progress."[6]

Cruikshank derided development on the speed and scale that underpinned the rise of Manchester, London, and other industrial cities. Purportedly inspired by the view from the rear of his house near King's Cross, his fantastic etching portrays the northeastward expansion of London and a countryside in retreat before the heedless advance of (sub)urban housing. The scene is bleak – as well as slyly droll. In the background, well-known London landmarks – Nelson's Column, the dome of St Paul's Cathedral, the Houses of Parliament – are shrouded in smoke belching from domestic and factory chimneys. Ranks of shoddily built houses spread from left to right in the mid-ground, barely distinguishable one from another and each ironically named "New Street." An army of builders – "rude mechanicals" with chimney pots for bodies, picks and shovels for legs, mortarboards, axes, and trowels for arms, and cowls and cement-filled hods for heads – marches forward determinedly, across a rough and despoiled field, anxious to erect the latest new street for their employer, "Mr. Goth." Kilns churn newly fired bricks into the air in an incessant stream, to rain down upon the countryside. Beneath the onslaught, disconcerted hay ricks, cows, sheep, and trees realize that fences will be no defence against the "Barbarians who threaten to enclose and destroy them" and beat disorderly retreat. Some lie, "mortarly" wounded, soon to be dismembered and buried as rubbish in newly excavated pits.

Yet few of Cruikshank's contemporaries found much untoward about cities devouring their surroundings. In the 1830s, Benjamin Love penned an account of Manchester and concluded that "wherever a country becomes populous, nature is always compelled to give way to the convenience or the caprice of man ... the whole forms a scene rich and magnificent, rarely equalled, perhaps nowhere excelled."[7] Decades later, in 1901, a historian of London life compared the city to "a great hungry sea, which flows on and on, filling up every creek, and then overspreads its borders, flooding the plains beyond."[8] As steam powered ever-more efficient factories, propelled locomotives over land and iron vessels across the seas, and allowed mineral wealth to be extracted from hitherto unimaginable depths, "Improvement" became the leitmotif of the age. The "hymns to 'progress'" sung by the citizens of Leeds harmonized with the convictions of countless thousands of other Victorians.[9] Despondent after a loss in love and contemplating the sublimation of his sorrow in toil, or retreat to some remote tropical isle, the protagonist of Alfred Lord Tennyson's "Locksley Hall" found his spirit lifted by the excitement and promise of his times:

> For I dipt into the future, far as human eye could see,
> Saw the Vision of the world, and all the wonder that would be;
> Saw the heavens fill with commerce, argosies of magic sails,
> Pilots of the purple twilight, dropping down with costly bales.[10]

Human ingenuity was remaking land and life, and – misunderstanding the basic engineering of the age's greatest transformer, the railway – Tennyson affirmed the value of letting "the great world spin for ever down the ringing grooves of change."[11]

Others were more cautious. The future might be a cause for wonder, but the present provoked alarm. Rapid growth, scant regulation, and an economic recession had brought British cities to the edge of crisis by 1840. Those who contemplated the darker side of the Victorian urban ledger shared Engel's outrage at the squalid conditions, broken health, and wasted lives of the vast and growing urban underclass. Turning their gaze, as Charles Dickens did in *Oliver Twist*, from "moonlit heaths" to the "cold, wet, shelterless midnight streets," novelists exposed readers to the wretched lives of those who occupied both the crowded, dilapidated, and decrepit inner sections of the city and the extensive surrounding districts built – like the "New Streets" of Cruikshank's etching – "on the cheap" and often in the shadow of noxious "works" or factories where, some felt, "the landscape of Hell was foreshadowed."[12] Still, local leaders were quick to defend their achievements and the opportunities offered workers in their factories. Even the *Manchester Guardian* took Elizabeth Gaskell to task for exaggerating the foibles of Manchester businessmen in *Mary Barton* and criticized her "morbid sensibility to the condition of the operatives."[13]

For all that, an 1842 report on the sanitary condition of the labouring population noted that the average age of death for Manchester tradesmen and their families was twenty years, compared with forty-one for those in rural Rutland, and showed that, on average, mechanics and labourers in the city died at seventeen, while their counterparts in Rutland lived to thirty-eight.[14] Today, we know that life expectancy at birth in the largest English cities fell from thirty-five years in the 1820s to twenty-nine in the 1830s, and that in the worst slums life expectancy in the 1830s and 1840s was lower than at any time since the Black Death (Plague) of the fourteenth century.[15] Writing on the importance of the politics of public health, historian Simon Szreter has identified the particular incidence of death, disease, deprivation, and disruption as a distinguishing characteristic of English cities in these decades.[16] Sanitary reformers, concerned about the effects of "secretions and miasmas," cast Victorian cities as "rotten, stagnant, putrefying" places – perhaps not inaccurately when one of their number, Henry Mayhew, estimated that animals dropped almost 40,000 tons of manure on City of London streets each year in the 1850s.[17] In Manchester, where at least 78,000 tons of manure were removed from the city in 1845, the most opulent streets were cleaned once a week, a middling group every fortnight, and a third class every month; the courts, alleys, and slums that housed the least fortunate were not cleaned at all.[18]

The fetid, malodorous, and insanitary conditions that resulted from such circumstances spawned anger and despair among those who noticed and endured them. In the 1830s, Elizabeth Gaskell and her husband (who ministered at the Cross Street Unitarian chapel in Manchester) published "Sketches Among the Poor," a 153-line poem, in *Blackwood's Magazine*.[19] A decade later, *Mary Barton* gave "utterance to the agony" of those "care-worn men, who looked as if doomed to struggle through their lives in strange alternations between work and want," and others among the voice-less thousands whom Gaskell encountered daily on the teeming streets of the inner city.[20]

Summing up the results of his wanderings through these and adjoining areas, Engels estimated that "350,000 working-people of Manchester and its environs live, almost all of them, in wretched, damp, filthy cottages," on streets that "are usually in the most miserable and filthy condition, laid out without the slightest reference to ventilation, with reference solely to the profit secured by the contractor." In his view, "no cleanliness, no con-venience, and consequently no comfortable family life" was possible in such settings where "only a physically degenerate race, robbed of all humanity, degraded, reduced morally and physically to bestiality, could feel comfort-able and at home."[21] Little wonder, then, that several nineteenth-century humanists and humanitarians – among whom we might number Thomas Carlyle, Benjamin Disraeli, A.W.N. Pugin, John Ruskin, and William Morris, as examples – were variously suspicious of industrial progress and deeply concerned about the damage inflicted upon the human spirit by conditions in burgeoning cities. Reading Cruikshank's etching allegorically, it is no great stretch to see the juxtaposition of his mute mechanical army and the despairing voices of the countryside as a parable that illuminates both the rise in anti-urban sentiment and Engels' sad conclusion, by re-minding us that "when the trees and haystacks are driven from the field, so will be the last trace of humanity."[22]

In the end, of course, debate over the greatness or otherwise of England's cities – over the balance between "progress" and "regress" – was not a simple matter of celebration or despair. Innumerable voices shaded the argument in countless ways. Recognizing and recounting such complexity is difficult. Asa Briggs went a long way to meeting the challenge in *Victorian Cities*, but such detailed and discursive narratives are no longer much in vogue. Although condemnation was only one in a broad spectrum of re-sponses to the Victorian city, some would argue that "dramatic images of social inequity, material degradation and decay" have dominated recent scholarship on the topic. In the words of English cultural historian Katy Layton-Jones, who finds "the anxious voice of despair" too prevalent in much historical commentary, "the demonic, Babylonian city described so vividly in Lynda Nead's *Victorian Babylon* has become a popular, almost inescapable idiom among urban, social and cultural historians."[23]

West Ham and the River Lea pulls few punches in detailing the "demonic" characteristics of late nineteenth-century West Ham, but it also offers a welcome corrective to the monocular tendency that sees little but ruinous squalor, injustice, and ugliness in Victorian urban development. By focusing equally on the social and environmental dimensions of his chosen territory, Jim Clifford places his work firmly within the traditions limned by Friedrich Engels and George Cruikshank early in the nineteenth century, but his attention to space and patterns on the ground, his use of a Geographic Information System (GIS) to acquire, store, analyze, manage, and present historical data, and his broad definition of the social all impart a distinct perspective to his concerns.

The River Lea rises in the Chiltern Hills and flows almost seventy kilometres to join the River Thames. Like the shorter Irk, its course and the clean, clear waters of its source are much changed along the way to its confluence. Both rivers have been subject to centuries of human use. There was a medieval corn mill on the Irk, and Romans, Danes, and English knew the Lea before small-scale diversions and dams were built to power medieval corn mills at several points along its length; by the sixteenth century, locks and canals aided navigation along the course of the Lea. In the middle of the following century, Izaak Walton's *Compleat Angler* told of Londoners making an excursion to fish the river in Hertfordshire.[24] Farms and market gardens lined the Lea and served the London market. Cloth works, lime kilns, and a few other relatively small-scale proto-industries appeared among them after 1700. Then, in the late eighteenth and nineteenth centuries, the lower reaches of both rivers were enveloped, and radically transformed, by urban and industrial expansion. Generally, these developments came later to the Lea than they did to the Irk, but just as the speed of Manchester's growth surprised people (the city almost doubled in size in the 1820s), West Ham was to the fore in the late nineteenth-century march of bricks and mortar out of London; it stood among the four fastest growing communities in the country between 1881 and 1891, and its population more than quadrupled in the thirty years after 1871.[25] Great environmental and social consequences ensued. Many of them were deleterious. But Clifford is more interested than Cruikshank in analyzing (rather than satirizing) the changing scene, and his use of GIS allows him to supplement, to good effect, the sort of focused optic available to Engels from Ducie Bridge with more general, but no less astute, insights into the rapidly shifting social and environmental circumstances of a West Ham buffeted by a "storm" of industrialization (see p. 8 of this volume).

At one level, the history of West Ham is broadly familiar: it is the story of the invasion – much as in Cruikshank's etching – of a receding country-side by industrial establishments and associated workers' housing. Simply put, fifty years saw the population of a rural parish increase from fewer than twenty thousand (in 1851) to more than a quarter million, as concerns about the growing regulation of noxious and dangerous trades in London itself (the eastern boundary of which was the River Lea) encouraged phar-maceutical, chemical, and food processing industries to move over the border. Along the way, the parish of West Ham secured incorporation as a municipal borough in 1886, to avoid being subsumed under the jurisdic-tion of the Metropolitan Board of Works, and then became a County Borough under the provisions of the Local Government Act of 1888. As the London *Times* saw it in 1886, "Factory after factory was erected on the marshy wastes of Stratford and Plaistow, and it only required the construc-tion at Canning Town of the Victoria and Albert Docks to make the once desolate parish of West Ham a manufacturing and commercial centre of the first importance and to bring upon it a teeming and an industrious population."[26] At the turn of the twentieth century, two large factories, one in Stratford and one near the Thames, each employed about as many people as had resided in the entire parish a century before.

Clifford divides his treatment of these striking developments into two broad parts. His first three substantive chapters (1, 2, and 3) chart the rapid industrial and population growth of the region, using photographs and archival evidence, as well as a series of maps derived from a Historical GIS database, to reveal the role of the environment in the industrialization of West Ham. Although marshlands gave way to factories and slums, and rivers that once meandered through meadows became polluted, partly canalized, arteries for the movement of coal, chemicals, and other industrial products, this was, by no means, a uniform or random transformation. Factories clustered along waterways to reduce their costs of access to coal, brought by barge up the Lea from distant coalfields. The Great Eastern Railway yards apart, large works located on the Thames to avoid tranship-ment costs, while smaller (though not necessarily less noxious) factories dominated upstream in the Stratford industrial zone. Although locks and canals improved navigation on parts of the river, several branches of the Lea remained tidal, their broad shallow banks alternately inundated and exposed by the diurnal rhythms of the sea. Economics and nature shaped housing development, creating a new, albeit fragile, urban ecology. Land prices in low-lying areas in the southwest of the parish/borough were relatively low, and the proximity of such marshy tracts to work places encouraged construction of cheap housing there. Back from the rivers, on higher ground to the northeast, more prosperous, better planned, less densely populated residential suburbs grew. When flood banks, both rudimentary and more robust, failed, as they did periodically, the poor suffered the dire consequences of the river's spread across its historical floodplain. These consequences were only exacerbated over time, as increasing suburban populations along the Lea upstream of West Ham added their effluent to the contributions of the fast-expanding borough. Stranded on the banks of tidal reaches by ebbing flows, sewage and other contaminants contributed to the insalubrity of the surroundings. Curiously muted after years of such accumulating indignities, including the reeking stench produced during the summer drought of 1884, the *West Ham Guardian* marked the early days of 1899 by lamenting that "offensive smells are far too prevalent in various parts of West Ham."[27]

Dirty though the river and its back channels were, polluted as the air might have been by local emissions and particulate matter carried across the Lea from London on prevailing westerly winds, and difficult though sanitary conditions remained in the marshland slums, the landscape of West Ham was not all of a piece. Clifford's Chapter 3, which discusses the challenges of living in the borough, fills an important pivotal function in this book, turning its focus from spatial and environmental to more social concerns. Here Clifford explores the implications, not only of living with periodic flooding, pollution, and insanitary conditions, but of the fact that large areas of West Ham remained undeveloped, even into the twentieth century. Difficult as the lives of industrial workers and their families were, people still farmed between Canning Town and Stratford; allotment gardens allowed those who lived in crowded houses along narrow streets to grow vegetables and flowers – and more importantly, find some release from workplace and dwelling. Men and boys took fish from the river, seemingly oblivious to the perils of bioaccumulation and biomagnification, and relative ease of access to open space and sunlight (compared with London's East End) reduced the incidence of vitamin D deficiency and rickets among West Ham's children. Life on the rural-urban interface offered benefits, even as urban expansion magnified the problems of crowded, poorly built, and unhealthy housing. As Clifford notes, even the journalist Henry Morley, rightly indignant at the worst of the insanitary excesses he encountered in the marshy slums of the 1850s, conceded that a re-oriented gaze revealed "pleasant belts of trees, with here a spire, there a church-tower, upon the horizon; and in the foreground, groups of cattle feed" (p. 56).

Continuing to explore the social consequences of steadily worsening environmental conditions in the borough, the remaining chapters of *West Ham and the River Lea* ask why more was not done to alleviate them. As industries expanded and population increased through the latter half of the nineteenth century, floods, drought, disease, and poverty wracked residents of the borough. But this was not a simple declensionist story of environmental degradation and growing human misery. Public expectations changed as scientific knowledge of the causes of disease and various advances in technology opened new possibilities for intervention and remediation.

Beginning with an analysis of a serious water shortage in the last years of the nineteenth century and its social and political consequences, Clifford finds that fragmented jurisdictional authority over the Lea watershed, an ineffective response to the dry conditions of 1898, and inadequate scientific understanding turned a drought into a crisis. Water rights on the River Lea were allocated according to the English legal tradition of prior appropriation, or "first in time, first in right." This meant, in essence, that the New River Company (actually the older of the two water companies with rights to the river) could take its usual allotment even though the river was running very low, leaving insufficient water for the East London Water Company (which also serviced West Ham) to meet its obligations after its storage reservoirs were depleted. When the ELWC announced supply restrictions, private control of the water system became a heated political issue. London's poor were deprived of running water for months while those who lived in more prosperous areas of London received regular service. Making the water crisis a key issue of their campaign, left-leaning candidates swept to victory in the 1898 West Ham municipal elections, marking the growing voice and political influence of the proletariat in the rise of social democratic politics at the beginning of the twentieth century.

Public officials – especially health inspectors and engineers – armed with a growing understanding of disease transmission as ideas about miasmatic diffusion gave way to germ theory, were enjoined, empowered, and (to some degree, albeit belatedly) effective in addressing the interconnected social, medical, and environmental problems of the suburb. Early in the twentieth century, deaths due to diphtheria and typhoid, and infant mortality rates, were down, largely due to such simple expedients as improving drainage and reducing the number and impact of flies by encouraging households to dump their rubbish in lidded containers. Government interventions in the form of house-to-house inspections, infrastructural improvements to reduce flooding, and the provision of relief for the unemployed were not uncontested. Then as now, many politicians, industrial leaders, and property owners were fixated on keeping tax rates as low as possible. But the sometimes faltering steps that were taken, led by a small group of increasingly respected and powerful municipal experts, worked almost literal (if sometimes spatially uneven) magic.

In the end, however, it was too little, too late. Changing economic and technological circumstances after the First World War initiated a long decline in West Ham's fortunes. The population of the borough declined as deindustrialization and heavy damage caused by bombing raids in the Second World War combined with the demolition of the worst slums to push those residents who could move to new suburban addresses further afield. Although West Ham was amalgamated with neighbouring boroughs and became known as Newham after 1965, residents of the area continued to face environmental and social challenges until preparations for the 2012 Olympics triggered another radical transformation of the Lower Lea Valley, revitalizing some areas but leaving others struggling with overcrowding, child poverty, and unemployment.

In sum, *West Ham and the River Lea* reveals the complexities of place-formation. Low-lying and swampy, much of the ancient parish east of the Lea and north of the Thames was an unpropitious site for industrial and residential development. But environmental limitations were of little immediate concern as the seemingly insatiable expansionary drive of the empire's metropolis – "the great wen," radical pamphleteer William Cobbett called it in the 1820s – drove London out of town.[28] Certain, ultimately transitory, advantages for transportation, and laissez-faire attitudes toward pollution and regulation laid the basis for a massive late nineteenth-century boom in this area. Of but not in London, the marshes and fields of West Ham were colonized in short order by George Cruikshank's march of bricks and mortar, with results that require little more than the substitution of Lea for Irk, and a slight stretch of the literary imagination, to characterize in the very terms called to Engels' mind by the view from Ducie Bridge.

Yet Clifford's account offers a perspective quite distinct from those provided by Cruikshank's etching and Engels' vignette, by virtue of its multifaceted, spatially sensitive, synoptic-scale view of the rise and demise of the liminal space that was West Ham. By making clear that bricks and mortar advanced unevenly across the marshy terrain of the eastern flanks of the Lower Lea Valley to produce a complex hybrid landscape, Clifford gives agency to those who produced this place. Abject though their living conditions may have been, difficult as their social and domestic circumstances often were, he refuses to see the people of the parish and borough as helpless victims or pawns of fate. Here we see a West Ham shaped in manifold ways by the intricate interactions of humans and nature. This is a story that encompasses and turns on ecology, hydrology, topography, prevailing winds, economics, politics, trade networks, industrial processes, engineering abilities, technological competence, human resilience, and chance. And it is, thus, a pertinent – and ultimately empowering – reminder of the point made by some students of modern-day globalization, that all transformative forces "are constituted, accommodated, mediated and resisted in social processes at multiple scales, from the national economy to the village and the household."[29]

Acknowledgments

N EARLY A DECADE IN the making, this book relied on the support of a lot of people and funders. Travel to archives and writing time in the early years were made possible by the Albert Tucker Award in Graduate British History, funding from York University, a St. George's Society Ontario Graduate Scholarship, and a second Ontario Graduate Scholarship. More recently, Social Science and Humanities Research Council funding contributed to the expansion of the historical geographic information systems database, and a Rachel Carson Centre for Environment and Society Fellowship provided time to revise the book. Finally, the Federation for the Humanities and Social Sciences Awards to Scholarly Publications Program and the University of Saskatchewan provided funding to aid with the cost of publication.

Stephen Brooke, Colin Coates, and Bernie Lightman at York University in Toronto all did a great deal to help shape this project. Peter Thorsheim asked a number of insightful questions. Colin Coates, as the principal investigator on the project that funded my postdoctoral fellowship, provided an opportunity to work on a very different topic for a number of years. The time away from West Ham, learning and writing about text mining and global commodities, allowed me to return to this project with a fresh perspective. I also offer a special thanks to Bill Turkel at Western University in London, Ontario, for convincing me that GIS was a useful tool for this project and to Marcel Fortin at the University of Toronto's Map and Data Library for helping me learn how to use it. More recently, I have continued to learn a great deal about GIS methods and cartography from my colleague

Geoff Cunfer in the Historical GIS Lab at the University of Saskatchewan. Two more lab members, Steven Langlois and Anne Riitta Janhunen, made a more direct major contribution to the GIS by tracing all of the factories across Greater London and error checking the database.

I owe a great debt to Richard Durack and Jenni Munro-Collins at the Newham Archives and Local Studies Library. Moreover, I found every archive and library in London incredibly helpful and accommodating, and I would like to thank all the staff at the London Metropolitan Archives, Guildhall Library, the British Library, the Wellcome Library, the London School of Economics Archives, and the British National Archives. It is a great pleasure to research in these institutions, and I really hope they survive the difficult funding cuts that many are facing. Durack and Munro-Collins in particular work with fewer and fewer resources, and their reduced opening hours will make a project like this one less viable in the future. This is a troubling trend with local archives that extends well beyond Newham.

This book has benefitted from countless readers at various stages of development in the past years, and it is unlikely that I can remember them all here. The remaining errors are mine alone, but many of my more insightful points were brought on by good questions from friends and colleagues. A writing group made up of Jennifer Bonnell, Ben Bradley, and Jay Young provided invaluable feedback on every chapter, and my friends Dan Bullard, Val Deacon, and Tom Peace read early drafts as well. Members of the Toronto Environmental History Reading Group, the Southern Ontario British History Reading Group, and the Network in Canadian History and Environment New Scholars Reading Group commented on selected chapters. Matthew Evenden provided a careful edit of a draft version of Chapter 1. James Elwick read Chapter 4 and offered feedback that helped me to refocus my argument in that chapter. John Maker and David Zylberberg helped identify some of the remaining errors that are inevitable when a dyslexic writer sets out to write a project of this length. I presented a revised version of Chapter 4 to the history department's research seminar at the University of Saskatchewan. Peter Cox, a visiting fellow at the Rachel Carson Centre, kindly read a new draft of my Introduction during the winter of 2015. My colleagues Erika Dyck, Matthew Neufeld, and Elizabeth Scott read parts of the book shortly before I submitted the manuscript to peer review.

I owe a great deal to the two peer reviewers, who made this book significantly stronger through their very constructive and helpful criticism. I greatly appreciate the effort they put into their comments. Randy Schmidt, my UBC Press editor, read a number of chapters and helped guide this book through the publishing process. Graeme Wynn, the series editor, also provided a very careful reading of a number of chapters and made the book better. I would also like to thank Katrina Petrik, the production editor, and Deborah Kerr, the copy editor.

Family and friends made the process of writing this book possible. My parents, Mary and Rod, and my brothers and grandparents were supportive through my time in graduate school, and I owe them a great deal. My dad read a full draft and offered helpful comments, as he did on many essays starting in high school. My partner, Katie Burns, has lived with the River Lea, West Ham, and nineteenth-century industry just as long as I have. This included reading drafts of grant proposals, chapters, and job cover letters, as well as listening to me practise presentations. She has even walked the valley on a number of occasions, most recently with our first child, Cameron, in tow. Hopefully, we will soon have the chance to bring Desmond, his younger brother, to visit the new playgrounds at the centre of the Olympic Park and the wonderful little nature reserve at the old East London Waterworks filter beds.

West Ham
and the River Lea

Introduction

London does not end at the limits assigned to it by those
acts of Parliament which take thought for the health of the
Londoners. More suburbs shoot up, while official ink is
drying. Really, there is no limit to London; but the law must
needs assign bounds; and, by the law there is one suburb on
the border of the Essex marshes which is quite cut off from
the comforts of the Metropolitan Buildings Act; — in fact, it
lies just without its boundaries, and therefore is chosen as a
place of refuge for offensive trade establishments turned out of
the town, — those of oil boilers, gut spinners, varnish makers,
printers ink makers and the like. Being cut off from the
support of the Metropolis Local Managing Act, this outskirt
is free to possess new streets of houses without drains, roads,
gas, or pavement. It forms part of the parish of West Ham.

       — *"Londoners over the Border,"* Household Words

H ENRY MORLEY, A STAFF writer working for Charles Dickens's weekly
Household Words, visited West Ham in 1857 and wrote an unattrib-
uted lead article for the magazine about people living in what he described
as squalid and unhealthy conditions. Morley recognized the profound
transformations that were beginning to take hold in the industrializing
Lower Lea Valley and contrasted the "many tall smoking chimneys that
mark out the line" of the River Lea with the "broad green Essex plain"
that on a sunny day still appeared to be "master of the situation."[1] When
he turned from broad vistas to the pockets of settlements growing on
the marshlands of southern West Ham, he found a landscape that was
inundated with sewage. Medical knowledge during this period associated
marshlands, decomposition, and bad smells with disease, so Morley, a
university-educated author whose work had appeared in the *Journal of
Public Health,* reasoned that these conditions posed a serious danger to

West Ham residents. He described, for example, a "pestilential ditch" with "three ghostly little children lying on the ground, hung with their faces over it, breathing the poison of the bubbles" and "fishing around with their hands in the filth."[2] Although Morley's concern was not grounded in our present-day conceptions of environmental health, he clearly understood that rapid suburban development on increasingly polluted marshlands contributed to harmful social conditions. London's unhealthy expansion was a significant political issue, and his article concluded with a call for West Ham's recently formed local board of health to improve the sanitary conditions in the suburb.

In the half-century that followed Morley's visit, the "green Essex plain" increasingly gave way to heavy industry and crowded housing. Between 1851 and 1901, the population of West Ham grew from 18,817 to 267,358. In the decade that followed, it grew by another 21,672, maintaining West Ham's status as the largest suburb in Greater London and one of the most populous independent municipalities in England and Wales.[3] Political independence meant that West Ham was both part of and separate from London. As a book reviewer for the *Economic Journal* put it in 1908, the suburb "was vaguely known as that of a spot somewhere near London to which people went with reluctance if they had business there, and from which they returned with joy as soon as the business was over."[4] London's industrial economy migrated east and concentrated in West Ham during the second half of the nineteenth century, but the independent borough remained both physically and conceptually beyond London's East End.

People moved to West Ham because of the employment opportunities at its docks and the many factories that lined its rivers.[5] In 1855, the large Victoria Dock came into operation, transforming the remote marshlands of southern West Ham into a major transportation hub and workplace. Before the construction of this dock, the scattered settlements in West Ham stood on higher ground, avoiding the wetlands adjacent to the Lower Lea and the Thames. The dock drew workers to southern West Ham, establishing new residential districts on the low-lying marshes. Marshland housing was built along the drainage ditches, which quickly became the stagnant open sewers described by Morley. In the decades that followed, the local board of health and municipal borough built a piped sewer network and alleviated the foul conditions of 1857, but the interrelated challenges of poverty, insanitary and crowded housing, pollution, and flooding continued to plague this industrial suburb, built within the unstable riverine environment at the intersection of the Lower Lea and the Thames Estuary.

For readers of the *Economic Journal*, West Ham may have been little more than a vaguely known and unpleasant "spot somewhere near London," but for those who were concerned with the labour movement and labour politics, it stood at the forefront of social and political transformations at the end of the nineteenth century. New Unionism grew in and around the suburb, which housed a large number of low-income workers. The Bryant and May match factory, where female employees organized a strike in 1888 and helped start the New Unionism movement, was in Bow, on the London side of the Lower Lea Valley. Many of the dockers who were involved in the 1889 strike lived and worked in southern West Ham. Will Thorne, who led the unionization of the gasworkers in 1889, lived in Canning Town and became an important municipal and national politician. The India Rubber, Gutta Percha, and Telegraph Works factory in Silvertown was the site of yet another major strike in the summer of 1889.[6] In 1892, three years after the upsurge of New Unionism, West Ham South elected J. Keir Hardie as the first independent labour MP, a year before he helped found the Independent Labour Party. Six years later, a labour and socialist coalition took control of the municipal government, which was another first for labour politicians in Britain. Social segregation, the concentration of large factories, and unionization all contributed to the rise of working-class politics, but labour politicians also echoed Morley and articulated grievances regarding the unhealthy and unpleasant local environment.

Dirty and crisis-prone urban conditions reinforced the social and economic divisions in Greater London and helped enable the rise of social democracy in West Ham. From an environmental or social perspective, the marshlands in the Lower Lea Valley and Thames Estuary were not an ideal locale for rapid suburban expansion. The speed and scale of industrial development and population growth completely transformed the environment and severely damaged the River Lea. As with the many other shock cities of nineteenth-century industrialization, economic factors drove urbanization in the Lower Lea Valley, and many decades would elapse before the environmental, public health, and social consequences of crowded living conditions and polluted landscapes were addressed. Environmental instability played a role in the social and political volatility of West Ham. The expansive marshlands and constant threat of flooding created considerable fiscal challenges, as everything from drainage to social services had to be funded from local rates (property taxes).[7] During the early period of rapid growth, from the 1850s to the 1880s, local politicians focused on balancing ratepayers' demands for low taxation with the increasing costs of public health, education, and civic infrastructure.[8] West Ham's disagreeable and in many cases deadly environment eventually stimulated political change during the 1890s, as voters increasingly called for costly government interventions to ameliorate it. In West Ham, the failure of the political elite to respond facilitated the victories of labour and socialist politicians, and made the suburb a testing ground for interventionist public policies. West Ham was certainly not unique – unhealthy urban conditions prompted political change throughout England during the later nineteenth century.[9] However, it was an acute example, with the combined challenges of draining marshlands, heavy industrialization, serious social problems, and jurisdictional independence.

Greater London led a wider transition in Britain, which became significantly more urbanized during the nineteenth century, a development that contributed to dramatic social and political transformations. Cities were not simply the backdrops for social and political change.[10] The nature of urbanization was a major factor influencing the population's standard of living and health. Environmental conditions, urban morphology, and economic stratification played an increasingly important role in creating new social and cultural identities. This in turn shaped democratic politics as a series of franchise reforms, combined with mass migration to cities, transferred increasing power to the major centres.[11] By the end of the nineteenth century, new and effective demands for improved urban conditions arose from increased attention to widening environmental, public health, and social divisions between the best and worst districts of cities.

Environmental history, with its focus on both the ecological consequences of human activities and the social or cultural response to changing environmental conditions, provides an important approach to better understand the history of West Ham. Environmental historians go beyond chronicling increased pollution and ecological degradation to study the many ways in which humans relied on and were a part of the wider ecosystem.[12] After all, they were just as vulnerable as plants and wildlife to the effects of air pollution, and they contracted diseases transmitted by dirty water supplies.[13] In the British context, environmental history builds upon the excellent literature on the history of urban public health, which focuses on the negative health impact of poor environmental conditions in nineteenth-century cities.[14] Urban environmental history blends the methods and questions of urban social and medical history with a greater focus on the environment.[15] It provides a new lens to explore the many consequences of rapid urbanization in nineteenth-century Greater London.[16]

Population growth and industrialization caused a wide range of environmental problems throughout Greater London and other major British cities during the nineteenth century. Coal enabled urban development on an unprecedented scale, heating the homes and fuelling the steam engines that carried raw materials into the city and pumped the wastes away. It also powered Greater London's expanding industrial sector. The hundreds of thousands of coal fires filled the air with smoke, and human and industrial waste poured into the waterways and seeped into the land. The city spread outward, transforming its hinterlands as it did. Rural landscapes became sprawling residential neighbourhoods, crowded commercial centres, teeming docklands, expansive rail yards, and towering industrial districts.[17] Across Britain, cities and towns outgrew their urban infrastructure, and from the 1840s onward local governments struggled to find technological solutions and sufficient finances to remove human waste and other pollutants.[18] In many cases, cities failed to fully solve their drainage problems, and coal smoke pollution persisted in major centres through to the mid-twentieth century.[19]

Although urban environmental problems were a collective challenge, Londoners did not equally share their negative consequences. The waterways, floodplains, and topography influenced the development of the built environment and the flow of pollution. The streams and rivers carried waste down to the Thames and east to the sea, though tides prolonged its circulation through the city. The prevailing winds also generally blew smoke and other air pollutants eastward, though inversions occasionally suspended the smog in place for days at a time. Hills protected the northwest and south of London from flooding, but the lowlands were regularly inundated by the Thames and the Lea. Not surprisingly, pleasant and green residential suburbs such as Hampstead and Wimbledon stood on higher ground, and dense and crowded housing for workers clustered around the docks and factories near the rivers.

Living with unhealthy environmental conditions was often a defining feature of social marginalization in Greater London during the nineteenth century. Residents of the eastern neighbourhoods experienced urban pollution most acutely. Poplar's Isle of Dogs and southern West Ham, for example, suffered from a combination of low topography, concentrations of heavy industry, and the influx of pollution from the rest of London. Just as Morley observed in 1857, poor environmental conditions correlated strongly with impoverished social conditions. Moreover, they produced an increasingly homogeneous social geography, as people with means moved to more pleasant areas, and the economically vulnerable clustered in the industrial floodplain districts.[20]

Many people have written about London's remarkable growth and the resulting political, technological, social, and cultural changes, beginning with individuals who lived through the process themselves and continuing with generation after generation of historians.[21] However, this literature overwhelmingly focuses on the centre of the city and the older East End, paying lesser attention to the suburbs.[22] In addition, until recently, the literature downplayed the significance of industrialization. J.L. Hammond suggested in 1925 that the industrial revolution was "like a storm that passed over London and broke elsewhere."[23] Small workshops remained prominent in central London's manufacturing sector before and during the industrial revolution, leading historians to conclude that the revolution never really took root in the city. Furthermore, the old manufacturing core of London began to experience a protracted decline during the 1860s, suggesting the diminishing importance of industry in the capital.[24] A number of historians have challenged the perceived absence of the industrial revolution in London, and general histories now mention the industrial suburbs in passing, but Greater London's importance as a major nineteenth-century industrial city remains underappreciated.[25] Map 1 highlights the extensive industry that lay just outside of London and in South London, and shows the problem of focusing on the centre of the metropolis and the decline of particular industries. (This book relies on historical Geographic Information Systems [HGIS] maps; see the Appendix for a short overview of HGIS methods and the Map Credits section for source material used to create the database and maps.) This narrow perspective misses the "storm" of the industrialization that struck the Lower Lea Valley and the floodplains of the Thames Estuary during the second half of the nineteenth century.

Urban industrial development on the West Ham marshlands was part of a more general nineteenth-century process in which urban growth spread onto the lowlands of the Thames Estuary. Map 1 shows the extent of the low-lying parts of the estuary. During the nineteenth century, urban and suburban development increasingly encroached on low ground, including the marshlands and floodplains along the Rivers Thames and Lea. Docks were concentrated on the lowlands near the Thames, east of the City of London. Urban industrial development on floodplains transformed the environment and shaped the social geography of the metropolis. West Ham, Poplar, and Bermondsey were at the centre of this trend, with the

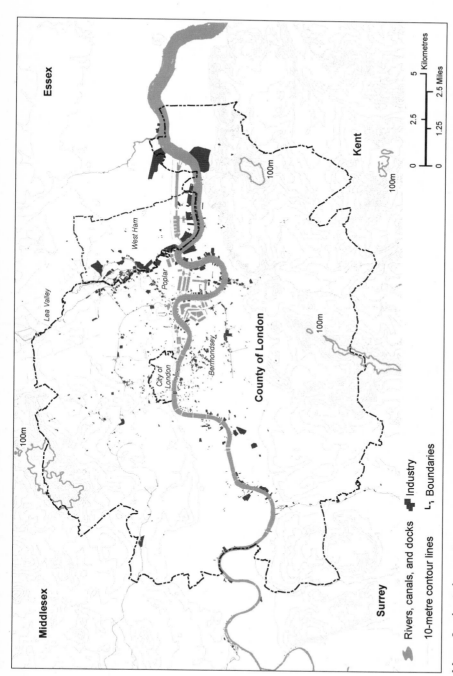

Essex

Kent

Middlesex

Surrey

West Ham

Poplar

City of London

Bermondsey

County of London

Lea Valley

100m

100m

100m

100m

Rivers, canals, and docks

10-metre contour lines

Industry

Boundaries

0   1.25   2.5   5
0   2.5   5   Kilometres
              2.5 Miles

Map 1 London industry, 1893–95

major concentrations of factories and largest docks in the London region. This expansion facilitated economic development, but it also elevated the risk of natural disasters. These rivers proved difficult to constrain, particularly after the extensive reclamation of Greater London's floodplains, leading to regular and damaging flooding throughout the century. The Lower Lea Valley and the Thames Estuary provided an economically advantageous but unstable landscape for rapid industrial and residential development.

West Ham became a prominent industrial suburb due to the economic advantages afforded by the Lea and the Thames. The Lower Lea's braided "back rivers" and the Thames itself provided numerous waterways to supply factories with coal and other raw material.[26] Most factories required access to the rivers to transport raw materials, and the majority were built near the Thames, Lea, Wandle, and Ravensbourne or along one of London's canals. Map 1, which depicts all the factories identified on Ordnance Survey maps updated between 1893 and 1895, shows that the Lower Lea Valley and the land along the Thames in West Ham had emerged as the heart of London's industrial economy by the end of the century.

The Lea and the Thames provide a particularly useful lens to explore the changing relationship between nature and society in Greater London.[27] Major engineering projects transformed these urban rivers.[28] Cities relied on the rivers to supply drinking water, facilitate transportation, and carry sewage and storm water, and they became so polluted that they could no longer support most forms of aquatic life.[29] At the same time, Greater London's rivers often frustrated the efforts of engineers to control them. Extreme weather contracted or expanded their flow and threatened the city with either a shortage or an excess of water. The Thames, Lea, Wandle, Brent, and other rivers also defined the geography of Greater London and remained some of the most significant semi-natural features in the built environment. There are numerous popular and environmental histories of the Thames but significantly less material on the Rivers Lea, Ravensbourne, and Wandle.[30] Although they are significantly smaller than the Thames, they still played important roles in Greater London's development, supplying water, disposing of sewage, and enabling transportation. Significant clusters of factories were established along their banks, but only the Lower Lea, with numerous braided back rivers and extensive level marshlands, developed into a major industrial centre. Industry and population growth polluted all of London's rivers, and again, the Lower Lea was a particularly acute example.

During the late eighteenth and early nineteenth centuries, the purity of the River Lea had drawn calico cloth printers to West Ham. By the 1880s, however, little more than sewage effluent trickled down the Lower Lea during the warmest weeks of summer, and chemical factories stood on the former calico grounds along the riverbanks. The population outpaced the infrastructure in West Ham and other Lea Valley suburbs, with the result that raw or partially treated sewage regularly flowed into the river. During heavy rains, overflow valves dumped a mix of sewage and storm water from London's sewer system into the Lea, which simply intensified its long-term pollution. Public health officials and engineers increasingly recognized the dangers of contaminating the water supply with sewage effluent, an understanding that began with John Snow's 1854 identification of a Broad Street water pump as the main vector in the spread of cholera. Concern about contaminated water supply intensified in the 1880s with the discovery of the existence of germs. Moreover, sewage pollution was easily recognizable: the public could smell it and see the dark effluent oozing down the riverbeds of the Lea. Industrial expansion also played a significant role in polluting the Lea. Map 1 shows the concentration of factories on the alluvial floodplains of the Lower Lea Valley. Limited legislation and lax enforcement make it difficult to identify particular examples of industrial pollution, but there is no doubt that the heavy industry in the Lower Lea marshlands significantly degraded the environmental conditions of the valley. The increasingly polluted Lea, along with the industry that transformed its marshlands and the population that lived with regular flooding and unhealthy conditions, shaped both the environmental and social history of West Ham during the nineteenth century.

The first three chapters of this book explore the environmental consequences of rapid industrial and population growth in West Ham and the Lower Lea Valley. Chapter 1 uses a series of maps from the HGIS database to confirm the important role of environmental conditions in aiding and hindering industrialization in West Ham. The maps show the process of industrialization along the Lower Lea, and they also identify the limits of this expansion and the areas that remained open at the turn of the twentieth century. Chapters 2 and 3 also use HGIS maps to chart the rapid development of the built environment and to explore the ongoing connections between urban morphology, environmental decline, and social problems. The burgeoning population contributed to the environmental troubles, and the people, in turn, suffered the consequences of living in a polluted landscape. Population growth upriver from West Ham produced a series of disasters, as new suburbs dumped their sewage into the Lea. Fractured jurisdiction in the Lea watershed, an ineffective legislative response, and scientific uncertainty meant that no comprehensive political or engineering solution to the sewage problem was applied until the twentieth century. Chapter 3 explores what it was like to live in West Ham during this period of dramatic and disrupting growth.

Chapters 4 to 6 focus on the social consequences of deteriorating environmental conditions at the height of suburban development in West Ham between 1890 and 1910. Chapter 4 begins with an analysis of the complex relationship between a prolonged drought, a major water shortage in East London and West Ham, the monopoly control of the water supply, and the first victory of a labour and socialist coalition in British municipal politics. The outcome of this election demonstrates that environmental analysis enables a fuller understanding of the shift from nineteenth-century liberalism to social democracy.

Chapters 5 and 6 explore the influential role of public officials, as residents demanded increased government intervention to resolve public health, economic, and environmental problems. The medical officer of health and the borough engineer used new powers and resources to improve both human health and the environment in the marshy portions of West Ham. The medical officer strove to balance popular assumptions regarding the cause of disease with the new scientific consensus that focused on germs. The borough engineer pushed the boundaries of local government further in an attempt to mitigate the endemic problems of flooding and unemployment.

As the public pressured politicians to address the tangled web of environmental and social challenges, including providing a constant flow of water, effective flood defences, solutions for unemployment, and healthier living conditions, the medical officer and the engineer gained new levels of managerial power. Over time, they were tasked with administering, regulating, and inspecting the growing array of government interventions in West Ham.

However, these interventions did little to alleviate the ecological damage to London's second river, whose long-term devastation epitomizes the environmental consequences of urban industrial development. Londoners and their governments privileged diverting water, dumping sewage, and reclaiming wetlands for industry and housing over the well-being of rivers and marshlands.[31] In West Ham, industrialists took advantage of the abundance of waterways and converted wetlands into a heavily industrialized landscape. The larger factories facing the Thames mostly continued to thrive into the twentieth century. In the Lower Lea Valley, decades of neglect damaged the tidal rivers, which in turn decreased the economic advantages of the nearby marshlands and ultimately contributed to the industrial decline of the region.

I

The River Lea and Industrialization in West Ham

NINETEENTH-CENTURY URBANIZATION accelerated the modification of the riverine environment in Greater London as docks, warehouses, factories, and housing converted reclaimed marshlands into new or expanded districts, and most of the rivers were constrained or buried to various degrees. The large-scale Thames Embankment and Main Drain project, completed during the 1860s in the aftermath of the Great Stink of 1858, engineered the flow of the Thames and sewage through central London while reclaiming land for transportation corridors and further urban development.[1] This costly government-funded project converted the river into a revered marvel of civil engineering. The Lower Lea also experienced a major transformation, becoming a working river, peripheral and disagreeable but essential in shaping Greater London's new industrial heartland. Topography mattered in its development. West Ham was a "river suburb," bounded by the multiple streams of the Lower Lea in the west and the Thames in the south. Its advantageous location attracted hundreds of factories and more than a quarter million residents during the nineteenth century. However, its economic advantages were as fragile as the river itself, and decades of rapid growth significantly damaged the health of both the Lea and the industrial economy that it enabled.

The Lea's capacity to fuel the industrial economy with coal and its proximity to and distance from central London contributed to the nineteenth-century industrialization of its marshlands. Noxious and polluting industries remained close enough to supply the London market, but their location on relatively inexpensive wetland, which was both downwind from the city and outside the jurisdiction of the increasingly powerful London government, shielded them from most public health and environmental regulations.[2] In addition, the old manufacturing core of London experienced a decline, further enhancing West Ham's industrial importance.[3]

The transportation network created in the Lower Lea Valley encouraged the growth of industry at a particularly significant moment in the development of Greater London's industrial economy. The combination of the high cost of transporting coal on land and the relatively small scale of most factories made the waterlogged marsh an attractive locale during the second half of the nineteenth century. The temporal factor was essential, as a few decades later, electricity, cheaper rail costs, the need for larger factories, and the growing importance of roads would increasingly free industries from their reliance on waterways, and the appeal of the Lea Valley, with its cramped and flood-prone marshlands, would decline.[4] As a result, the marshes and riverbanks of West Ham never fully industrialized, and some pockets of undeveloped marsh and farmland remained well into the twentieth century.

Flooding, mills, and drainage projects continually remade the West Ham landscape throughout the centuries.[5] The growth of coal-fuelled industry vastly amplified the scale of change, and this accelerated after the first railway arrived in 1839. The river carried the fuel of the industrial economy and directly or indirectly supplied water for industry.[6] As a result, the banks of the Lower Lea were encased with factories, and its streams were filled with barges, sewage, and other forms of pollution.[7] By century's end, the conflicting uses of the Lea had diminished its capacity to support industrial development. River pollution and sedimentation had made transportation increasingly difficult. Both intentional and accidental human intervention, along with the varied flow of the Lea and the tides, created a high level of disruption and instability in the new industrial landscape. The failure of the government and the Lee Conservancy Board to adequately regulate environmental conditions in the Lower Lea Valley meant that the river became an obstruction to the industrialization it had once enabled.

MARSHLANDS AND EARLY INDUSTRY

The first Ordnance Survey map, published in 1805, depicted the marshlands of the Lower Lea Valley and Thames Estuary (Map 2). It suggested an overwhelmingly wet and rural landscape. The large marshes in the south of the parish, the site of major development after 1850, were devoid of buildings. Scattered buildings lined the Stratford High Street as it crossed the marsh between Bow and Stratford, and a few more stood on the eastern banks of the Channelsea River at the former site of the Stratford Langthorne Abbey (labelled W. Ham Abbey on the map). The map did not indicate which buildings were devoted to industry and did not capture the extent of the calico-printing ventures and mills that were already well established along the Lea. West Ham remained significantly less developed than Stepney and Poplar, located a little closer to London.

By 1805, much of the River Lea had been changed into canals, reservoirs, and flumes to ease transport, supply water, and provide power for mills. Even at this date, the Lower Lea was a hybrid creation of the natural flow of water and human efforts to manipulate that flow. On the western edge of the marshes and flowing south from Hackney, the relatively straight Lee Navigation canal network, first constructed in the fifteenth century, was vastly expanded during the canal-building boom of the late eighteenth and early nineteenth centuries.[8] The canal craze of that period added the Limehouse Cut in the 1760s. This canal created a second mouth for the River Lea and provided a direct route to London that avoided the long bend in the Thames around the Isle of Dogs. Improvements continued in the 1770s, with the construction of the Hackney Cut, which forms the western edge of the Hackney Marsh (Map 3). In 1830, the Hartford Union Canal linked the Lee Navigation network at the southern end of the Hackney Cut with the Regent's Canal as it travelled across North London. Locks controlled the water level throughout the Lee Navigation canals. As these became integrated with England's wider canal network and expedited transportation between the Lea Valley and London, the "improved" western sections of the Lower Lea became increasingly separated from the remaining tidal streams.

The Lower Lea's tidal streams, which flowed through marshes to the east of the Lee Navigation, included the meandering Old Lea and a number of distributaries known as the back rivers. These encompassed the Channelsea, Waterworks, City Mill, and Pudding Mill Rivers in the north of the Stratford Marsh (see Map 3 for a more detailed look at the rivers as they were represented in the 1893–95 maps).[9] The Waterworks, City Mill, and Pudding Mill Rivers reconnected north of the Stratford High Street

Map 2   Lower Lea Valley and East London, Ordnance Survey map, First Series, 1805. *Inset map cartography by Eric Leinberger.* ▶

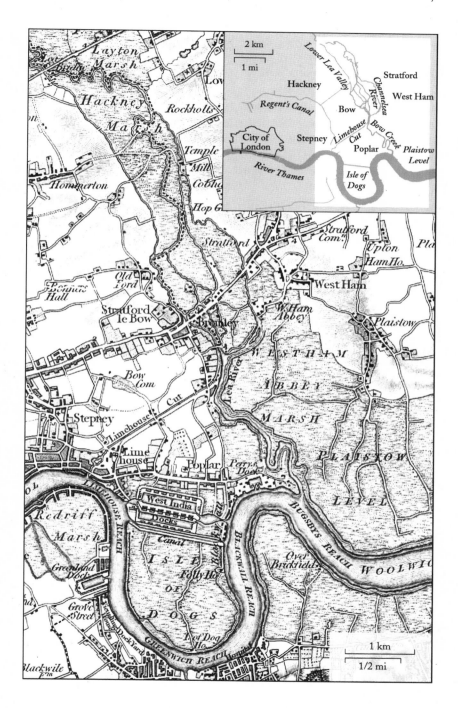

(labelled High Street on Map 3) and continued through the mills and under the bridges, where they became two streams, the Three Mills Back River and the Three Mills Wall River. These merged and flowed through Three Mills, after which they joined with the Channelsea River and the southern locks of the Lee Navigation to form a single River Lea, often called Bow Creek, which drained into the Thames.

These tidal streams were not carefully maintained canals, but humans had modified them over thousands of years. The various names of the back rivers confirm that they were millsreams and had been manipulated to various extents by mill owners and waterworks companies. In this low-lying topography, it is also likely that the bed of the Lea meandered during the centuries, as siltation and regular floods shifted channels and created new streams.[10] As a result, it is difficult to distinguish the natural riverbeds from the artificial ones.

Watermills began the industrial alteration of the rivers on a small scale by harnessing tidal energy during the early Middle Ages, and a large-scale drainage program transformed the marshlands and increased the height of riverbanks centuries before the railroad arrived. The *Domesday Book* recorded five tidal watermills on the Lower Lea at the end of the eleventh century. One-way gates opened to allow the flood tide to roll up the Lower Lea and then closed, redirecting the ebb tide through the watermills. This technology enabled millers to harness water power in this flat landscape, first to grind cereals and later to mill other goods such as oil seeds and gunpowder.[11] A number of windmills were built in the region during the early modern era, such as the example in Figure 1, which dates from around 1800.[12] As long as mills and other industries remained restricted to the tides and the wind for their sources of energy, there was a limited capacity for industrial expansion in the Lower Lea Valley.[13]

In the sixteenth and seventeenth centuries, Stratford and West Ham attracted a number of silk weavers. No detailed maps record the location or size of their workshops, but some were concentrated around the Bow Bridge, the main crossing of the River Lea on the road that connected London and Colchester (known as Stratford High Street within West Ham).[14] Calico printing replaced the waning silk-weaving trade in the late seventeenth century, and by 1747 calico works occupied thirty-two hectares (eighty-one acres) of marshland.[15]

As Map 3 indicates, the Lower Lea was not heavily industrialized at the start of the nineteenth century. A few tidal mills, calico-printing grounds, a recently established chemist (drug) factory called Howard and Sons, and a few lime kilns were the sum of regional industry. The calico grounds

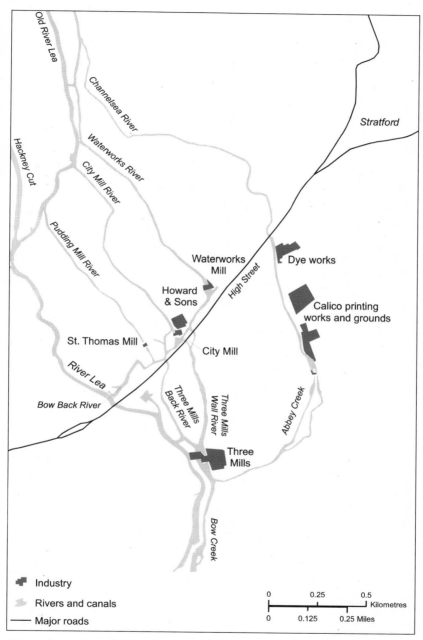

MAP 3 Lower Lea industry, c. 1810

Note: This map is an approximation: some industrial sites are missing, and others appear larger or smaller than they actually were during the first decade of the century.

FIGURE I View of West Ham Mills by the River Lea in West Ham, c. 1800. |
Wakefield Collection, London Metropolitan Archives. Reprinted with permission
from the London Metropolitan Archives.

were on the site of the former abbey, east of the Channelsea River, and
were probably more extensive than this map shows.[16] These developments
aside, the landscape and economy of West Ham and the Lower Lea remained largely agricultural through the first decades of the nineteenth
century. Plaistow produced potatoes, and livestock were assembled and
fattened on the reclaimed marshes before delivery to the London market.[17]
According to the census of 1801, about 6,500 people lived in West Ham.[18]
This made it the second most populous parish in Essex, after Colchester,
suggesting that suburban expansion from London had already begun.[19]

The landscape transformations produced by early modern farming
and gardening laid the basis for later industrial growth in West Ham. After
responsibility for flood defence and land drainage passed from Stratford
Langthorne Abbey to the Court of Sewers with the dissolution of the
monasteries in the sixteenth century, the extent of drained marshlands increased from 7.07 square kilometres in 1563 to 9.59 square kilometres in
1850.[20] This replicated a more general trend of marsh reclamation in the
Thames Estuary after drainage works and flood defences fell into disrepair
following the population crisis of the fourteenth century.[21] The ditches

created for agriculture provided an early (and inadequate) sewer system in the marshy sections of West Ham. Furthermore, the shape of the ditches structured the residential spaces, in much the same way as the rivers influenced industrial areas, as early builders erected housing along the ditch banks.[22]

EARLY DAMAGE

The modest growth of manufacturing during the early decades of the nineteenth century caused a major conflict after a severe flood occurred in 1824. A series of reports record a prolonged clash between mill owners and the upstream communities over an improved embankment that was built during the eighteenth century to trap more of the tide for the large Three Mills and Four Mills.[23] Three documents from the Committee of the Floods of the Lea (1824–30) provide useful, but one-sided, insights into this early struggle over the industrialization of the river. According to one report,

> a flood more devastating than had occurred for some time, attended by a loss of £10,000 in 1824, aroused the attention of the inhabitants; they investigated the cause of this calamity, and observed it did not extend below the mill dams, and on inquiry into the right of the millers to inflict these cruel injuries, found that this damming and penning up of the Lea was not only in opposition to the laws of the realm, but specifically prohibited by the 39th of Elizabeth, statute of sewers.[24]

The plaintiffs argued the new embankment increased the frequency and severity of flooding, limited the transportation potential of the Lower Lea, and threatened the health and property of the upstream neighbours.[25] The last of the reports suggests that the millers won this case, leaving a deep rift in the community between the two large mills and the upstream landowners and tenants. After the 1820s, the ability to retain large amounts of tidal water to power mills was no longer a major limiting factor in industrial development. The Lea remained essential to local industry, but instead of moving the waterwheels, it facilitated the transportation of coal and filled boilers. Three Mills, one of the two mills targeted by the Committee of the Floods of the Lea, remained operational, and the distillers who owned the property continued to protect their legal rights after many more floods damaged the growing number of factories and homes upstream.

Travel narratives from the early 1840s note the distasteful changes that accompanied coal-fuelled industrial development. Charles Mackay's *The Thames and Its Tributaries* (1840) describes a walk along the Lea, which ended in West Ham:

> Bromley-le-Bow ... is the last of the pleasant villages that ornament the Lea, which is then lost amid the ship-yards, manufactories, and long straggling outskirts of the shipping districts of the metropolis. Divided into several branches, aided by canals, polluted by gasworks, and other useful but un-fragrant factories, it loses its character of a retired and rural stream. Its very name is taken from it at the end of its useful career, and it unites itself with the Thames, neglected and unhonoured, under the name of Bow Creek.[26]

Four years later, James Thorne published a similar description, observing that below Bromley "our river has ceased to be either picturesque or interesting: lime-kilns, calico-printing, and distilleries are the most prominent objects ... and however useful these may be, they are not agreeable to either nose or eye."[27]

During the middle decades of the nineteenth century, the renewable but limited energy of the tides was largely replaced by the abundant but polluting energy of seaborne coal. Industrial expansion began to accelerate, and the rural countryside gave way to a productive landscape shaped by factories, railways, and dockyards, all of which consumed large amounts of coal. Mackay and Thorne underlined the trade-off involved, noting the negative consequences of this trend while acknowledging its importance. Their reactions to the Lower Lea reflect a wider cultural tension between enthusiasm for economic and technological development and the growing awareness of the "heaps" of pollution and otherwise blighted landscapes left for the future by industrial innovations.[28]

RAILWAYS AND DOCKS

Although manufacturing in West Ham predated the arrival of the first railroad that connected the area with central London in 1839, that crucial transportation infrastructure helped accelerate industrialization in the Lower Lea Valley. Figure 2, an 1837 print commissioned by the railway company before the construction of the line, gives a view of the region at this crucial moment. Perhaps the railway promoters hoped to ease anxiety about the destruction of the pastoral Lea Valley by showing that the advent

FIGURE 2 *View of the Proposed Stratford Viaduct on the Eastern Counties Railway, Showing Two Figures Fishing on the Bank of the River Lea, and a Windmill,* lithograph by George Harley, 1837. | Wakefield Collection, London Metropolitan Archives. Reprinted with permission from the London Metropolitan Archives.

of the railway would not be disruptive. Although change was not immediate, the arrival of the railway did mark the start of a dramatic transformation of this landscape in the decades that followed. The bucolic scene of the print was replaced by the damaged industrial landscape that appears in photographs taken at the turn of the twentieth century (see Figures 3 and 4). In 1851, the population of West Ham was 18,817, three times that of 1801, and new factories had been developed at points where the rivers met either the main road or the new railway.

G.W. Colton's 1856 map, "The Environs of London" (Map 4), captures the construction of docks and railways that made West Ham a transportation hub and fuelled its subsequent industrial development. The map includes an ambitious vision of the future Victoria Dock, a large rectangle that parallels the Thames; only the western half was completed between 1850 and 1855.[29] The dock was built on these remote marshlands because they were topographically lower than the high-water level of the Thames, which reduced the cost of excavating a large deep-water dock. The undeveloped Plaistow Level also provided enough open land, in a good location on the edge of London.[30] The Colton map also shows the southern railway line of 1847 that connected Stratford to North Woolwich (labelled N. Woolwich); the main line was rerouted north of the docks after 1855,

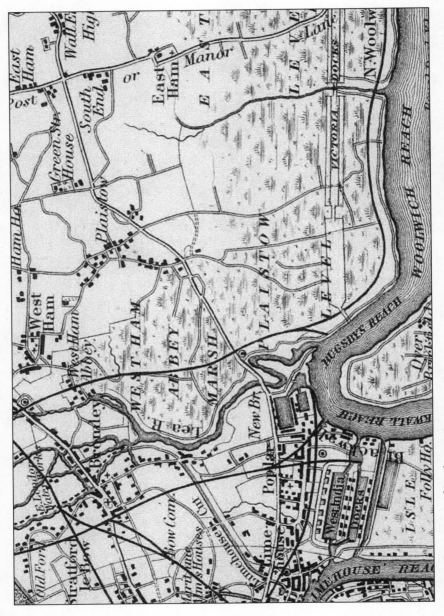

MAP 4 The Environs of London, 1856

but the southern branch opened the area south of them to industrial development.[31]

The Victoria Dock played a crucial role in the industrial expansion of the Lower Lea Valley. The William Cory and Son coal depot installed hydraulic cranes in the dock to transfer coal from ocean-going vessels to river barges, creating the key link in the energy regime of the Lower Lea.[32] An early historian of West Ham's industrial development, Archer Philip Crouch, found that Cory and Son reduced the price of seaborne coal in the mid-1850s to "7s. 6d. per ton, while the railborne coal remained at 12s. 6d. per ton."[33] In 1859, Cory and Son commissioned a local shipyard to build a floating river wharf so that ocean-going ships could be unloaded without paying dock fees, further decreasing the cost of coal.[34] The use of coal barges, like the 1902 examples in Figure 3, allowed the Lower Lea River network to supply energy to any riverside factory that they could reach. The Lea remained integral in supplying the energy for industrialization, as steam engines became the main source of power. The Lower Lea was a ready-made transportation network for coal barges in the immediate proximity of the docklands, which reduced the cost of energy in West

FIGURE 3 Coal barges on the Channelsea River. | Abbey Mills Ingham Clarke & Co 1902. Reprinted with permission from Newham Archives and Local Studies Library.

Ham. As a result, it was more competitive with northern England than were the older industrial landscapes in London proper.[35]

Late in the nineteenth century, most of West Ham's largest and most valuable factories were in Silvertown, where direct access to the Thames further reduced the cost of transporting coal and other raw materials.[36] Maps 5 through 9 suggest that the economic significance of development along the smaller River Lea still deserves careful attention, as it was the crucial incubator for industry on the edge of London, and collectively, the many factories along the Lea created an important industrial landscape decades before the success of Silvertown.

MAPPING INDUSTRIAL EXPANSION

Map 5 depicts the industrial landscape of the Lower Lea during the 1850s. The cloth printers have been joined by a gasworks, the Great Eastern Railway's Stratford Works (labelled as GER Works on the map), a soapworks, and a number of chemical factories. The map also captures a large shipyard, renamed the Thames Ironworks in 1857, at the Lea's mouth and an early chemical factory on the Thames, south of the Victoria Dock's lock. This fertilizer plant and Samuel Silver's rubber factory, established farther east and off the map, began the industrialization of Silvertown. The basic configuration of West Ham's industry was in place by the mid-nineteenth century, stretching from the GER Works in the north to Silver's rubber factory in the southeast, but a great deal of marshland remained undeveloped between the two sites.

Map 6 shows a number of industrial clusters in London during the 1860s and 1870s.[37] The numerous tanneries and curries in Bermondsey predate the steam-powered industrialization of the nineteenth century. Tanneries had been established in Bermondsey by the Middle Ages and were thriving by the seventeenth century. The leather industry continued to develop to the mid-nineteenth century, after which it began to shift to Liverpool and oversea competitors.[38] In West London, the banks of the Thames housed an important industrial cluster during the nineteenth century. Railroad works and candle making led development in this region. The docklands were another important centre of industry. Shipbuilding boomed on the Isle of Dogs during the mid-nineteenth century before declining in the 1860s. The Limehouse, Surrey, and Regent's Canals and Deptford Creek (the lower reaches of the River Ravensbourne) all attracted factories to their banks, reflecting the importance of waterways in assisting

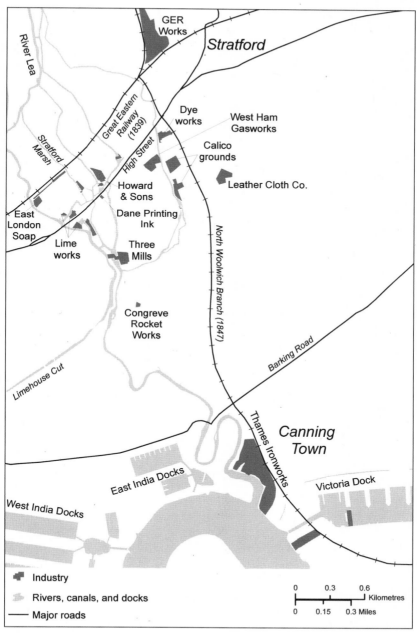

MAP 5 Lower Lea industry, 1850s
Note: This map is again an approximation, albeit with better source material than
Map 3. See Map Credits for more information.

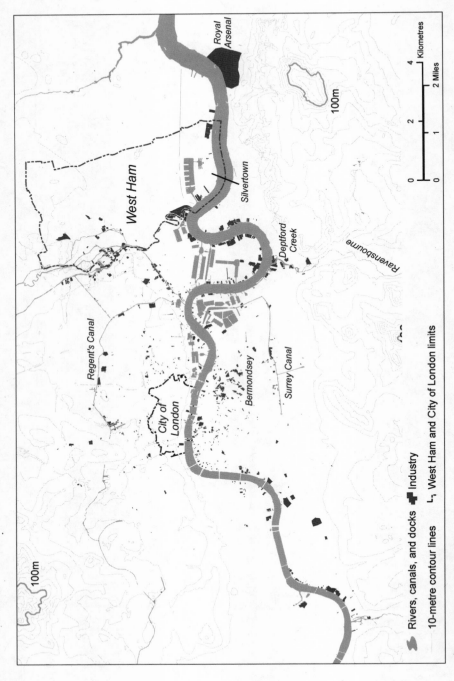

MAP 6 Industrial London, 1863–73

industrial development. In the far east of Greater London, industry was expanding, with additional chemical works, a sugar refinery, an ironworks, and a gasworks established in Silvertown by the end of the 1860s. South of the Thames, the Royal Arsenal in Woolwich was one of the largest industrial sites in Greater London, but the Ordnance Survey maps left this strategic location blank, so they cannot be used to gauge its extent. The Lower Lea was emerging as an important industrial landscape. There were dozens of small and medium-sized factories between the heavy industrial sites of the Thames Ironworks shipyard and the Great Eastern Railway Stratford Works.

The first detailed surveys of the Lower Lea's built environment date from the 1860s. Map 7 relies on the first Ordnance Survey maps (1867–70) and presents the early stages of rapid industrialization, as factories expanded along the banks of the Lower Lea River network north and south of High Street and on the old calico grounds at Abbey Marsh. Further clusters established themselves at Old Ford and Hackney Wick. The map highlights the growing importance of the chemical industry among the smaller factories that lined the braided streams of the Lower Lea. These included a tar and printing ink works, a number of lye producers, the Howard and Sons fine chemical and drug works, and producers of bleach and sulfuric acid.[39] The map also reveals that the Lower Lea Valley continued to be a dynamic patchwork of riverine environment, agriculture, and urban industrial concerns. Three decades after the railway reached West Ham, much open marshland remained extant. There were working farms in the south, where only one small rocket factory had been established between Three Mills and the Thames Ironworks. The back rivers north of High Street also remained essentially undeveloped.

Most of the large factories built in London between 1870 and the 1890s produced coal gas (Map 8). Situated to the north of the expanded Royal Docks in East Ham, Beckton Gasworks was the largest gasworks in the world. A number of major railway works also expanded, and the Thames Ironworks remained an important industrial site even as shipbuilding waned elsewhere in East London. The Bermondsey Leather District was also in decline by the 1890s. The Isle of Dogs was still a significant industrial region, and the Greenwich Peninsula grew in importance. West Ham housed the most prominent industrial districts in Greater London, as Silvertown and the Lower Lea Valley experienced major growth, with two large sugar refineries, jam factories, numerous chemical works, a large-scale soap factory, a gasworks, and an expanded underwater telegraph cable and rubber works.

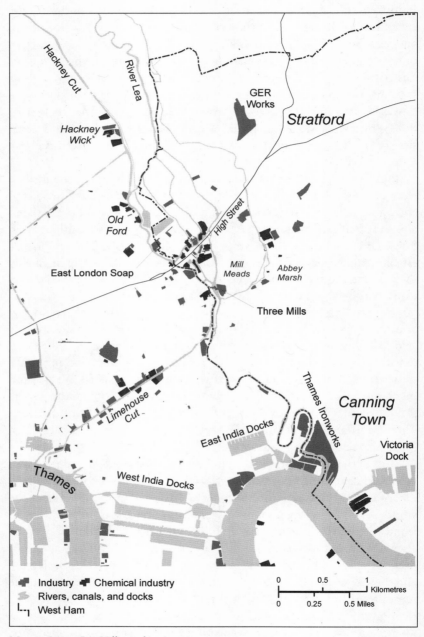

MAP 7   Lower Lea Valley industry, 1867–70

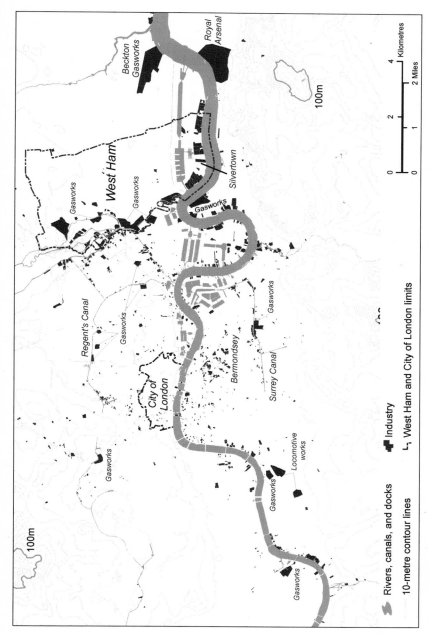

Rivers, canals, and docks

Industry

10-metre contour lines

West Ham and City of London limits

100m

100m

Beckton Gasworks

Royal Arsenal

West Ham

Silvertown

Gasworks

Gasworks

Gasworks

Regent's Canal

Gasworks

Gasworks

City of London

Bermondsey

Gasworks

Surrey Canal

Locomotive works

Gasworks

Gasworks

Kilometres

0   2   4

0   1   2 Miles

Map 8 Industrial London, 1893–95

The development of the docks, railways, and related heavy industry clearly contributed to rapid industrial growth in West Ham, but many contemporary commentators, including the Outer London Inquiry Committee, attributed it to the suburb's freedom from the new regulations that governed noxious trades in London.[40] However, many offensive and polluting industries remained within the County of London, which suggests that the lower cost of transporting coal was a more important factor than West Ham's independence.[41] Nonetheless, we should not entirely discount West Ham's jurisdictional freedom, and the concentration of polluting industries in the suburb suggests that it did play a secondary role.

Map 9 portrays industry in the Lower Lea Valley from 1893 to 1895. Compared with Map 7, it shows that factories have significantly increased along all the branches of the Lower Lea, where they drastically altered both the rivers and the landscape. The map shows the continued reliance on the Lower Lea for transportation. Except for the Stratford Rail Works, very few factories were distant from a navigable river. New small and medium factories spread across Stratford Marsh north of the High Street. Factories also sprang on Abbey Marsh, along the southern banks of the Channelsea River and south of High Street. Expansion also occurred along the west side of the River Lea, between the Poplar Gasworks and Hackney Wick.

During an interview with the author of a travel narrative that explored London's industrial landscapes, industrialist Edward Cook explained that the Lea aided transportation at his East London Soap Works:

> "That is our highway," he remarked, following my gaze "that and the railway that runs into our own siding, though we find sufficient road-work to justify us in keeping fifty horses and vans in constant use." Steam cranes hoist the material on to the wharf, and a system of rails serves to bear it to any part of the works. The tallow and fats used in soap-making, however, find their way by a steam lift to the top of the main factory, where they are started on their evolutionary journey.[42]

The East London Soap Works Factory was situated on the Lee Navigation canal at Bow Bridge, so Cook had the advantage of a well-maintained water "highway" to supply it. Most West Ham factories had to rely on the back rivers, and their declining quality limited industrial development. The largest addition to Map 9, the Bromley Gasworks, was the last significant industrial site constructed along the Lower Lea, and it was the first major failure.

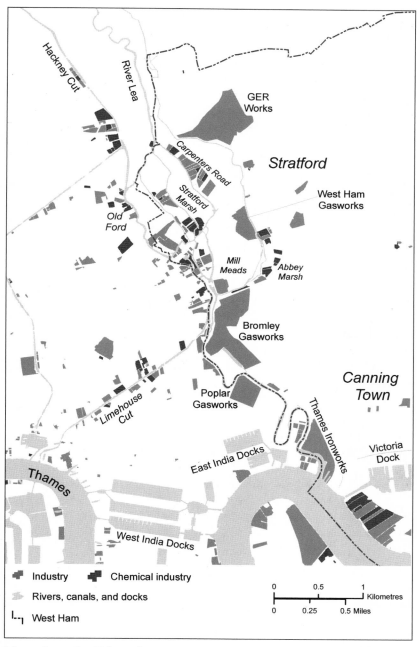

MAP 9 Lower Lea Valley industry, 1893–95

NEGATIVE FEEDBACK LOOP

The Bromley Gasworks compared unfavourably with the Beckton works. Its technology was inferior, and whereas Beckton could unload coal directly from ocean-going vessels, Bromley incurred the cost of transferring it to smaller river barges.[43] In 1876, a few years after the Bromley works was built, the Gas Light and Coke Company, owners of the Beckton plant, bought the Imperial Gas Company, which owned the Bromley works.[44] After investigating the cost of installing a direct rail link between Beckton and Bromley, and failing to find ocean-going ships that could pass up Bow Creek, the company resigned itself to the cost of filling barges at the Beckton pier to serve Bromley.[45] The economic disadvantages of the Bromley site limited its expansion, and large adjoining areas remained in use for market gardening, growing osiers for basket making, and later for allotment gardening.[46]

The example of the Bromley Gasworks reflected a wider trend in the economic development of the Lower Lea Valley. The river's natural transportation network created an economic advantage for smaller factories, but as the scale of industrial production continued to expand in the late nineteenth century, locations with access to the Thames held a significant edge over those on the Lea. This pattern arose during the mid-nineteenth century, with the growth of large factories in Silvertown, and it continued to the 1930s, when a massive five-hundred-acre Ford factory was built on the Dagenham marshes.[47] The scale of industrial development and its demand for larger amounts of energy outgrew the capacities of the Lower Lea.

Industrialization also led to deteriorating conditions on the back rivers. Although much of Stratford Marsh and Mill Meads remained undeveloped (Map 9), the accumulation of garbage, pollution, and sediment in the Stratford back rivers and the conflicting demands on the whole of the River Lea decreased the utility of this water network as the century wore on. Photographs, including Figure 4 of Abbey Creek (on the right) and the Channelsea River (on the left), provide some indication of the poor state of the rivers at the turn of the twentieth century. The open landscape of Mill Meads appears at the right of this photograph, directly across from the chemical factories on the banks of the Channelsea.

The decline in the water quality had many causes: the towns of Leyton and Walthamstow dumped their sewage into the Channelsea; London's sewer overflow pipes discharged into the Old Lea and Abbey Creek; garbage from dust heaps (dumps) spilled into the northern portion of the streams; and the Lea carried silt from up the valley through straight and

Figure 4　Channelsea River, south of Abbey Mills, 1900. | Reprinted with permission from Newham Archives and Local Studies Library.

deep canals to the lower streams.[48] During dry summers, the waterworks companies diverted most of the Lea's water, and little more than sewage effluent trickled down to meet the tide in the Stratford back rivers. As a result, the upper reaches of the back rivers became increasingly congested and difficult to navigate.[49]

Factories also dumped waste into the rivers or onto the adjacent land. Until 1901, West Ham's sewers disgorged partially treated effluent into Bow Creek, which probably also carried industrial waste. A local newspaper, the *West Ham Guardian,* reported in January 1899 that West Ham had finally prosecuted a large Silvertown firm, Burt, Boulton and Haywood, for dumping waste into the municipal sewers. The paper implied that the borough had turned a blind eye to this practice in the past. Whereas Burt, Boulton and Haywood's waste flowed to the Silvertown treatment plant and then into the Thames, other firms probably dumped their waste into the main sewer network that ended up in Bow Creek.[50] The minute books of the Public Health Committee regularly refer to problems with river pollution. In 1899, for example, the committee received complaints about the polluted condition of the Channelsea, Waterworks, City Mill, and Thames Rivers.[51] Moreover, present-day environmental monitoring shows that the

Waterworks River and sections of Bow Creek are among the worst contaminated in Greater London, and the Lea remains one of the most polluted rivers in England.[52] In sum, the back rivers experienced a precipitous environmental decline during the period of rapid industrial growth in the Lower Lea Valley.

The Lee Conservancy Board (LCB) and the Corporation of West Ham shared jurisdiction over the back rivers, but neither wanted to shoulder the responsibility of upkeep, as the streams were toll-free and both bodies were limited in what they could do by the millers' long-standing rights to use the tidal flow to generate power.[53] From the 1880s onward, the LCB engineer, Joseph Child, planned to canalize the back rivers, and in 1892 he attempted to work with the affected interests, though without success.[54] The rivers continued to deteriorate during the last years of the century, as sewage in the Channelsea threatened public health and the back rivers became progressively more difficult to navigate.[55]

In 1908, J.G. Morley, West Ham's engineer, approached Charles Tween, the new LCB engineer, complaining that the rivers were increasingly ineffective waterways. According to the lengthy correspondence between the two men, all the rivers had problems with excessive silting, causing significant delay in traffic in the Bow Back River and an almost complete reduction in flow down the Pudding Mill River, even during floods.[56] This threatened the economy of West Ham, as the rivers became hard to navigate, and the congestion increased the frequency of floods.[57] Together, these factors partially explain why large sections of marshland remained undeveloped in the mid-1890s.[58] The poor state of the rivers, the growing scale of industry, the freedom of location provided by electricity, and improved overland transportation all combined to end the industrial boom in the Lower Lea Valley during the early twentieth century. As the Thames Ironworks fell on bad times, finally closing in 1912, and William Ritchie and Son's jute factory shut its doors in 1904, West Ham transitioned from a vibrant economic centre to the symbolic heart of Britain's unemployment crisis in 1904–05.[59]

2

Population Growth

BETWEEN 1801 AND 1911, the population of Greater London mushroomed from slightly more than 1 million to over 7 million and spread out across the region (see Figure 5 and Maps 10, 11, and 12). This dramatic increase changed the environment. Air pollution worsened as the number of inefficient open coal fires used for heat and cooking corresponded closely with the number of households. Quantities of sewage and other domestic waste also spiked in lockstep with the population. Roads, railways, and buildings spread out from central London and brought major environmental transformations, converting agricultural land into urban and suburban landscapes. Population growth and the importance of rivers for transportation led to significant urban and suburban development on marshlands and floodplains, devastating these ecosystems and their ability to absorb water.

Map 10 shows that eighteenth-century urban development remained concentrated around the City of London and on the higher ground in the north and west.[1] Map 11 shows that as London's population more than doubled in the half-century that followed, mostly by expanding onto the hills in the north and south. But, the marshland districts including Bermondsey, Poplar, and West Ham, also started to attract tens of thousands of residents. Maps 10 and 11 also highlight the difficulty in defining nineteenth-century London, as its jurisdictional boundaries did not match the urban limits and the City of London remained independent from the new upper-tier London government. The City of London, which dates from the Anglo-Saxon period, controlled only a square mile in the heart

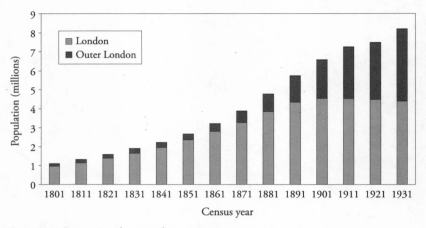

FIGURE 5 Greater London population, 1801–1931
Source: R. Haywood, "Railways, Urban Reform and Town Planning in London: 1900–1947," *Planning Perspectives* 12, no. 1 (1997): 38.

of Greater London. A series of reforms during the 1850s and 1880s created a new two-tier system of municipal government for much of the rest of the metropolis. The Metropolitan Board of Works (1855), later replaced by the London County Council (1889), formed the upper tier and governed London as it was defined for the 1851 census (the hash-mark boundary labelled County of London on Maps 10, 11, and 12). Population growth was already starting to spill beyond the new census definition of London: in 1851, more than 300,000 people lived in the outer suburbs, with concentrations in Brentford, Croydon, Edmonton, and West Ham.

London, as it was defined in the 1851 census, experienced growth until the first decade of the twentieth century, but as Figure 5 shows, the growth rate began to level off in the 1890s. This reflected a new trend in which central districts, such as the City of London, became significantly depopulated, even as some of the outlying areas in the County of London continued to grow. The City of London dropped from almost fifty-six thousand inhabitants to under twenty thousand between 1851 and 1911, while Lambeth doubled in size. Map 12 shows that people spread across Greater London, with large populations living on the marshlands and floodplains of the Thames Estuary and the tributaries. Outer London, the suburban districts outside of the 1851 boundaries, accounted for most of Greater London's population expansion after 1891.[2] The Lea Valley suburbs, along with Croydon and Willesden, were the early centres of this growth.

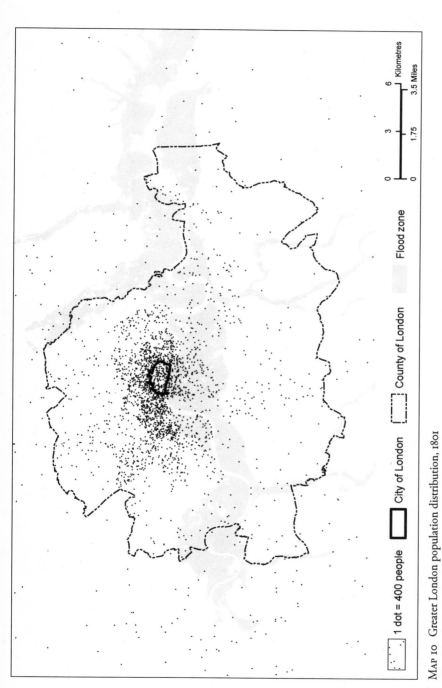

MAP 10 Greater London population distribution, 1801

Note: The dots outside of the County of London boundary do not reflect the real situation; the population would have been more concentrated along the border.

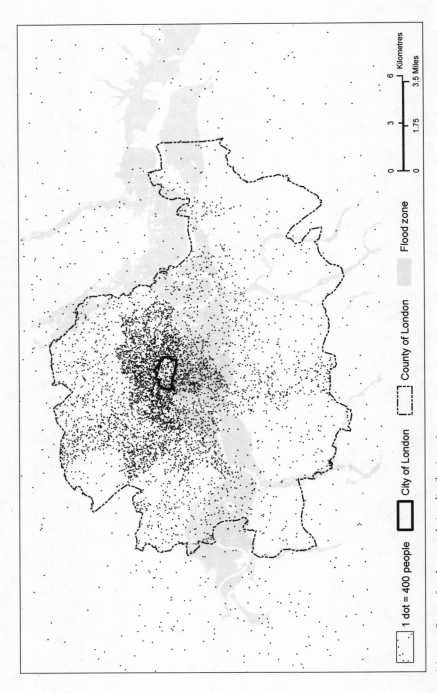

MAP 11 Greater London population distribution, 1851

1 dot = 400 people

City of London

County of London

Flood zone

Kilometres
0   3   6

Miles
0   1.75   3.5

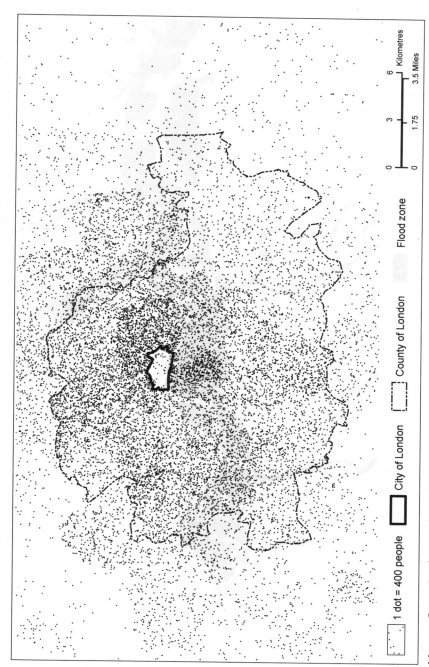

City of London

County of London

Flood zone

Kilometres

0　　　　3　　　　6

0　　1.75　　3.5 Miles

MAP 12　Greater London population distribution, 1911

The new suburbs were less equipped than central London to address the environmental challenges that accompanied this trend. Croydon struggled to process increasing quantities of sewage in the south, just as Tottenham contended with the same problem on the northeast edge of London.[3] Similar issues arose in the River Brent watershed, as the population of Willesden exceeded 150,000 by 1911. Plans to divert the sewage by large intercepting drains failed due to the fractured nature of suburban governance and the limits of local taxation. Downstream from new suburbs, Wandsworth, Brentford, Hackney, and West Ham struggled with increasing accumulations of sewage that floated down the Rivers Wandle, Brent, and Lea from the growing populations upstream.[4] This problem was most pronounced in the Lea Valley, where the combined population surpassed 1 million by 1911 (see Map 13).

The Lea supported this growth in East London and northeast Outer London. The East London Waterworks Company diverted much of the river and delivered its water to homes and factories through a network of pipes. Local sewer systems then returned some of this polluted, offensive, and hazardous water to the Lea as partially treated effluent whose solid waste had been removed. In instances when the system failed to keep pace with population growth, the effluent was not treated at all. And during periods of heavy rain, a mix of storm water and sewage was flushed into the river. Long before deteriorating river conditions reduced the viability of industry, the people who lived near the Lea suffered from disease and the general unpleasantness of their surroundings. The network of pipes connected the human and natural ecologies of the region. Fish and other forms of life that relied on oxygen in the water suffered along with the human residents, as the quantities of sewage resulted in eutrophication, which significantly reduced biodiversity.

The Lower Lea and its adjacent marshlands began to smell badly, the river turned black at times, contaminated water spread disease, and the Stratford back rivers became more difficult to navigate. This helped to shape the social geography of the Lower Lea Valley as low-income and socially marginalized people concentrated in its tainted marshland districts, and those with greater means occupied higher ground away from the rivers and factories. The Lea's dilemma was simple: too little water and too much sewage.[5] Solving it proved far less simple, as the structure of suburban municipal politics complicated the funding of large public works projects. Co-ordinating multiple suburbs in the counties of Essex, Middlesex, and Hertfordshire was a major impediment, as the numerous demands on municipal government budgets ensured that protecting downstream

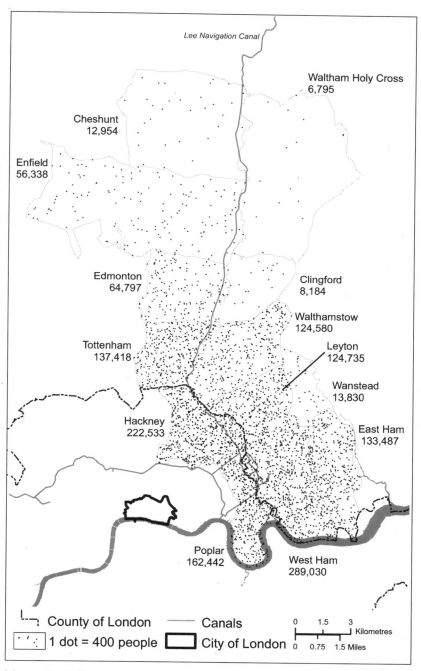

Lee Navigation Canal

Waltham Holy Cross
6,795

Cheshunt
12,954

Enfield
56,338

Edmonton
64,797

Clingford
8,184

Walthamstow
124,580

Tottenham
137,418

Leyton
124,735

Wanstead
13,830

Hackney
222,533

East Ham
133,487

Poplar
162,442

West Ham
289,030

⌐⌐⌐ County of London   ⎯⎯ Canals

∴ 1 dot = 400 people   ☐ City of London

0   1.5   3
Kilometres
0   0.75   1.5 Miles

MAP 13   Lea Valley population distribution, 1911

populations from sewage remained a low priority. Although pollution was a pressing issue, and the Lea became a focus of national concern twice during the second half of the nineteenth century, political leaders responded with investigations, a conservancy board, further investigations, and some partial solutions, without addressing the underlying causes of damage to the river.

Local people did not need scientific or medical experts to confirm the environmental degradation that they saw and smelled in the Lower Lea Valley. They complained to investigators and the press about the situation. Science played an important role in the legal conflicts and public policy debates that arose from a series of crises between the 1860s and the 1880s, as experts debated the significance of pollution in the river. Numerous local governments, the Lee Conservancy Board, scientific experts, and the courts could not agree whether the River Lea was dangerous or simply offensive to the eyes and nose.[6] Disagreement and inaction meant that West Ham had to deal with both local water pollution and the waste of hundreds of thousands of people in upstream communities.

SEWAGE AND THE WATER SUPPLY

Pollution in the River Lea began to invoke significant public health concerns during the mid-nineteenth century.[7] Residents who were interviewed for a public health report of 1855 and Henry Morley's article in *Household Words* identified the sewage-filled back rivers and miasmic marshes as causes of disease.[8] The miasmic paradigm remained influential in medical circles through to the 1850s, and the bulk of rotting organic matter in the river prompted people to blame the resulting gases for the high rates of disease in the area.[9] In subsequent decades, the zymotic theory of disease and later the germ theory concentrated expert attention on drinking water as a major vector for the spread of disease, whereas much of the general public remained focused on bad smells.[10] During the second half of the nineteenth century, proponents of the three paradigms struggled for ascendancy. This conflict destabilized expert and public knowledge concerning the health consequences of polluted rivers. Some powerful experts challenged the link between such rivers and human disease. Scientists who espoused the miasmic theory doubted that upstream sewage endangered the health of downstream consumers. They argued that diluted sewage became safe when it had enough time to oxidize as it flowed down the river.[11] With little evidence on how much contamination rendered a water supply dangerous and no tests that were capable of confirming the zymotic or germ theories, the proponents of the miasmic theory, some of whom were connected with water companies, remained influential in the courts of law.[12] This scientific uncertainty, together with the constant pressure to keep municipal rates low and the stresses created by rapid growth, delayed a long-term solution to improve the condition of the Lea.

The river was a major disease vector in London's final cholera epidemic, which killed 5,548 people in July and August 1866. The outbreak centred on districts whose drinking water was supplied by the East London Waterworks Company; deaths were particularly frequent in "Bethnal Green, Whitechapel, St George-in-the-East, Stepney, Mile End and Poplar."[13] The possible connection between the Lea and the epidemic resulted in two major reports: one was commissioned by the board of trade on the responsibility of the East London Waterworks Company for the outbreak, and the other emerged from an already established royal commission on river pollution, which shifted its attention to the Lea after the cholera deaths.[14]

Captain H.W. Tyler carried out the first investigation and confirmed that pollution from the Lower Lea contaminated the adjacent drinking water reservoirs, owned by the East London Waterworks Company, near Old Ford. However, Tyler was unwilling to assign full blame to the waterworks company, as the medical community was uncertain regarding the causes of cholera. The disease struck districts with poor drainage and impoverished social conditions, suggesting that miasmic gases and poverty might have done more damage than the tainted water system.[15] The company was nonetheless guilty of breaking the law because it distributed unfiltered water and because it continued to use open reservoirs in the Lower Lea. In the aftermath of the cholera outbreak, it moved its water storage and filtering facilities farther north.[16]

The royal commission on river pollution concluded that the Lea needed a conservancy board to manage its conflicting functions. "The rapid growth of the metropolis during the last half century," it wrote, "has caused a large increase in the population of the lower part of the valley of the Lee; and as no effective means have been taken to prevent pollution, this has also increased with the growth of population and the extension of trade and manufactures." To make matters worse, suburban growth intensified demands for drinking water, and the commissioners reported that "at present, the entire dry weather volume of the river over and above that required for navigation is taken for domestic and trade purposes."[17] This diminished the river's capacity to dilute the increased volume of sewage: "Thus whilst the pollutions tend to multiply, the water wherewith they might be diluted tends to fail."[18] Too much sewage and too little water produced a noxious result: "At neap tides the river is reduced to a small foul stream, oscillating at the bottom of a muddy creek, and there exposes an area of eight acres of oozy mud and sewage deposit, verging into a state of putridity."[19] During the hot summer months, the Lea was little more than an open sewer.[20]

The commissioners were well aware of the practical difficulties entailed in addressing the issue, as the suburban governments were openly indifferent to the harm done to downstream communities. They quoted an official from Bishop Stortford, who described sending sewage mud downstream, to exemplify this problem:

> The nuisance of which the inhabitants have complained from the smell of the river was during last summer and the summer before, but it was very much abated in consequence of our having wet seasons, and a plan was adopted that succeeded remarkably well, and that was this: during the summer ... the filth will sometimes almost crop up to the mouth of the drains, and when there has been a flood in the winter this accumulation has been stirred ... so that we have passed it on to our neighbours to some extent. We thought we had kept it long enough.[21]

This kind of localism led the commissioners to recommend a new form of river government that would manage the entire watershed and regulate the pollution of the Lea. This resulted in the Lee Conservancy Bill, legislation that created the Lee Conservancy Board (LCB) in 1868.[22] The LCB was allocated new powers to manage the river, but in practice it had limited jurisdictional control over the municipal governments that were largely responsible for the degradation.

The LCB engineer concerned himself with maintaining the transportation network, and the LCB sanitary engineer worked to reduce the flow of pollution into the Lea. Both reported to a board that represented the City of London, the Metropolitan Board of Works, two water companies, barge owners, and landowners.[23] The Lee Conservancy Bill was a direct response to the royal commission's recommendations, but the population and associated problem grew faster than anticipated, and the LCB was unable to cope with the constant increase in municipal sewage. It did not have the financial resources to police the river or to pay for expensive litigation when it identified a source of pollution; nor did it have the full legal jurisdiction to force municipalities to stop dumping sewage into the Lea.[24]

The Lea's "Great Stink"

In the mid-1880s, sewage in the Lea attracted national attention, generating months of regular coverage in the *Times*. A major drought in 1884 turned the already polluted river south of Tottenham into a major crisis. This was the Lea's "great stink" moment, but unlike the more famous 1858 Great Stink on the Thames, it did not prompt the construction of an intercepting sewer. There was simply not enough political will in the Lea Valley to take this step.[25] This crisis made the ineffectiveness of the LCB clear to the public.

On August 1, 1884, the *Times* published a letter from B.B. Marston under the heading "State of the River Lea below Tottenham." Recounting a recent ramble along the river near the Tottenham outfall, Marston wrote that "it was like walking by an open sewer – in fact, the river is now nothing but an open sewer from Tottenham to the Thames."[26] He identified the social consequences of the pollution: "This horrible, fetid stream passes through a thickly-populated, poor district, and is frequented by thousands who go for recreation in boats and on the banks."[27] These residents, Marston continued, "are almost without exception of the lower classes, and are doubtless in too many cases used to bad drainage; but the one thing I heard talked about both by young and old was the horrible smell."[28]

Three weeks later, on August 21, Thomas Francis also wrote to the *Times*, drawing public attention to the disgraceful state of the Lea. His letter gave some details about the legal obligations of Tottenham and the LCB to mitigate pollution in the river, but his most memorable statement dealt with its appearance and odour: "The river is now as black as ink. The Stench emitted causes everyone to sicken who inhales it."[29] Francis extended Marston's argument and suggested that the river was a danger to public health. He also asserted that the economic health of the region was threatened: "The boating is entirely suspended, and the boat builders, who have had a succession of bad seasons, all but ruined."[30] He concluded with the dire warning that if "an epidemic break out of cholera, typhus, typhoid, or diphtheria the ravages would be fearful."[31] Four days later, another contributor to the *Times*, George Singer, confirmed that "the atmosphere for miles is poisoned, all healthful recreation is stopped, or become so dangerous that boating or bathing is a peril few will risk."[32] These three letters on the crisis in the Lower Lea were the first of many that the *Times* printed in 1884 and 1885. They made clear that its causes were simple: significant population growth in Tottenham increased the flow of sewage into the river, and a severe drought in 1884 reduced the flow of water during the summer months and left the sewage undiluted.[33]

The letters increasingly blamed the LCB and the Tottenham Local Board for failing to remedy the problem.[34] In late August, George Corble, the clerk of the LCB, wrote to defend his board against the charges of inaction. Corble provided historical context by describing the protracted fight between the LCB and Tottenham: "Ever since 1868 the conservators have been pressing the Local Board (Tottenham) on the question, and certain enlargements and improvements at the sewage works have taken place."[35] He explained that the LCB had referred the issue to the home secretary in 1875, but the minister had sided with the Tottenham board. When the problem recurred, the LCB again referred it to the home secretary, who had commissioned a public inquiry in January 1884.[36]

The findings of the inquiry, presented to the board in early June, finally allowed it to give the Tottenham Local Board notice. In July, the local board was informed that if it did not act within twelve months, legal proceedings would commence. Because the home secretary's recalcitrance had delayed the sanction of Tottenham, Corble insisted that the public should not blame the conservancy:

> Your correspondents have not exaggerated the filthy condition of the river below Tottenham in the least, but, bound down as the conservators are by certain clauses in an Act of Parliament, they feel that they cannot be justly charged with failing to fulfil their public trust in the face of the increasing attention they have given to this nuisance and their anxiety to bring the river back to the pure condition it was in about 20 years ago.[37]

He failed to mention that the LCB's powers had been further curtailed earlier in the year, when it had gone to court in hopes of stopping Hertford from dumping its poorly treated sewage into the Lea above the East London Waterworks intake. It had lost its case.

In early September, Hertford's town clerk, C.E. Longmore, wrote to the *Times,* responding to the letters that condemned the upstream towns. He defended Hertford's right to dump sewage effluent into the Lea. A provision in the 1868 legislation that created the LCB allowed towns that had historically discharged their sewage into the river to continue doing so, as long as they treated it to the "Best Means Possible." In practice, this language made litigation very difficult, as it was open to interpretation and no scientific consensus existed. To prove that Hertford was not guilty of contaminating the Lea, Longmore referred to the recent case in which it had defeated the LCB. Justice Williams had found that if the town "thoroughly and efficiently subject the Hertford sewage to the best practical process of purification they are not liable to an action for discharging the effluent into the river."[38] The judge accepted that Hertford did meet this standard of treatment and concluded "that this action ought to be dismissed, and dismissed with cost."[39] The case left the LCB with a large legal bill and few options to stop others from polluting the river.[40] It did not have the financial resources to persist with such expensive litigation and could not improve the condition of the Lower Lea until the national government and the courts ceased siding with the polluters.

This court decision went against the opinion of a growing number of sanitary engineers, led by Edward Frankland, who questioned the effectiveness and safety of the settling tank purification methods used along the Lea and throughout Britain.[41] In their opinion, dumping sewage effluent into rivers that supplied drinking water posed a major risk to public health. However, a number of influential experts rejected these concerns and downplayed the implications of the newly emerging germ theory for engineering safe water systems. Dr. Charles Tidy was the principal opponent of those who sought tighter regulation of water quality in the 1880s.[42] Tidy may have lacked influence among other scientists, but he was very articulate and effective at debating Frankland in public. He worked closely with the water companies and opposed Frankland at every turn: "He believed chemical methods of water analysis were adequate to pronounce waters safe, doubted germs caused disease, and maintained that rivers purified rapidly."[43] Tidy testified on behalf of Hertford in their successful defence against the litigation brought by the LCB. He employed chemical analysis to confirm that the town's purification techniques worked, and argued that its sewage effluent would be rendered harmless by natural oxidation and would not endanger downstream consumers.[44] The scientific uncertainty introduced by Tidy and other chemists reduced the effective legal power of the LCB and slowed its campaigns to prevent sewage effluent from entering the Lea.

In yet another letter to the *Times*, R. Willis identified the lack of a unified suburban government as the real problem that allowed the pollution of the Lea. The fragmented jurisdictions in Outer London allowed sewage and toxic waste to flow into the river: "Along the valley of the Lea are the boundaries of numerous parishes – artificial districts – but whose limits nature disregards." He elaborated: "I venture to think the heaviest portion of the burden arises from the limited parochial area, within which all its sanitary requirements have to be dealt with, as though it was an island

without any natural connexion with its next door neighbour."[45] Willis
hinted that natural regions, such as the river watershed, should be united
to manage a combined sewage infrastructure. The letters and the failure
of the LCB in the court together demonstrated that the political structures
implemented in 1868 to regulate the pollution of the Lea were largely
ineffective in dealing with the crisis resulting from the drought.

In 1886, a Parliamentary Select Committee on river pollution investi-
gated the crisis in the Lower Lea of the two previous summers. It interviewed numerous experts and stakeholders, including Corble and the LCB
sanitary engineer, Lamorock Flower. These two LCB officials testified that
the significant population growth since 1868 and the inadequacy of existing
sewage treatment options had made the mounting tide of effluent, treated
or not, excessive for the small river. Flower suggested that all sewage should
be diverted out of the Lea. As he and Corble explained, population growth
caused two problems. First, it often outpaced the construction of new
treatment facilities, which meant that some untreated or hastily treated
sewage inevitably entered the river. Second, the constant growth resulted
in too much sewage effluent flowing into the Lea at the same time as water
companies diverted much of its water during the summer.[46] In any event,
even the best chemical treatment did little more than deodorize the sewage. Obviously, the valley needed an intercepting sewer, comparable to
the London Northern and Southern Outfalls, designed by J.W. Bazalgette
and built in the early 1860s (Figure 6), or it would remain an open cesspool
during the hotter months.

A year earlier, Bazalgette had intervened in the public debate. In a letter
to the *Times,* he suggested that his 1860s proposal for an integrated sewer
in the Lea Valley be reconsidered. Bazalgette feared that politicians would
take the easier solution of connecting Tottenham to the London system.
The suburbs around London were continually expanding, and he felt that
the London system could not cope with their sewage: "At the beginning
of the present century the population of London was not a million, whereas
it is now four millions, and is increasing at the rate of about 70,000 per
annum. The result of this is that our intercepting sewers, reservoirs, and
pumping establishments have ample work to do for the metropolis alone."[47]

Bazalgette suggested that because the Metropolitan Board of Works
sewers were already nearing capacity, the various local governments in the
Lea Valley needed to work together to implement their own long-term
solution. Their failure to co-operate was the sole factor that delayed the
implementation of his proposed solution: "This is the only difficulty in

FIGURE 6 J.W. Bazalgette's Northern Outfall Sewer under construction, November 1861. | Newham Archives and Local Studies Library.

the way to accomplishing what I venture to think is the only means of thoroughly purifying the River Lea and effectually draining the towns in that valley."[48] He encouraged one of the suburbs to take a leadership role and present his 1860s plan to Parliament. Bazalgette recognized the difficulties facing these suburbs, chiefly that leading the effort would be costly for one municipality. Nevertheless, he stated that "without some such combination and works the River Lea will continue to be a foul stream, and the polluting sewage a constant source of litigation."[49] In the end, Lamorock Flower proposed a short-term compromise solution in which Tottenham diverted all its sewage to London during the summer months.[50] This alleviated the worst of the unpleasantness, but it did not eliminate the problem of pollution in the Lea.[51] Local governments remained unwilling to acknowledge the major challenge posed by population growth, and they continued to delay paying for an integrated sewer system.

Efforts to deal with Tottenham's sewage did not solve the wider problems, and by 1898 suburban growth in Leyton and Walthamstow again sent a regular flow of sewage effluent down the Channelsea River through the heart of Stratford. As with all the previous cases, West Ham's location at the bottom of the valley put it at the receiving end of pollution from the upstream communities. A local Conservative MP, Ernest Gray, rose in Parliament and asked the Conservative president of the Local Government Board "whether his attentions has [sic] been drawn to the condition of that part of the Channelsea river which lies within the county borough of

West Ham; whether he is aware that, under certain conditions of tide and
of weather, this water is little better than an open sewer, and therefore
dangerous to the public health." The president responded that he knew
of the "far from satisfactory" conditions, but he claimed that his ministry
had little power to solve the problems and no "authority to determine the
local responsibility."[52] The national government remained unwilling to
acknowledge that suburban municipalities could not address the issue of
urban river pollution.

IN 1900, AN ARTICLE in the *British Medical Journal* considered the continuing problem of sewage in the Lea Valley. It listed as a source of pollution
the sewage farms in the valley, which irrigated and fertilized agricultural
land with sewage to divert the waste from the rivers, but remained a threat
when the waste seeped back into the river. The article also listed other
sources of pollution, from malting and sewage effluent generated by
Hertford and Ware, through to the run-off from skin-dressing establishments and garbage at the "West Ham Tip" that flowed into the Lea at
Carpenters Road. The article confirmed that sewage remained a major
problem throughout the Lea Valley and echoed Bazalgette's call for the
installation of a Lee Valley Main Drain.[53] A similar proposal surfaced
during the 1930s, but the challenges of developing an intercepting sewer
in the Lea Valley persisted until the 1950s, when the development of New
Towns in the river's catchment area forced the national government to
organize and help finance a comprehensive scheme. With significant
population growth planned in the upper reaches of the watershed, the
importance of the Lea as a supply of drinking water finally provided the
motivation for an advanced engineering solution, almost a century after
Bazalgette first developed his plan for the valley.[54]

3

Living in West Ham

WEST HAM FACED considerable environmental and social challenges during the second half of the nineteenth century. Heavy industrialization and rapid population growth remade its landscape. Many people lived on the marshlands and in close proximity to the factories and the polluted rivers, with daily exposure to smoke, sewage, and other contaminants. The early residential development in these new suburban outposts was haphazard, unregulated, and without sufficient sanitary infrastructure. Visitors and locals recognized the unhygienic conditions and voiced their concerns about the living situation. The unhealthy environment was a major factor in defining the social hierarchy of West Ham and London more generally. Discerning the low standard of living in Canning Town or west Stratford was not difficult. Local people could see and smell the squalor and pollution. Official reports confirmed and reinforced the connections between disagreeable social and environmental conditions. Commentators and politicians, in turn, used vivid descriptions of the urban environment to critique social inequality in London.

The lack of effective regulations and resources available to municipal governments in West Ham exacerbated the role of population growth in transforming the ecosystem. Laying out a network of streets and constructing houses, shops, and municipal buildings created a very dense landscape that increased the threat of and damage done by flooding. The network of water pipes, sewers, canals, and natural rivers produced a hybrid hydrologic system in the Lea watershed. Ineffective sewage infrastructure compounded the environmental transformation brought by suburban development and created an unhealthy landscape for people, plants, and animals.

The hybridity of the landscape extended well beyond the rivers in the Lower Lea Valley. The factories and homes formed a patchwork, with surviving green space in the form of farms, gardens, parks, and wetland.[1] As a result, West Ham's location on the edge of the receding countryside provided some positive opportunities, as people were able to use the remaining open spaces for recreation and agriculture. The extensive marshlands and numerous rivers constrained urbanization, and green corridors connected the densely populated and industrial core of West Ham with rural landscapes in the Lea Valley and the Thames Estuary. Hybridity also caused problems, as much of the intensely developed portions of West Ham lay on former marshes and were subject to regular flooding. The environmental flux was matched with economic and social instability. Living in West Ham presented numerous challenges, with environmental and social problems overlapping, and the population suffering the consequences of the unhealthy environment.

Londoners over the Border

During the mid-nineteenth century, the pace of development began to accelerate in West Ham, and its environment soon showed signs of degradation. The parish had no municipal government when the railway arrived in 1839, and there were no planning regulations or building codes to restrict the development of Hallsville and Canning Town when they grew up alongside the Victoria Dock during the early 1850s. These remote suburban outposts showed evidence of dramatic environmental and social problems from the start. The insanitary conditions came to the national government's attention in 1855, when more than eight hundred West Ham ratepayers petitioned it to extend the 1848 Public Health Act to their district and provide them with a local board of health.[2] The government responded by sending a civil engineer, Alfred Dickens, to investigate and write a report on the sanitary conditions of West Ham. The region's environmental and health problems received wider attention two years later, when *Household Words*, a weekly paper published by Alfred's brother, Charles, printed the lead article titled "Londoners over the Border," written by Henry Morley.[3]

Alfred Dickens identified the growth of housing on the marshes in the west and south as the major problem in the parish. His report described the appalling situation in districts near the Lea and its back rivers. He often mentioned the complaints of the inhabitants, which suggests that not only middle-class visitors, but also local residents, sensed the disturbing smells and connected them with poor health.[4] His discussion of the ten homes at Wood's Yard highlighted individual concerns:

> There is a privy in the end house in a room under a sleeping apartment. Mr. Duck informed me that this was used, to all intents and purposes, as a public privy. It is in a most foul and filthy condition, and smells most offensively. The tenant of the cottage (Mrs. Applethwaite) says the smell in the bedroom is almost unbearable, and her children have frequently suffered from it.[5]

Many homes were built along the pre-existing marsh drainage ditches, with their privies overhanging the sluggish waterways. Alfred described an example that lay behind New Street, on the marsh near the Channelsea River: "At the backs of the houses are privies emptying into an offensive ditch, which gets a little water through it at certain times of the tide. It was, when I saw it, nearly dry, and words cannot describe its foulness."[6] Using marsh ditches for household drainage was normal throughout the district, where it produced numerous stagnant open sewers. When they did drain, the raw sewage went directly into the Lea.[7] However, the bowl-like shape of these former marshlands, with drainage intended to reclaim land for agriculture rather than housing, meant that much of the sewage remained in place. This resulted in terrible smells and created a constant threat to public health. Alfred also pointed to the arrival of noxious industries along the rivers, which further damaged the environment and health. In the worst cases, the same streams that transported sewage and industrial waste also supplied drinking water because a significant number of homes remained unconnected to the East London Waterworks in 1855.[8] Regular floods also spread the contents of the ditches and rivers across the land and into the homes. In the aftermath of Alfred Dickens's report, Parliament extended the Public Health Act to West Ham and created a new local board of health.[9]

Morley's article, published two years after Alfred's report, argued that Canning Town and Hallsville remained foul and neglected by the new board of health. He claimed that the board focused its resources on less pressing issues in Stratford, where the majority of this elected body lived. His portrayal of West Ham at the start of the population boom remains evocative and provides one of the most descriptive sources on its social and environmental state. After noting the futility of using legal boundaries to define the limits of London and discussing the concentration of noxious factories in the Lower Lea Valley, Morley described his first visit to southern West Ham, which occurred in wet weather. He highlighted the boggy conditions, suggesting that "it is a district, at such times, most safely to be explored on stilts."[10] During this period of London's expansion, marshlands were commonly transformed into residential and industrial landscapes, but what Morley observed at West Ham was that residential development on drained marshes created an unhealthy and flood-prone environment.[11] He pointed out that Canning Town and Hallsville had been built seven feet below the high-water level in Bow Creek and that only "very ancient banks of earth" held the river back during high tides.[12]

The rest of his article described a second trip, taken in dry weather, which initially concealed the many environmental problems of the area. As mentioned above, Morley focused on the agreeable rural character of West Ham before contrasting it with the insanitary housing on the marshlands: "There are pleasant belts of trees, with here a spire, there a church-tower, upon the horizon; and in the foreground, groups of cattle feed."[13] This description was reminiscent of the railway print (Figure 2) of the region from two decades earlier, which also highlighted rural continuity.

While Morley borrowed familiar romantic rural sentiments, his positive description of the mixed agricultural and industrial landscape was punctuated by his central theme, that the wetlands constituted a danger to health: "The district, on such a day, seems more inviting than repulsive. The wide plain of valuable pasturage – for the marshes that give ague to men, give grass to beasts."[14] His reference to ague, a term for malarial fevers, underlined the health threats posed by the marshland.

Morley deployed some of the analysis in Dickens's report but with considerably more literary licence:

> We come to a row of houses built with their backs to a stagnant ditch. We turn aside to see the ditch, and find that it is a cesspool, so charged with corruption, that not a trace of vegetable matter grows on its surface – bubbling and seething with the constant rise of the foul products of decomposition, that the pool pours up into the air. The filth of each house passes through a short pipe straight into this ditch, and stays there.[15]

Noticing a small flock of ducks in the ditch, Morley reinforced the social consequences of the sewer-infused landscape: "Upon its surface, to our great wonder, a few consumptive-looking ducks are swimming, very dirty; very much like the human dwellers in foul alleys as to their depressed and haggard physiognomy, and to be weighed by ounces, not pounds. Some of them may be ducklings, but they look like the most ancient ravens."[16] Animals and humans both suffered in the unwholesome environment.

Like most people of his day, Morley connected foul smells with disease. He explained that the parish surgeon "was himself for a time invalided by fever, upon which ague followed," and he linked the surgeon's ill-health with the degraded environment of West Ham: "Ague is one of the most prevalent diseases of the district: fever abounds. When an epidemic comes into the place, it becomes serious in its form, and stays for months. Disease comes upon human bodies saturated with the influences of such air as this breathed day and night, as a spark upon touchwood."[17] Although the miasmic theory would be superseded by the germ theory, Alfred Dickens and Morley were nonetheless correct in linking insanitary conditions with human disease. Malaria had been a threat in the Thames Estuary through to the mid-nineteenth century, and the standing sewage that accompanied residential development increased the risk of diarrhea, typhoid, and cholera, all of which were transmitted via the fecal-oral route.[18]

The remainder of the *Household Words* article dealt with the inaction of the local board of health. Despite its newly granted powers, it had failed to act except for spreading some deodorizing chemicals. Morley urged that more of the recommendations in Alfred Dickens's report be implemented and ended with, "We need hardly say, that the level of the marsh ought to be no obstacle to the proper drainage of a town built over it. If it be worth while to put a pump over a coalmine, certainly it is worth while to put one over the place by the river-side to which the sewage of a little town may fall."[19] Instead of arguing that the marshlands should have been exempt from suburban development, the article demonstrated a faith in technological progress and a belief that coal and steam engines should have been used to drain the area for human habitation.

HOUSING FOR A QUARTER MILLION

Dickens's report and the Morley article both show that extensive harm had already been inflicted on the Lower Lea and its marshland during the early years of suburban development, in the decade before the influx of a quarter of a million people between 1861 and 1911. Better drainage significantly reduced malaria in the Thames Estuary by the end of the nineteenth century, and a proper sewer system eventually removed the standing raw sewage from residential districts.[20] However, diseases that arose from

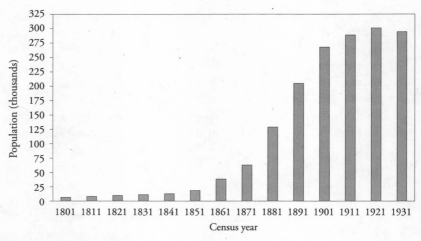

FIGURE 7 West Ham population, 1801–1931.
Source: Great Britain GIS project at the University of Portsmouth, "West Ham CP/AP through Time: Census Tables with Data for the Parish-level Unit, 1801–1961," A Vision of Britain through Time, http://www.visionofbritain.org.uk/unit/10241388/cube/TOT_POP.

overcrowding and poverty remained a major challenge to the end of the nineteenth century, as the scale of growth between the 1860s and the 1890s overwhelmed the local government.

Between 1801 and 1911, the population of West Ham increased from approximately 6,500 to almost 300,000 (see Figure 7), and residential building dominated the landscape. The early-nineteenth-century population congregated in three villages – Stratford, West Ham, and Plaistow – on the edge of the marshlands (Map 2). Stratford, which straddled the road between London and Colchester, was the largest. The small village of West Ham stood to the east of the old abbey grounds, a short distance south of Stratford; Plaistow lay a little farther southeast.

Map 14 depicts West Ham as it was in 1867–70, immediately before three decades of rapid population expansion. It shows significant growth away from the marshlands in the north of the parish. Stratford expanded around the Great Eastern Railway works, which provided many jobs. The railway also enabled the development of Forest Gate, a small middle-class suburb in the northeast, which had good connections on the Great Eastern into the centre of London. A second commuter railway service contributed to the expansion of Plaistow during the mid-nineteenth century. The growth farther south was more remarkable, as Canning Town

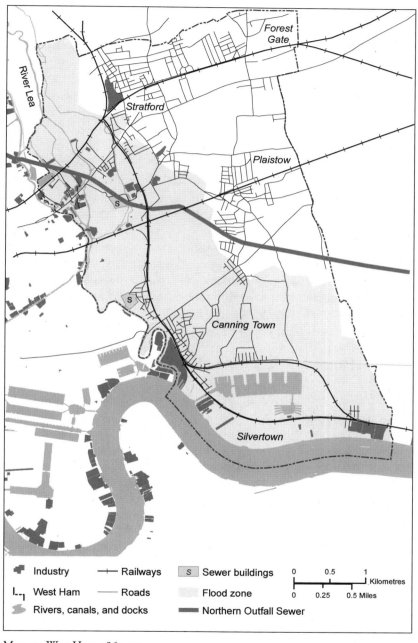

Map 14 West Ham, 1867–70

developed in twenty years into a major population centre near the docks. Silvertown remained very remote in the late 1860s, with just one cluster of houses for company employees at Samuel Silver's India Rubber, Gutta Percha, and Telegraph Works.[21]

Map 15 shows the 1893–95 landscape transformed by the influx of new inhabitants. The 1880s saw the single biggest increase in a decade, as the population reached 204,903 in 1891. Residential development filled in the gaps between Stratford, Forest Gate, and Plaistow, and spread out across the marshlands. The Ham House estate was protected from this incursion, as the Corporation of the City of London acquired the land and created West Ham Park in 1874.[22] New residential developments also appeared near the factories in west Stratford. In the south, Canning Town grew considerably and accounted for a large proportion of the population increase. Most of the available land in Silvertown between the railway line and the docks also filled in with housing, creating remote communities near the large factories.[23]

The maps reflect the social differences between the various regions of West Ham. The flood zone roughly corresponds with the original marshland, showing the division between low and high ground. The maps do not fully capture the unique topography of the region, in which the Northern Outfall Sewer stood "higher than the adjacent houses" and divided West Ham in two.[24] The most impoverished communities established themselves on the former marshlands at the south and west. Their more prosperous suburban counterparts, which housed regularly employed railway workers and middle-class commuters, sprang up in the northeast, where the land rose away from both the rivers and industry. This distinction was not uniform, and as with much of London, even the better neighbourhoods contained impoverished streets and homes.[25] The street network also reflected the social divisions, with the early streets in Canning Town laid out in a haphazard web, originally determined by the drainage ditches, whereas those in Forest Gate, northern Stratford, and even the newer examples in the south were more orderly and spacious. The old disorganized streets were the most socially disadvantaged by the early twentieth century. Figure 8 shows housing in an unidentified street in Canning Town during the 1890s.

In 1906–07, the Outer London Inquiry Committee completed a housing survey of West Ham. The committee surveyed the housing types, rents, and levels of subletting in each of the new wards, but because of limited resources, it did not perform a house-by-house census with the same detail

River Lea

West Ham
Park

S

Mill
Meads

Farm

East London
Cemetery

Farm

Farm

Farm

Recreation
Ground

S

Allotments

Cricket
Grounds

S

Industry	Railways	S Sewer buildings
West Ham	Roads	Flood zone
Rivers, canals, and docks		Northern Outfall Sewer

0   0.5   1
Kilometres

0   0.25   0.5 Miles

MAP 15 West Ham, 1893–95

FIGURE 8 Living conditions in Canning Town, c. 1890. | Newham Archives and Local Studies Library.

as Charles Booth's earlier investigation of London.[26] Nonetheless, its report provides a detailed picture of the social divisions in West Ham.[27]

West Stratford and the southern marshland districts contained the majority of the low-quality housing, cheap rents, and subletting. The state of the housing often corresponded with the age of the street and its proximity to the rivers. The areas adjacent to the Lower Lea River were built first, and thus many of the most rundown streets were located there. The report's authors clearly associated poor housing with immorality, noting that the "lowest class of loafers and very irregular workers" in the older parts of Canning Town lived "in the short streets and culs-de-sac off the Victoria Dock Road":

> In one short street were six different types of houses; at the end a block of half-a-dozen were ruined and uninhabited; some six-room houses, in very bad repair, were let in halves at 3s. 6d. each half. They were in a filthy condition with wet walls and paper peeling off, and were inhabited by tenants who only had sacks for bedding. In some of these houses four families have lived at one time.[28]

The investigators reported on a few locations in which dilapidated buildings stood on poorly drained marsh, creating the worst possible conditions. Hermit Road featured "houses and shops of an old type, many of which seem to have been built on a marsh without adequate foundations, and are gradually subsiding into the soil."[29] Many dwellings in southern West Ham were newer and of better quality than these extreme examples. Rents in the working-class districts varied from about 3s. 6d. per week (£9.1 a year) for half a house in the worst streets to 12s. a week (£31.2 a year) or more in better neighbourhoods. Crowding, however, was a widespread problem, and many homes were either converted by the landlord into halves or sublet by the tenants, in which case one of the flats often had inadequate kitchen facilities.[30] Overcrowded, old, and poorly built homes contributed to the social and environmental instability of the marshland section of the suburb.

The northeast region was developed as a middle-class area, with parks and better-quality housing. The best homes were either owner-occupied or rented annually for between £28 and £80 a year. Some of the homes near West Ham Park were very large and housed the remaining wealthy elite in the suburb. As the demand for housing continued to expand in the late nineteenth century, new infill development surrounded the older large homes, which reduced social distinctions.[31] Residents in the northern end of the borough also had access to Wanstead Flats, a large park just north of Forest Gate.[32] In terms of formal parkland, the north held a clear advantage over Canning Town in the south, but in terms of access to open land, everyone in West Ham was better off than most residents of East London.

PATCHWORK LANDSCAPE

In contrast with the older East End on the London side of the Lea, West Ham did not transform as completely into an urban-industrial landscape. In the late nineteenth century, houses and factories co-existed with farms, gardens, and marshes in a hybrid landscape (Map 15). When population growth slowed significantly during the early twentieth century, large sections of this open land were converted to parks and allotment gardens.[33] These areas were affected by suburban and industrial development; parks were carefully managed landscapes, clay was mined for brick making, fields were used for intensive gardening, and large amounts of household garbage were collected and deposited in the peripheral wetlands. Public health reports record that two garbage dumps were situated near the brickyards in the remote northwest Temple Mills area during the early twentieth century.[34] The minutes of the Public Health Committee chronicle an ongoing search for dumpsites as the town decided whether to build a dust destroyer (incinerator). As the population increased, so did the amount of household waste. Late in the 1890s, the borough corporation collected more than thirty thousand tons of waste each year.[35] Discarded on the marshlands, it filled holes and raised the level of wet ground.

A number of farms survived in West Ham through the second half of the nineteenth century (see Map 15), although most disappeared before 1914. Piggeries and allotment gardens persisted. Pig barns are not clearly identified on maps, but reports from the veterinary inspector to the Public Health Committee recorded outbreaks of swine flu at various places throughout West Ham in 1898–99. Most of the barns seem to have held a few dozen animals and were located either among the housing in Canning Town or on the edge of the built environment in Plaistow and Temple Mills.[36] Allotment gardens became important spaces for recreation and for working-class men and their families to supplement their wages with small-scale agriculture.

The slow decline of farming and the continuity of food production in West Ham point to its location between the city and the countryside. Even after major industrial and population growth, two corridors of open agricultural and marshlands directly connected the heart of West Ham with the countryside: the Lea Valley, running north-south, and Plaistow Marsh, which linked West Ham with green space in the Thames Estuary. Because these corridors survived, West Ham remained distinct from the more densely crowded East End. Neither Whitechapel nor Poplar had large open spaces for new parks and allotment gardens at the end of the nineteenth century. Instead, urban reformers turned the graveyards of East End churches into small parks to create little parcels of open space in these crowded neighbourhoods.[37]

Living with Industry and Polluted Rivers

In a 1902 pamphlet written in response to a series of *Times* articles that critiqued the first Labour government in West Ham, J.J. Terrett, a local socialist politician, provided geographical and social context for what the local government faced in the suburb. Like the *Household Words* article from a half-century earlier and the 1880s letters to the *Times* concerning

FIGURE 9 Channelsea River and Abbey Mills Pumping Station. | Newham Archives and Local Studies Library.

the state of the Lea, his pamphlet focused on the disagreeable aspects of the suburb. It explained that West Ham was "built in a vast marsh, a considerable portion of which is below high-water level, and is intersected by numerous tidal backwaters, on the banks of which factories of every description are erected."[38] The *Times* attacked the Labour government's extravagant spending, and Terret responded by highlighting the major challenges the suburb faced. Terrett sarcastically characterized the walkway built on top of the Northern Outfall Sewer that passed through the industrial landscape as "West Ham's 'boulevard'" and asked why the *Times* series did not "severely censure the extravagance involved in this outlay."[39] He continued that the *Times* had missed an opportunity to draw a picture of a "working man, rolling in ill-gotten gains ... recreating himself by promenading along this embankment with a gasworks on his right, a sewage pumping station on his left, two chemical works behind him, and a soap factory in front."[40]

Figure 9 shows the industrial landscape Terrett had in mind, with the Northern Outfall Sewer and the Abbey Mills Pumping Station (the chemical factories were located behind the photographer).[41] This was just one of the clusters of heavy industry that West Ham residents might have seen though their back windows or passed on their way to work. Smokestacks, gasometers, and polluted rivers were simply a fact of life for them.

In conclusion, Terrett focused on areas near the Thames: "In the south of the borough are Victoria and Albert Docks, with their huge attendant army of semi-casual workers, and beyond that the industrial district of Silvertown with its collection of immense factories and wharves fronting on the River Thames – a desolate region." At Silvertown, "the atmosphere is blackened with smoke and poisoned with the noxious fumes of chemicals, and the stench of bone manure and soapworks, and the only sounds to be heard are the shriek of railway engines and the mournful foghorn hoots of the steamboats coming up the river."[42] Terrett connected the docks with the social problems of underemployment and the chemical factories with air pollution. He then evoked the sounds and smells in this landscape in contrast to the more wholesome sections of London. Figure 10 shows an open sewer in Silvertown at the turn of the century, confirming the picture painted by Terrett of this particularly unpleasant region. Like Alfred Dickens and Henry Morley before him, Terrett linked the social and environmental problems of West Ham.

Turn-of-the-century concerns about pollution were not limited to socialists like Terrett. The local conservative newspaper, the *West Ham Guardian,* also expressed anxiety over the air quality and the polluting industries in the borough. Its editorial pointed out in January 1899,

> Offensive smells are far too prevalent in various parts of West Ham, and it is high time the council authorities commenced a crusade against the offending parties. Of course, West Ham benefits by the situation of factories in its midst and must be prepared to suffer some little inconveniences. But these stenches are no trifling annoyance; and can surely be abated if not abolished.[43]

An earlier editorial of December 7, 1898, suggested that a noxious environment was a danger to health: "So far as West Ham is concerned, we are afraid that the condition of public health is even worse than in other parts of London. Filthy streets and crowded slums are not the conditions which have been found to be favourable to longevity, nor do they assist in the maintenance of a high moral tone."[44] The *Guardian* went further than Terrett had a few years later, by suggesting that a degraded environment was also a factor in the demoralization of the poor.[45] The editorial concluded with a hopeful view of the future: "A city without smoke, a river

FIGURE 10 An open sewer in Wilton Street, Silvertown, c. 1900. Although sewers were improved in West Ham during the late nineteenth century, some open sewers remained at the turn of the century. | Newham Archives and Local Studies Library.

as pure at Canning Town as it is at Richmond; the substitution of electric for steam traction; of cremation for burial; and of motor cars for horse vehicles – these with some other reforms would enable London to become the healthiest and pleasantest and brightest city in the world."[46] Conservatives and socialists agreed that high levels of pollution threatened public health in West Ham.

Despite its many disadvantages, people who grew up in West Ham remembered some positive aspects of its environment. At a time when urban children often suffered from rickets due to vitamin D deficiencies that arose from a lack of exposure to sunlight, access to open spaces significantly improved the quality of life in parts of West Ham.[47] The River Lea was also a recreational site; north of West Ham, its waters sustained enough fish to support angling.[48] Figure 11, though it may have been staged, provides some evidence that children fished the back rivers in West Ham.

According to the few oral histories left by individuals who grew up in West Ham before the First World War, allotment gardening and raising poultry were popular pursuits.[49] So, for example, the father of the Mahoney family in Canning Town kept a very productive allotment that allowed him

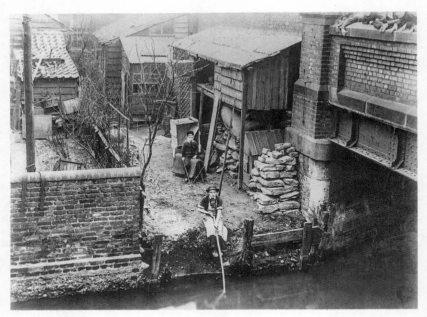

FIGURE 11   Unknown boy fishing. | Newham Archives and Local Studies Library.

to sell some of the surplus to neighbours and to supplement his irregular work as a stevedore at the docks.[50] Some employers provided allotments on spare land near the factories. Mr. Bushnell gained an allotment through his employer, the Bromley Gasworks, which passed to his son after he died in 1930.[51] The undeveloped lands also provided space for children to play. The Bushnells lived near one of the large open spaces that remained along the Lower Lea through the early decades of the twentieth century, and the son remembered playing games and catching birds south of the Bromley Gasworks.[52] But West Ham was by no means a garden city. To augment the limited access to open spaces and parks, families and charities occasionally provided opportunities for urban children to travel out of the borough. Most interviewees remembered escaping the crowded streets of Canning Town with trips to Epping Forest, rural Barking, and Woolwich Commons.[53] A few recalled trips to the seaside and summer vacations that were paid for by Country Holiday Fund.[54] These interviews hint at how Canning Town residents felt about the area in which they lived. As London spilled outward, transforming fields into industrial and crowded residential zones, they still sought out green spaces during their limited leisure time. None of the interviews echo the harsh critique that informs Terrett's pamphlet, but the fact that so many childhood memories focused on the few brief trips out of this manufacturing suburb suggests an awareness of its negative aspects.

THE MAPS AND PHOTOGRAPHS of West Ham illustrate a hybrid landscape created through intensive industrial development and shaped, aided, and hindered by a waterlogged natural topography. The rivers changed, as new factories crowded their banks and human and industrial waste fouled their waters, but the streams continued to play an active role, both supporting and damaging the newly built environment and local economy. The rural landscape of drained wetland, market gardens, pastures, and small pockets of industry, mills, and housing gave way to densification. The burgeoning population produced an abundance of sewage and other household waste, contaminating the newly built areas and the remaining open spaces. The geographic, economic, and environmental conditions in West Ham set it apart from both London's declining industrial core and the expanding commuter suburbs elsewhere in Outer London.

The close correlation between social and environmental problems was a constant theme in nineteenth-century descriptions of West Ham. In the worst cases, families shared small homes that were slowly sinking into the mire and in the immediate vicinity of heavy industry. Although the situation of West Ham residents was slightly better than that of the residents of the even denser East End, their marshland districts were overcrowded, poorly built, and very polluted. West Stratford, Canning Town, and Silvertown were predominantly working class and were often plagued by high levels of underemployment. Poverty and a degraded environment went hand in hand. People who possessed sufficient resources decamped to healthier locations, a pattern that constantly reinforced the social divisions in West Ham and London more generally.

Close attention to the distinctive geography and environment of West Ham provides a foundation to reconsider the history of rapid urban growth on the eastern edge of London. By assessing the extent of the environmental decline in these first chapters, we have developed a new understanding of the spatial context from which we can re-examine West Ham's social and political transformations in the remaining chapters. The environmental and social divisions established by the mid-nineteenth century and reinforced during the decades of population growth shaped the politics of the borough. The south provided early support to independent labour and socialist candidates. These southern marshland districts also confronted public health officials with major challenges during the 1890s and were the centres of the unemployment crisis during the early twentieth century.

4

The Labour Group
and the Water Question

O N AUGUST 20, 1898, the East London Waterworks Company (ELWC)
announced that for the third time in four years, it was limiting the
water supply in the East End, West Ham, and other eastern suburbs to
six hours a day. During the hot, dry summer of that year, the ELWC had
depleted its reservoirs in the Lea Valley, and by mid-August it was clear
that the supply would not last if the amount of water flowing into the East
London network were not reduced. The company tried from the start to
deflect criticism by pointing to the prolonged and unprecedented drought
that led up to the shortage, but the public remained unconvinced. Most
newspapers, municipal politicians, and water consumers identified the
greedy monopoly, not the weather, as the real culprit.

A few months later, in early November, with the water restrictions still
in place, West Ham held a municipal election. This was won by the Labour
Group, a coalition of labour union leaders and socialists, who campaigned
on a diverse range of issues, from core labour matters like the eight-hour
workday to municipalization of trams, gas, bakeries, markets, and water.
The Labour Group won power more than a year before the formation of
the national Labour Party, initially called the Labour Representation Committee, and resulted in the first Labour-controlled municipal government
in Britain. An editorial in the *West Ham Guardian,* a conservative newspaper, pointed to the water supply problem to explain this triumph: "By
taking advantage of the water question, and playing it for all it was worth,
the labour party succeeded in calling the large number of voters. This, with

the lavish promises which can never be filled, was the means of winning the support of the fickle ratepayers."[1] This quote clearly links the Labour Group's breakthrough victory with the water question, but was the *Guardian* correct in its analysis?

Throughout Greater London, the consumer-driven attack against the water monopolies crossed class, party, and ideological lines. A coalition of progressive Liberals, labour union leaders, and socialists in East London and West Ham worked to channel the anger of consumers and reclaim the advantage in a decade-long struggle to establish municipal control of the water supply.[2] In West Ham, the 1898 crisis highlighted the wider problems of social inequality, particularly when local conditions were compared with the wealthier and cleaner regions of Greater London, which enjoyed a constant supply of water throughout the drought. This helped create a shared experience of inequity and provided the Labour Group with an effective political narrative to unify the diverse voters of West Ham.[3] The shortage enabled the Group to broaden its electoral coalition, supplementing its existing supporters with enough angry water consumers to outnumber a depleted Conservative vote.[4]

The Labour Group victory in West Ham was an example of urban environmental instability playing an important role in Britain's broader transition from laissez-faire liberalism to a more interventionist social democratic politics during the late nineteenth and early twentieth centuries.[5] The struggle over the water system in Greater London during the previous decade and the growing critique of natural monopolies help explain why the water shortage developed into a major political issue. In West Ham, consumer anger translated into electoral support for a coalition of labour leaders and socialists. This was crucial, as even in this heavily industrialized suburb, with its large population of manual workers, the limited franchise meant that the Labour Group needed the crisis to break through electorally.

CONSUMER EXPECTATIONS AND THE ROOT OF THE CRISIS

Numerous factors caused the water crises of the 1890s. Among them was population growth: in 1851, the East London Waterworks Company serviced a little over 400,000 residents. By 1891, this number had expanded to more than 1 million. As the supply failures of the 1890s demonstrate, the ELWC did not respond quickly enough to this change.[6] Simple arithmetic, however, only partly explains the shortages.

Three decades earlier, an investigation of the 1866 cholera epidemic had highlighted the inadequate and intermittent water supply in much of the East End. Many families relied on a shared tap in the street, which often provided water for only a few hours each day.[7] It should be noted that most homes had water tanks or cisterns, so the intermittent daily supply did not inconvenience people who lived in adequately equipped and well-maintained homes.[8] By the 1890s, in contrast, metropolitan consumers expected the ELWC to maintain water pressure throughout the day. Many household cisterns had been removed for sanitation reasons and had not been replaced, because continuous water made them redundant. In the poorest neighbourhoods, including the low-lying districts of West Ham, the lack of cisterns intensified the crises of the 1890s, as people could no longer store water.[9]

The expectation of a continuous supply, and more generally that the urban environment would remain stable, was grounded in a new outlook that arose from living in the leading "modern" city of the late nineteenth century. Due to a wide range of economic and social changes, people felt that they were "living in a particularly 'modern' age."[10] The enormous growth of cities, scientific knowledge, European imperialism, the mounting scale of manufacturing, mass advertisement, and regular availability of consumer goods all set the late nineteenth century apart from earlier times. Moreover, due to the efficiencies brought by expansion of the networked city and the arrival of electric and gas lights that replaced the dull illumination of oil lamps and candles, the "manmade tempo of great cities" began to supplant the "diurnal, seasonal and annual rhythms of the natural world."[11]

Britons increasingly believed that rational scientific planning and capable engineering could bring consistency and stability to more and more aspects of modern life. Expanded consumption not only amplified the volume of goods they could buy, it also created a steady supply of a wider range of products. Expanding knowledge allowed experts to engage in rational planning. This could result in a well-organized supply of food, water, and energy, more affordable life insurance, and state intervention in the economy to stabilize the labour market. The public believed that social problems would eventually be resolved by science and technology: "Past ages of ignorance, scarcity, and irrationality were deemed, not to be wholly done away with, but to be working themselves out like a long-division sum."[12] This modern sensibility made the water supply failure of the 1890s into a larger political issue than it might have been a few decades earlier. The ELWC failed to live up to the new expectations of the public, who were

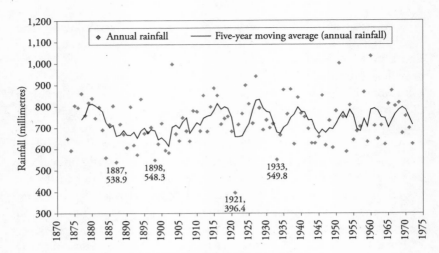

FIGURE 12 Annual rainfall data for southeast England, 1873–1972.
Source: Met Office Hadley Centre Observation Data, http://hadobs.metoffice.com/
hadukp/data/download.html.

increasingly willing to support governments that would take control of
the water supply, putting it under the management of publicly employed
experts instead of market forces.

By the mid-1890s, after decades of rapid population growth, the East
London water system had begun to fail. Its inadequacy became evident
during a winter frost in 1894 and the hot and dry summers in 1895 and
1896, all of which caused short periods of intermittent supply. Then, in
1898, a prolonged drought and hot summer contributed to the near collapse of the system and more than three months of supply limitations.
The weather was a contributing factor, but the private ownership of
the Greater London water system was the primary cause of the prolonged
crisis.

Rainfall data confirm that 1898 was the fourth driest year between 1873
and 2014, supporting the ELWC claim that a severe drought had caused
the shortage. Moreover, the five-year moving average trend line in Figure
12 shows that a dry period spanned the mid-1880s to the first years of
the twentieth century. The Lea's reduced flow could not meet the needs
of both the ELWC and the New River Company, which supplied central
London. At its lowest level in September, the Lea was flowing at between
23 and 25 million gallons a day.[13] The New River Company diverted about
16.5 million gallons each day, leaving only about 7.0 million gallons for
the ELWC. As the two companies normally relied on the river for between

50 and 60 million gallons a day, the reduced flow led to the near collapse of the East London water system.[14]

The monopoly control of Greater London's water supply created a crisis out of the drought. The historical rights held by eight monopolies, rather than a rational distribution of available resources, managed the region's water. The New River Company's right to divert water from the Upper Lea dated from the seventeenth century, obliging the younger ELWC to rely on the remainder of the flow. During a drought year, the older company was still entitled to divert its full amount, leaving the ELWC in crisis. If Greater London had not been divided into eight zones that were controlled by independent monopolies, the surplus from other areas could have been used to remedy East London's shortfalls in the 1890s. Unfortunately, the water networks were not connected until September 1898, when engineers built the pipes that would transfer surplus water to East London.[15]

The ELWC was in a difficult situation because of the limited supply in the Lea and because there was no other major water source in the east of Greater London. As the population expanded in East London and the northeastern suburbs, the company needed to find other means of supplying its product. Piping Thames water from the west side of Greater London was a costly venture, and sinking deep wells was an expensive gamble, as the extent of the groundwater resources was unknown. Reservoirs provided the only viable solution, as they could store water during the winter for use in the summer. Their drawback was that they required large and expensive infrastructure for the rare instances of major drought. The Lea Valley reservoirs, which had been significantly expanded after the 1896 shortfall, were sufficient for most normal dry years but were not enough for 1898.[16]

THE IMMEDIATE PUBLIC RESPONSE TO THE "WATER FAMINE"

On June 20, 1898, the ELWC's 1.2 billion gallon reservoirs were full, but after a few weeks of dry weather, the River Lea dropped significantly, and the company began to draw heavily on its reserves. By the end of July, the reservoirs were down to 550 million gallons, so the ELWC turned to the New River Company to boost its supply. Between July 19 and August 15, it bought between 4 and 12 million gallons a day from New River, slowing the depletion of its reservoirs.[17] The drought persisted, however, and the limited rain in August, most of which came in short, heavy bursts, did little to alleviate the situation. To prevent pollution from entering the system, the ELWC could not collect the first rush of water after a storm, so a prolonged rainfall was needed to begin refilling the reservoirs.[18] By mid-month, New River's own supply had come under pressure, and it decreased its daily assistance to 4 million gallons.

On August 17, William Bryan, the ELWC engineer, and I.A. Crookenden, the company secretary, began planning to limit the water supply. These two men understood that shifting to an intermittent supply would be a public relations disaster. Bryan wrote to Crookenden on August 18, saying that all he needed was a little more sleep and he would be ready to "tackle the whole of the press and 1,290,000 irate consumers in addition."[19] They knew from the 1895 and 1896 experiences of restricting the supply that the ELWC would encounter a major backlash of public criticism. Moreover, they could foresee that the progressives on the London County Council (LCC) would use this third supply crisis in four years to bolster their demand for municipal control of the water network, which dated back to the 1880s.[20] Bryan and Crookenden publicized the restrictions via posters and letters to the press, and attempted to counter their opponents by framing the problem as a weather event. The ELWC notices and posters of August 18, which announced the discontinuous supply, blamed the "severe and continuous drought" (see Figure 13). Unfortunately for the ELWC, Bryan and Crookenden could not control the message. From the beginning of the reduced supply, they dealt with a hostile public and press, largely determined to end the private control of water in Greater London.

The resulting prolonged water famine was a major political issue in both West Ham and East London. The crux of the argument focused on whether a greedy monopoly or the weather were to blame. The return to intermittent supply in 1898 provided new fuel for the fight between the progressive government of the LCC and the national Conservative government over municipal control of London water.[21] George Shaw-Lefevre, a leading member of the LCC and former president of the Local Government Board in Rosebery's Liberal government, held that people were suffering because of the inefficient monopoly control of the water system. There was "no doubt," according to Shaw-Lefevre, "that if in 1895 the purchase Bills of the County Council had passed through Parliament, there would have been no water famine in the autumn of that year, none in the year 1896, and none in the current year."[22] In 1898, London lagged behind many other major cities in Britain, the United States, and Canada, where the water supplies had come under municipal control during the middle decades of the century.[23]

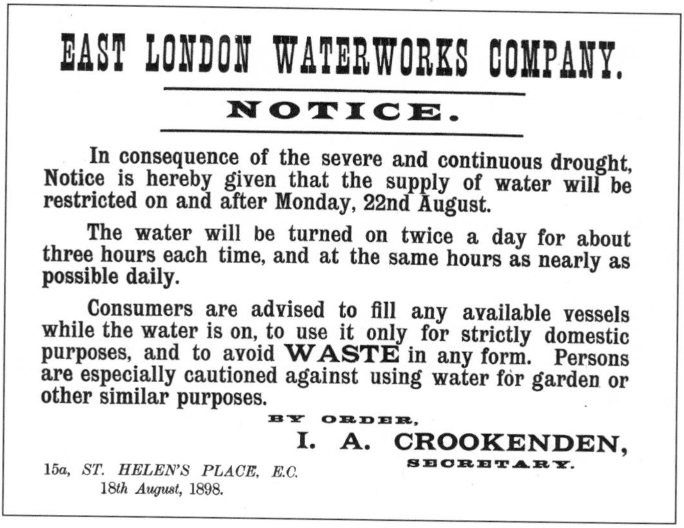
EAST LONDON WATERWORKS COMPANY.

NOTICE.

In consequence of the severe and continuous drought, Notice is hereby given that the supply of water will be restricted on and after Monday, 22nd August.

The water will be turned on twice a day for about three hours each time, and at the same hours as nearly as possible daily.

Consumers are advised to fill any available vessels while the water is on, to use it only for strictly domestic purposes, and to avoid WASTE in any form. Persons are especially cautioned against using water for garden or other similar purposes.

BY ORDER,

I. A. CROOKENDEN,

SECRETARY.

15a, ST. HELEN'S PLACE, E.C.
18th August, 1898.

FIGURE 13 ELWC flyer announcing the intermittent water supply, August 18, 1898. | Poster in Public Notices, Bills and Posters Concerning Water Shortage and Saving including 2 Bills in Yiddish, Files on Droughts, East London Waterworks Company Corporate Records, ACC/2558/EL/A/16/002, London Metropolitan Archive.

The campaign to end private control of London's water began in the late 1880s, when the newly formed LCC became dominated by a coalition of progressive councillors. The LCC agitated for municipal control on both ideological and practical grounds. Fabians and Liberal progressives believed that municipal control of basic services was a key means to improve urban conditions, and they associated utility monopolies with vestiges of undemocratic privilege.[24] They were also concerned that the Thames and the Lea could not provide enough clean water for the rapidly growing population. In the early 1890s, the LCC engineer, Alexander Binnie, recommended that a massive public works project bring water from the hills of Wales. The cost of this endeavour necessitated public control and provided a practical reason for the LCC to take over the water system.[25]

A royal commission led by Lord Balfour, a banker, Conservative peer, and occasional cabinet minister, rejected the dire warnings of the LCC and reported in 1893 that Greater London's water supply was safe until 1931.[26] The Balfour Report supported the water companies' contention that expanding the reservoir network in the Thames and Lea Valleys would provide enough water for the growing metropolis.[27] The efforts to bring London's water under municipal control took another blow with the defeat of Rosebery's Liberals in the 1895 election. The incoming Conservative government, headed by Salisbury, wanted to avoid increasing the power of the left-leaning LCC and opposed both municipal control and the Welsh scheme. With the support of the Balfour Report and the national government, the water monopolies appeared to be winning their struggle to maintain control. This changed with the ever-worsening series of supply failures in East London between 1894 and 1898, which demonstrated the failings of the privately controlled monopoly system.[28]

Water emerged as a political issue in West Ham immediately after the late August announcement of the supply restriction. Two local newspapers responded with anger to the news of yet another shortage. In a lead editorial titled "The Water Scandal: Our Annual Famine," the conservative *West Ham Guardian* blamed the ELWC, arguing it was "a public scandal that such matters as water supply should still be in private hands and that we should still be at the mercy of persons who are working for dividends only."[29] Three days later, the local Radical and pro-temperance liberal newspaper, the *Herald,* provided a similar perspective, asserting that West Ham residents were "in the grip of a scandalously immoral monopoly." It suggested that the ELWC should "be wiped out of existence" but, citing the experience of previous years, predicted that "everything will be forgotten directly [when] the company announces the resumption of full supply."[30] The *Herald* identified the shortage as a political issue, imploring readers not to forget that the monopoly had caused hardships once the full supply was reinstated. As it turned out, the full supply did not return until after the local election in 1898, so the subject remained at the forefront of voters' minds. These newspapers gave little attention to the drought and hot weather, placing the blame squarely on the ELWC.

West Ham's Labour politicians also engaged with the shortage soon after it began. On August 27, the Labour Group sent an open letter to West Ham mayor William Ivey, a moderate, asking him to take a number of steps. It demanded that information should be gathered on the public health dangers caused by the intermittent water supply, that "a town's meeting should be held at once in view of joining other authorities in providing a proper and continuous municipal supply of water," that "money should be spent by the Mayor to a limited extent to provide the poorer residents with storage utensils," and that the local MPs, both of whom were in the Conservative government, should be invited to help find a solution.[31] Tying the water famine to public health concerns and poverty helped expand the issue beyond consumer politics by linking it to the wider social problems of West Ham.

Mayor Ivey responded with an open letter of his own, answering each of the Labour Group's points. He stated that he was already dealing with the immediate problems by instructing the medical officer of health to monitor the health effects of the shortage. He had also met with William Bryan of the ELWC to develop a scheme to assist the poorest residents of West Ham. Ivey was more reluctant when it came to holding a public meeting and concocting a plan to supply municipal water. He explained that the meeting would have no legal standing and therefore would merely be a venue to express opinions, but he made the town's halls available to the Labour Group to organize its own meeting. Ivey's letter also appeared to downplay the significance of the shortage. He referred to the "difficulties caused by the present spell of dry weather," which suggests that he accepted the company's excuse for the scarcity. He pronounced himself satisfied that the ELWC was "willing to do everything in their power to prevent inconvenience or trouble being caused by the existing shortness of supply" and concluded, "I do not think myself that any more can be done than has already been arranged."[32] Ivey's tone made it clear that he was not willing to lead West Ham in the struggle to replace the water monopoly with municipal control; nor was he interested in endorsing the inflammatory statements made by other politicians in West Ham and East London. His reluctance to join the fight against the ELWC probably damaged his fellow moderates who were up for re-election that November and established the Labour Group as the local political faction that was willing to take leadership on the water issue.

As the final days of August merged into September, the newspapers became a site of conflict between differing representations of the "water famine" or "drought." The *Times* defended the ELWC, whereas the two West Ham papers maintained a regular attack on the company for its irresponsible management of the water supply and for putting profit before people. On September 3, the *Herald* published a parody of the ELWC posters, which undermined the company's public relations campaign:

Notice.

To E.L.W.W. Shareholders

In consequence of the depression of trade and serious lack of money experienced by many householders, the shareholders of the East London Water Company are hereby warned that the supply of dividends will be restricted. For the next ten years dividends will therefore be shut off, and at the end of that time one-twentieth of the former annual percentage may be turned on for a short while. Shareholders and directors are, however, STRICTLY WARNED not to waste the money supplied to them, as it is very scarce, and difficult to obtain. For all common purposes they will be able to purchase farthingsworth [sic] of food and other articles at many shops in the East End. Workhouses have also been placed at convenient intervals. It is hoped that these advantages will be appreciated, and that there will be no devilment or spending half-pennies all at once, or other wanton extravagance or riotous living on the part of the shareholders, which might lead to a further curtailment of the supply.[33]

The *Herald* published two regular political columnists, one expressing Radical and Liberal views, and the other Labour and socialist perspectives. Both commented on the water issue. The socialist and Labour columnist, who wrote under the pseudonym "Proletaire," noted on August 27 that the socialists were the first to take up the matter and suggested they were gaining credibility by championing it.[34] The *Herald's* parody, along with the more serious editorial comments and the content of its two political columns, suggested to readers that company greed was the cause of the famine.

The *Times,* in contrast, portrayed the situation in a very different light. Its special correspondent and editors depicted the shortage as the "failure" of the Lea, blaming nature instead of humans for the crisis. The pages of the *Times* expressed a plurality of views, as the almost daily coverage of public meetings and protests communicated the regular attacks of public bodies and local leaders against the ELWC, but the paper's special correspondent regularly challenged these perspectives. This reporter, who was not identified by name, wrote with the authority of an expert and used this superior knowledge to support the company against its many critics.

His lengthy articles were better informed than the limited reporting of the local papers, and they openly set out to correct what he argued was misinformation concerning the supply failure. In his first report, published on August 29, he rejected the language used to convert an unfortunate drought into a social justice issue. He argued that the inconvenience and minor hardship produced by the intermittent supply did not justify the hyperbole of local papers and politicians: "To speak of a famine is ridiculous."[35] His second report proclaimed, "The cause of the present difficulty is the failure of the river Lea in consequence of the prolonged drought."[36] This report provided a close examination of where the company got its water and why the prolonged drought had caused the intermittent supply. Subsequent articles dealt with the substantive effort to connect the ELWC network with those of other water companies and consistently attacked the social arguments made by other newspapers, politicians, and the public in mass meetings.

Two weeks into the crisis, the *Times* published an editorial that defended the ELWC: "The so-called 'water famine' in East London has given rise to a good deal of descriptive reporting and to loud complaints of the neglect and greed of water companies in general."[37] The editorial lauded the articles of the paper's special correspondent, claiming that they had provided a "better idea of the real facts than many of the sensational utterances of ill-informed indignation by which it is attempted to guide public opinion."[38] The *Times* attempted to deflate the social critique and show that the ELWC had done everything humanly possible to avoid the shortage.

The press in West Ham, however, never accepted the drought argument and represented the shortage as a social problem caused by an irresponsible monopoly. Obviously, the reporters and their readership would have known that rainfall had been scarce and the weather unusually hot, so it is interesting that they refused to see the drought as at least a major cause in the failure of the water system. The popular primacy of social and political rather than environmental causes of the shortage resulted from a complex mix of factors, including the social geography of East London, the ELWC's disastrous public relations throughout the shortage, vocal politicians, and finally the broad faith in progress and engineering that made it difficult to believe the supply could fail in late-nineteenth-century London.

THE POLITICAL RESPONSE TO THE FAMINE

The geography of the water shortage was significant, as the people of East London and West Ham saw the famine as yet another injustice inflicted upon them because the rest of London continued to enjoy regular service despite the drought. The *West Ham Guardian* linked the famine with the wider environmental and social problems that beset East Londoners. In its first editorial on the crisis, it asserted that "city life, even at its best, has many disadvantages, compared with that of the open country, but in the East End, in sultry weather, it is marked to an unnecessary extent by conditions fatal to health and happiness."[39] The *Guardian* connected the water problem to the established sense of urban inequality. The fact that service was not disrupted in the rest of Greater London, even as East London and its suburbs endured more than three months of shortages, made the company's drought argument increasingly untenable.[40]

For its part, the ELWC did little to better its public image. During the mid-1890s, it had blamed droughts so often that the public had become distrustful of such assertions. The "droughts" of 1895 and 1896 were less severe than the one in 1898 (see Figure 12); in reality, population growth and inadequate reservoirs caused the intermittent supply of those years. The company further damaged its image in late August and September 1898 by suggesting that consumers were wasting water. It complained about waste in the press and published yet another leaflet to promote conservation among its customers (Figure 14). Unfortunately for the company, this coincided with its announcement that the water supply would be reduced to two periods of two hours each day, with the result that public anger merely intensified.[41]

Much of the "waste" arose simply because people left their taps on, positioning tubs underneath them to ensure that they collected whatever water happened to flow during the day.[42] Given the circumstances, this tactic was entirely rational, but the *Times* special correspondent chastised those who employed it, charging that they were "really helping to bring disaster on themselves and their neighbours by this criminal behaviour."[43]

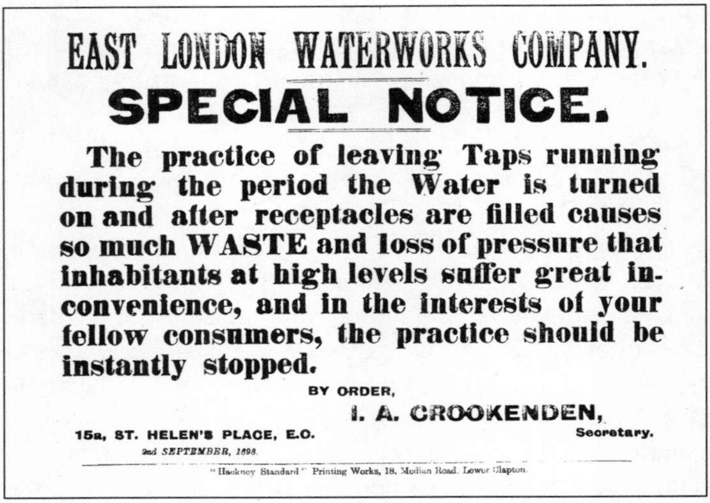
EAST LONDON WATERWORKS COMPANY.

SPECIAL NOTICE.

The practice of leaving Taps running during the period the Water is turned on and after receptacles are filled causes so much WASTE and loss of pressure that inhabitants at high levels suffer great inconvenience, and in the interests of your fellow consumers, the practice should be instantly stopped.

BY ORDER,
I. A. CROOKENDEN,
Secretary.

15a, ST. HELEN'S PLACE, E.C.
2nd SEPTEMBER, 1898.

"Hackney Standard" Printing Works, 18, Median Road, Lower Clapton.

FIGURE 14 ELWC flyer on water wastage, September 2, 1898. | Drought 1898, Files on Droughts, East London Waterworks Company Corporate Records, ACC/2558/EL/A/16/015, London Metropolitan Archive.

Finally, a public letter from a cabinet minister, Henry Chaplin, the president of the Local Government Board, condemned the waste of water in East London, providing official support for this attack on consumers.[44]

Local politicians and the public reacted with outrage when the ELWC and the national government began blaming consumers for worsening the crisis. Months later, the Whitechapel District Board of Works remained upset and raised the issue in Parliament. An East London Waterworks Company memorandum noted, "the Whitechapel District Board of Works are very much offended at the Circular letter issued by Mr. Chaplin during the Drought stating that considerable waste existed in the East London District, and mentioning among other places, Whitechapel."[45] The *Herald* printed a similar concern from a local consumer: "I never 'waste' water, but while I am swindled out of what I pay for I shall use what I'd get just as I think best."[46] The issue of waste became a potent symbol of the ELWC's contempt for its consumers.

The company's practice of billing customers in full during the period of intermittent supply confirmed its greed and substantiated the impression that it put money before its consumers. It was legally entitled to demand full payment, and it argued that it could not be expected to suffer financially because of a drought. On this point, even the *Times* special correspondent demurred, and he called on the company to voluntarily decrease its billing during the supply failure. The London Metropolitan Archive possesses a large bundle of letters complaining about improper or unjust bills from the months after the famine.[47] These public relations mishaps created a receptive audience for the anti-monopoly critique.

Finally, as discussed above, many people believed they were living in the world's most advanced city and simply could not accept that a water shortage was possible. Given this, company greed must be responsible for it. The *Herald*'s Liberal and Radical columnist summed up this feeling on September 10: "It is somewhat amusing to read the books on the advances made in the Victorian era, and then look back and find that the old Romans supplied 300 gallons per head while we have to be content with the dribble which the shareholders of a company think fit to squeeze out."[48] Similarly, the chair of the public meeting at St. George's-in-the-East vestry hall said, "it was strange, considering the strides science had made, that in London, the richest city in the world, they should, at the close of the 19th century, have to meet and complain of a shortness in the supply of water."[49] The efforts of the *Times* and the ELWC to blame the drought for the supply failure largely fell on deaf ears, and the public became increasingly mobilized in support of the municipal control of water in Greater London.

Consumer Anger and Political Leadership

In September, political movements developed to pressure the government for an end to monopoly control of the water supply. Two public meetings were called in West Ham, one organized by the Labour Group in Canning Town and the other in Forest Gate at the Liberal Hall. Neither drew massive crowds, but the one in Canning Town on September 12 was larger than its Forest Gate counterpart of September 14. Councillor Arthur Hayday, the secretary of the West Ham Trades Council and a gasworkers union leader, energized his listeners with a condemning speech against the water company. Hayday wondered why government regulators controlled coal and milk retailing but allowed the ELWC to cheat its customers out of twenty hours of daily service. He then focused on the company's changing excuses for the 1896 and 1898 shortages: "Last time it was that the London County Council tried to stop them from building reservoirs, and now they had a reservoir but had no water to fill it."[50] Hayday urged the borough council to bring a bill to Parliament that would put the water supply under municipal control. He concentrated on the injustice that consumers felt and attacked the mayor and the rest of the political establishment for their inaction. This meeting helped to establish the Labour Group as the local leadership of the growing consumer movement that demanded municipal control of the water supply.

On September 24, increasing public pressure in West Ham and across East London resulted in a public meeting between Henry Chaplin and a delegation representing water consumers. In attendance were spokespersons for the Social Democratic Federation (SDF), the London Trade Council, East London Water Consumers League, East London Water Consumers Association, Bow Vestry, and the council, guardians, and schoolboard from West Ham.

SDF spokesperson George Lansbury explained to Chaplin that the delegation represented the mass public meetings recently convened in Victoria Park, West Ham, and Trafalgar Square to demand that the government resolve the water famine and the resulting injustice imposed on East Londoners. The delegation constituted a blending of consumer activism with socialist politics, as the supply failure disproportionally affected working-class people. It presented a motion passed at a public meeting, calling on the government "to use such pressure as is necessary to compel the companies responsible for the water supply of the metropolis to connect their mains and so allow all classes to be treated alike" and "to place the whole water supply under public ownership and control."[51]

After listening intently to the delegation's words, Chaplin responded comprehensively to its requests. He respectfully acknowledged the anger of East Londoners and claimed that he too was deeply frustrated with the situation. Unlike the special correspondent of the *Times* or its editorial board, he made no attempt to downplay the issue of social injustice. In fact, he accepted the framing of the crisis as a social problem, acknowledging "the inconvenience and mischief, and in a great number of cases of positive hardship and suffering, which have been inflicted upon the poorest classes of the community owing to the period of hot weather in this country."[52] Although this comment subtly invoked the drought as a cause, Chaplin went on to recognize the demand for a permanent solution. He pointed to the ongoing Royal Commission on Water Supply within the Limits of the Metropolitan Water Companies as proof that his government understood the seriousness of the circumstances and was developing a plan to fix the structural problems created by the monopoly control of water. The remainder of his long response dealt with what the Local Government Board was doing to solve the problem in the short term; the causes of the supply failure and why East London suffered, whereas the rest of the metropolis did not; the problems that must be surmounted before the supply could come under public control; and a defence of his own actions and those of the government. He did not rule out taking over the water supply, but he insisted that this could not be done as swiftly as the delegation and public meetings requested. Chaplin also referred to his letter on the waste of water, apologizing for the harm and insult he had caused.[53]

This public assurance from a cabinet minister demonstrates the effectiveness of grassroots mobilization against the ELWC and the monopoly control of the water system. The government had little choice but to comply with the demand that it take control of the system. In 1902, it passed a bill to nationalize the water monopoles, which would take effect in 1904.[54] Nonetheless, the famine continued into early November 1898. In West Ham, it became a major election issue and helped decide the vote.

THE WATER QUESTION AND THE ELECTION

The intermittent water supply was only one factor in the rise of the Labour Group in West Ham, but it did play a crucial role in developing enough support to overcome the voting restrictions that privileged affluent and older men. The suburb was an important locus of working-class politics before the 1898 election. It was a centre of New Unionism from the start. In 1889, Will Thorne, a Canning Town resident, led the formation of the National Union of Gasworkers and General Labourers at the nearby Beckton Gasworks. In the same year, the employees at the Royal Docks were involved in the creation of the Dock, Wharf, Riverside and General Labourers Union and the London Dock strike. Many New Unionism leaders, including Thorne, were also committed socialists. The energetic efforts of the SDF from the 1880s and the Independent Labour Party (ILP) from the early 1890s helped heighten the level of class consciousness in the suburb. In 1892, a year after Thorne became the first labourer on the borough council, the voters of West Ham South made history by electing Keir Hardie, the first independent labour MP.[55] This early upsurge in labour politics ended three years later, in 1895, when the Conservative candidate, George Banes, defeated Hardie.[56] The Conservative victories in the 1895 and 1900 national elections in both of West Ham's seats provide an important reminder of the fragility of the "forward march of labour," even in centres of unionism and working-class politics. Contingent events, such as the water crisis, remained important for mobilizing labour supporters, as the Conservatives retained significant levels of support through the early twentieth century, and the restriction on the franchise remained a large disadvantage for labour politicians.[57]

THE FRANCHISE

To understand why the water issue was so crucial in the 1898 election, we must remember that voter registration was more restricted in urban boroughs such as West Ham than in other districts throughout England. About 50 percent of adult males, or 25 percent of adults, were registered to vote in the national elections of 1900.[58] Low turnout reduced the electorate even further: only 59 percent of registered West Ham voters cast a ballot in the 1900 parliamentary election. Even fewer voters appear to have participated in the 1898 municipal election.[59]

The urban franchise after 1867 was a complex mix of inclusiveness and restrictions.[60] It encompassed the full spectrum of occupational categories, all the way down to casual labourers. Instead of disenfranchising people due to their occupation, this system primarily excluded women, adult children who lived with their parents, aliens (immigrants), tenants whose landlords resided in the same building or failed to pay their rates, poor relief recipients (including those on medical relief), and individuals who moved frequently.[61] All household heads, including a limited number of widows and unmarried women who lived independently, could vote in local elections. Despite the fact that the system encompassed voters from across the socio-economic spectrum, in urban settings it still discriminated disproportionally against the poor, including those with unstable employment and younger people, who were highly likely to fall into one or more of the disenfranchised categories.[62]

Many East Londoners moved frequently, which made it difficult to get onto the voter registry even if they did qualify. Subletting also played a major role in limiting the franchise in the poorer urban districts of the East End and West Ham. Generally, the male head of the primary tenant's household was automatically listed on the registry, but the heads of the other households in the building were not. Depending on the size and cost of the house, a primary tenant could come from any occupational category. Normally, this individual and his or her family paid the bulk of the rent and occupied the most rooms. They then sublet a portion or portions of the building to boarders or poorer families.[63] Thus, the primary tenant tended to be a member of the lower middle class, an artisan with a higher paying and stable job, or an older labourer. Most labourers would become enfranchised only after a number of their children had joined the workforce but remained at home, which allowed the family to occupy the main part of a house. Typically, the father would lose his vote after most of the children left home and he was forced to downsize.[64] As a result, people from the lower-paying and casual labouring jobs got to vote only at the height of their family's earning cycle, whereas the more affluent received the franchise sooner and kept it longer.

In West Ham, there was a high proportion of unofficial subletting, in which the tenants became landlords to help cover the rent. This arrangement disenfranchised a large number of casual poor in the crowded districts of the suburb, as only the head of the family that held the lease would be listed as a ratepayer.[65] In 1899, despite an effort by the Labour Group to roll back this reform, West Ham's four municipal wards were divided into twelve new ones (see Map 16), based on the size of the electorate, not the total population, and provided more representation for the wealthier districts in West Ham where more of the population was able to vote.[66] Five of the new wards were concentrated in the northeast, and seven were spread across the rest of the borough. There was a much higher franchise rate in Park ward, where the 15,273 residents in 1901 had more than twice the political repersenation as the 31,652 residents in West Ham ward. The survey of the Outer London Inquiry Committee clearly associated higher population wards with intense poverty and high rates of subletting.[67]

The restricted franchise meant that the Labour Group could not rely entirely on members of the new gasworkers or dockers unions, the labouring poor, and the unemployed, as many of them were not eligible to vote. The Group needed a significant amount of support from older workers with stable employment, many of whom voted Liberal or Conservative in national elections. It managed to accomplish this in 1898, when many working-class people remained skeptical about socialism and the need for independent labour politics, even among the leadership of the labour movement itself.[68]

THE CAMPAIGN

The water crisis was the key issue that allowed the Labour Group to reach out beyond its core constituents. Its early leadership in the days after August 20, 1898, helped increase its legitimacy throughout West Ham. The support for municipal control of the water supply gave Labour Group members an entry to wards in the north of West Ham, where labour union issues held less of an appeal. The Group overcame voter apprehension regarding socialism and emerged as the leader of the progressive movement in West Ham by adopting a pragmatic and compromising approach.[69] Will Thorne, Arthur Hayday, and other members of the SDF worked closely with Percy Alden, a Christian Socialist, and John Bethell, a progressive Liberal. Labour Group candidates came from a wide range of unions and political parties, including the National Union of Gasworkers and General Labourers, the Amalgamated Society of Engineers, the West Ham School Teachers Association, the Crane Drivers Union, the SDF, and the ILP. Some of this unity sprang from another contingent event: the Amalgamated Society of Engineers, who had a large membership in the north of West Ham, "were embittered by their [1897] strike defeat" and "threw their important local influence behind the socialists."[70]

The water famine gave the Labour Group more than two months to demonstrate its leadership abilities. In early October, as the moderate (Conservative) and progressive (Liberal) candidates slowly began to prepare for the election, the Labour Group candidates carried the energy from their water monopoly campaign into the municipal contest. On October 16,

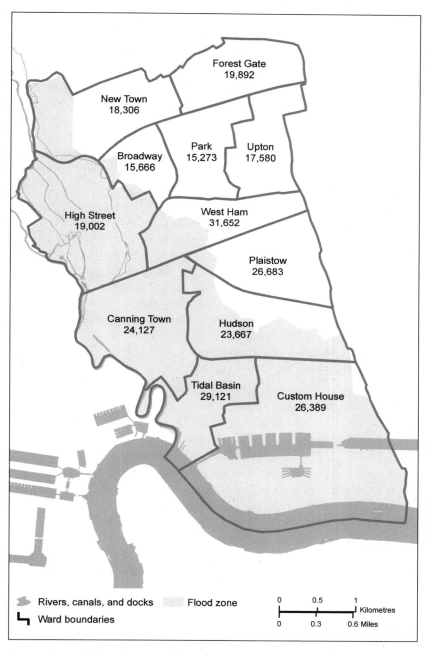

MAP 16   In 1899, West Ham was divided into twelve wards, based on electorate size, not population. The wards' 1901 population figures are shown.

the *Herald* listed the candidates who publicly supported municipal control of the supply. The Labour Group candidates and their progressive
ally, John Bethell, accounted for ten of the twelve names on this list. They
also made up ten of the twelve victors on election day.[71] By October 29,
most candidates from across the political spectrum had addressed the water
problem in their election platforms, and most supported municipal or
national control of the resource.[72] However, the early leadership shown
by the Labour Group in confronting the ELWC and the national Conservative government months before the election clearly gave it significantly
more legitimacy on this issue than its late-coming opponents. The correlation between the candidates who voiced unequivocal and early support
for government-controlled water and victory in the election reflects the
importance of the issue for the voters of West Ham.

As the campaign progressed through October, Councillor W.R. Athey,
the only Labour Group member running in the more prosperous Forest
Gate ward, pushed the water issue to the front of his platform, ahead
of working-class housing and the use of unionized labour for municipal
projects. Athey argued that municipal ownership could be a source of
revenue to reduce the pressure on ratepayers, making his public ownership
platform attractive to the wealthier voters in Forest Gate. He campaigned
for municipal control of the water supply, trams, lighting, and housing.[73]
Bethell had concentrated on the water issue earlier in October, and Athey
shifted his focus to the same subject, which suggests that it had significant
traction with the voters whom the two men encountered at their joint
rallies during the lead-up to the election.[74]

In the three remaining wards, candidates highlighted the water issue
to varying degrees. In the Stratford ward, Labour Group candidates J.J.
Terrett and Walter Scott were trying to break new ground. Terrett, a socialist
agitator and meat packer, and Scott, a schoolteacher and local ILP secretary,
capitalized on the sense that the Labour politicians were the only true
progressives in West Ham. They put water at the centre of their election
address, along with three labour issues: "Trade union wages, trade union
hours, no sweating, municipal water supply."[75] In this, they differed from
R. Mansfield and C. Pert, two of the three Labour Group candidates in
Canning Town, who buried the issue deeper in their platform. They focused
on stopping subcontracting for municipal work and providing union
wages, hours, and pensions for city employees. Moreover, they prioritized
improved housing, house-by-house sanitary inspections, and new restrictions on the collection of fish offal before the "municipalisation of trams,

gas, water, markets and bakeries."[76] Councillor C. Skelton, the third Labour Group candidate in Canning Town, followed the example of Scott and Terrett in according the water supply a prominent position. The *Herald* explained that Skelton "declares for trades union wages, hours, and conditions, useful work for the unemployed, and the abolition of the contractor wherever possible. He adds: 'I am in favour of municipalising the water supply, electric lighting extension, gas, tramways, and markets.'"[77] Skelton's message differed from that of Pert and Mansfield, reflecting the broad coalition of labour politics brought together by the Labour Group. He was the general secretary of the Crane Drivers Union and the secretary of the Labour Group, but unlike many of his colleagues he was not a socialist. This distinction prompted him to run his own campaign and to promote the water supply as a major issue, like the other progressives in Greater London, with whom he presumably aligned politically.[78]

When all the newspaper election coverage from October 29 is read together, the water supply failure clearly stands out as the most important issue in the contest.[79] The failure of Mayor Ivey and his fellow moderates to display leadership during the first weeks of the water famine had a dual effect in West Ham. First, it confirmed the growing sense that the political establishment lacked the conviction to follow the progressives of the LCC in tackling urban problems. Second, it allowed the Labour Group to firmly establish itself as a viable and responsible alternative, and as the only truly progressive voice left in West Ham. The Group was filling a void, as the Liberal Party had lost support in West Ham during the 1890s, and some of the remaining progressive councillors began to vote with the moderates on council to keep spending in check.[80]

The *Herald,* a liberal newspaper, endorsed the Labour Group in late October, after the North West Ham Conservative Association came out in support of Councillors Rippin and L.W. Spratt, who were affiliated with the Liberals. This confirmed for the paper that these councillors were not true progressives and thus no longer deserved the support of its readership.[81] In an editorial, the paper stated that though the Labour Group had "many faults," it had "been the sole representatives in West Ham of the policy and the aims represented in London by the Progressive party on the London County Council."[82] The paper urged its readers to vote for the Labour Group, despite its socialist affiliations, not because of them. The election results suggest that a significant number of progressive voters changed their allegiance for this election and helped sweep the Labour Group to victory.

The Results

The limited water supply persisted during the weeks leading up to the November 1 election and through to the runoff election, held three weeks later to replace councillors who were elected as aldermen.[83] On November 1, the Labour Group won nine of the twelve contested council seats, and its ally Bethell won the tenth, leaving only two for the opposition. In the runoff election of November 21, West Ham voters again demonstrated their resolve, choosing the Labour Group to fill five of the six seats. This gave the Group a majority of three on the borough council.[84]

The election records suggest that the Labour Group won its seats in Stratford and Forest Gate because Conservative voters either stayed home or temporarily switched their allegiance.[85] The *West Ham Guardian* blamed the Group's effective campaign, focused on the "water question," for swaying the electorate.[86] A few days later, on November 12, it acknowledged that the moderates had failed to develop a platform that dealt with the many problems of West Ham. It went on to admit that though their general theories were "wild and wrong," the socialists were the only faction that adequately addressed water, housing, and sanitation.[87] This failure of the political establishment to address the water issue and the wider urban problems of West Ham contrasted unfavourably with the early and energetic leadership shown by the Labour Group. By addressing the concerns of angry ratepayers while simultaneously using the water famine to develop a wider critique of social inequality in East London and West Ham, the Group broadened its appeal to the electorate. In contrast, the moderates and liberals, who had shared control of the borough council from its formation in 1886 to 1898, had made little headway in solving the many social and environmental problems of the suburb.

The Labour Group promised to address not only the water issue, but also the continued problems of sanitation, poor housing, lack of open spaces, inadequate public infrastructure, and unemployment, all of which had beset West Ham since the mid-nineteenth century. So, though its platform contained numerous promises that were directed at its core unionized supporters, it managed to expand and create a winning coalition of progressive voters. Its victory resulted from a combination of worsening disenchantment with established politicians and growing confidence in its leadership capabilities.

As London grew in the nineteenth century, the network of pipes, waterways, streets, and railroads that facilitated the flow of resources and waste in and out of the city became increasingly essential to supporting urban life. When environmental disturbances, such as floods and droughts, demonstrated the frailty of urban landscapes, individuals experienced the material consequences of too much or too little water. This collective suffering and the perceived inadequacy of the response by water monopolies and governments led to political repercussions. East Londoners' experience of dealing with weeks of an intermittent water supply was constrained and filtered by the available language, but this, along with the experience of hunger, changing employment markets, and polluted urban spaces, shaped public engagement with the increasingly varied discourses in the contested terrain of late-nineteenth-century urban politics.[88]

In 1898, the distress caused by a natural event, one of the worst droughts in southeast England on record, was magnified by the inefficient monopoly control of the water supply. Widespread focus by newspapers and politicians on the company's failure and rapacity amplified the political significance of the drought.[89] The increased solidarity between urban consumers helped expand the appeal of government intervention and social democracy. Clashes over the water supply changed during the nineteenth century from disputes over payment rates, which mirrored conflicts over taxation, to a new "politics of entitlement" that emerged during the 1894–98 shortages.[90] The shortage was a powerful force in the ongoing public debates about urban social conditions. Infectious disease, poor air quality, the lack of sunlight due to high levels of coal smoke, and unemployment were further examples of urban instability that increasingly shaped political language and practice at the end of the century.[91] The water crisis galvanized popular frustration and provided an opportunity to discuss the wider geographic divides between East and West London.

The water supply finally returned to West Ham and East London in late November and early December. The drought had subsided in October, eventually replenishing both the flow of the Lea and the ELWC reservoirs to the point where resuming full service became safe. However, repercussions continued to be felt, particularly through a spike in the number of infectious diseases, which the *Herald* linked with the prolonged shortage. On December 3, it published a short article in which it connected human health with the water famine. As it pointed out, the death rate from zymotic (infectious) diseases in West Ham was almost always high, "but the recent increase in the figures can be attributed with reasonable certainty to the defective water supply."[92] The paper reported on a motion presented to West Ham's council by Councillor H. Davis, condemning the ELWC for the rise in the death rate. The *Herald* stated that Davis "was in all probability right," as plentiful water was "essential for preventing the spread of typhoid from a patient," and nurses had confirmed that the hospital suffered from regular shortages. The writer felt that the situation was "enough to make one wish for a germ to destroy, not individuals, but the infernal system, which is the cause of so much disease in large populations."[93] West Ham's death rate due to infectious diseases, which the 1898 spike simply capped off, had escalated throughout the decade, a fact that helped elevate public health as a major priority for the borough council in the years that followed.

5
Environment and Health

D URING THE LATE NINETEENTH century, the prevalence of typhoid in
an urban region was a good indicator of the overall health of its adult
population.[1] Typhoid spreads via the fecal-oral route, meaning that insanitary conditions, ineffective sewers, and contaminated water or food produce
higher rates of the disease. The accumulation of human waste in the urban
environment was exacerbated during hot and dry weather, when there was
little rain to wash it away, and the number of flies increased significantly,
helping to spread the disease. Failing urban infrastructure, crowded and low-
quality housing, and dry summer weather all combined to create a very
unhealthy environment in many nineteenth-century cities.[2] In West Ham
during the 1890s, typhoid deaths increased at a faster rate than the population did. The socially marginalized inhabitants of the crowded marshland
districts suffered from higher rates of this deadly disease, but the local elite
were also at risk.

In early November 1898, the outgoing mayor of West Ham received a
letter from Ernest Baggallay, the stipendiary magistrate at the Police Court,
claiming that he had contracted typhoid due to the poor drainage and
insanitary state of the court building, which had also caused other serious
illnesses among his staff during the previous two years.[3] Baggallay, who
was forty-eight, had considerable standing in the community, both from
his position as a magistrate and as a former Conservative MP.[4] He refused
to return to work until the conditions at the Police Court improved.

In the weeks that followed, his concerns became a political issue, as some
councillors sided with him and questioned the findings of Lewis Angell,

the borough engineer, and Charles Sanders, the medical officer of health (MOH), who performed a joint investigation and found that the court's drains showed no evidence of sanitary problems.[5] The borough council commissioned Dr. John Thresh, the Essex County medical officer, to undertake an independent investigation, and his report suggested that insanitary conditions in the Police Court building "strongly predispose a person in frequent attendance, to contract" typhoid fever.[6] Undeterred, Lewis Angell firmly dismissed these findings. He was already on a collision course with the new Labour Group–led council because he opposed creating a works department. In his opinion, science demonstrated that "typhoid must be either eaten or drank." He reinforced this point by quoting the Bristol MOH: "The cause of Enteric fever must be looked for elsewhere than in occasional bad smells."[7] The experts of the day disagreed on the relative importance of environmental causes and the role of germs in the direct transmission of disease.

Like many members of the public, Baggallay associated disease with environmental conditions, so when he and his co-workers became ill, he naturally identified their shared workplace as the cause. Lewis Angell and Charles Sanders, who were proponents of the new germ theory, pointed to person-to-person transmission, perhaps from the low class of individuals who frequented the building, as the more probable vector. Like other public health experts, they increasingly shifted from "an 'inclusive' concern with the environment to an 'exclusive' focus on disease agents, people and their interactions."[8] In the end, the borough's Public Health Committee decided that there was insufficient "evidence to warrant the statement that typhoid fever was contracted in the precincts of the police court."[9] This public statement suggests that the committee had accepted the outlook of Sanders and Angell.

However, much of the public persisted in believing that observable environmental problems, such as filth and foul smells, caused what were known as the "zymotic" diseases – smallpox, scarlet fever, diphtheria, fever (typhoid and typhus), measles, whooping cough, and diarrhea. By the late nineteenth century, "zymotic" had become an anachronistic term, and its associated theory, that ferments caused infectious diseases, had been replaced by a more sophisticated understanding of micro-organisms. Medical officials clearly distinguished between distinct fevers such as typhoid and typhus, but MOHs continued to use "zymotic" to describe these infectious diseases in their official reports, as did the press. Popular associations between smells and illness dated back to the miasmic theory, which saw decomposition and the resulting gases as a major cause of disease. Although experts had long since dismissed the miasmic theory, the mechanics of germ transmission were not completely understood, which resulted in a protracted overlap between the old and the new approaches. Led by Robert Koch, scientists of the 1870s, 1880s, and 1890s identified many of the micro-organisms that caused deadly infectious diseases, but decades would elapse before they fully understood how these organisms moved through the population and the environment.[10] When health experts and engineers rejected the public's insistence that foul smells spread disease but were unable to provide a definitive solution to a deadly epidemic, tensions inevitably arose. The social context in which the experts operated limited their ability to embrace and implement the latest scientific findings.[11]

Focusing on micro-organisms provided a new way for public health officials to understand epidemics and prompted them to emphasize interventions, including mandatory notification, disinfection, isolation, and hospital care, to nurse individuals back to health – and more importantly, to stop the spread of disease. However, crowded and insanitary urban districts with poor housing and elevated death rates provided ample evidence for the public to connect environmental conditions with sickness. Recognizing this correlation, Charles Sanders and the borough council began in late 1898 to devote considerable resources to cleaning up the worst streets of West Ham. With the backing of council, Sanders pursued a highly successful multifaceted approach, in which he improved the sanitary condition of the borough while also expanding hospital resources and their ability to isolate sick children from the community.[12]

West Ham provides an interesting example of a wider trend in which urban districts struggled with high levels of infectious disease before finally achieving remarkable strides during the early twentieth century. For the past half-century, historians have debated the relative importance of the rise of scientific medicine, urban sanitary reforms, and the improved standard of living in increasing life expectancy over the long term. Thomas McKeown downplays the role of scientific medicine and suggests that urban sanitary reforms accounted for only about a quarter of the gains, most of which he attributes to a bettered standard of living.[13] This explanation remains useful in understanding the enhanced life expectancy, as malnutrition was certainly a contributing factor in the high death rates caused by numerous infectious diseases.[14] However, national economic development did not translate directly into better conditions in socially marginalized urban districts. There was a long delay between the significant economic growth of the mid-nineteenth century and the improvement in urban health, which became significant only during the final three decades of the century. Disruptive urbanization that corresponded with rapid economic growth in British cities caused high rates of death and disease for decades before political and social change brought about healthier conditions. Unstable urban environments "critically required mechanisms of collective action to solve expansive problems," but the prevalence of laissez-faire ideology limited government action.[15]

Joseph Chamberlin's three terms as mayor of Birmingham (1873–76) marked a turning point in municipal politics. Progressive Liberals increasingly used government intervention to ameliorate urban conditions and public health. However, this was not consistently implemented throughout England and Wales, and progressive mayors of larger cities proceeded faster than politicians in smaller districts and suburbs.[16] Long-standing political and legal structures insisted that those who directly benefitted from upgraded infrastructure should pay through local rates, based on property values.[17] This meant that impoverished districts in London and suburbs across England and Wales struggled to fund the necessary infrastructure and social services to provide healthy conditions for their growing populations.

West Ham lagged significantly behind the leading progressive cities during the final three decades of the century, as its local government grappled with the cost of draining storm water and sewage from the former marshlands, building and running schools and hospitals, and all its other responsibilities. The suburb lacked the broad tax base of Birmingham and could not rely on the national government for much beyond guaranteeing loans.[18] The constant tension between keeping rates low and addressing the real and pressing threats to public health remained at the heart of the borough's politics. The turning point for West Ham came in the late 1890s, during a diphtheria epidemic that coincided with a series of hot and dry years that elevated the health consequences of its dirty environment. A new political consensus emerged that supported increased public health intervention and spending.

THE SOCIAL CONTEXT OF HEALTH AND ENVIRONMENT

Between 1895 and 1900, diphtheria ran increasingly rampant in West Ham. This childhood throat infection creates a deadly toxin and sometimes leads to death from organ failure or asphyxiation. Reported cases in West Ham climbed from fewer than nine hundred in 1895, 1896, and 1897 to more than twelve hundred in 1899 and 1900.[19] Fortunately, the use of a new anti-toxin after 1896 and the fact that a disease strain of lesser virulence was at play kept the death rate from escalating as rapidly as the reported cases.[20] The diphtheria epidemic and reports about the growing number of deaths from zymotic disease in West Ham made public health a major political issue in 1899. Charles Sanders confirmed that during the two weeks ending on February 18, the zymotic death rate had risen in the borough.[21] On February 25, the *Herald* reported on a rumour, which suggested that up to fifty children were being treated for diphtheria in the Forest Gate District School.[22] This story raised alarm, as the middle-class residents of Forest Gate believed that they were sufficiently removed from the widespread disease found in the marshland districts of West Ham. They and their political representatives demanded action to address the spread of infectious disease into their healthy enclave. This created a challenging social and political context for Sanders, who knew that diphtheria spread through personal contact but recognized the need to appease people who still focused on controlling the sources of bad smells. In the longer term, however, heightened concern about public health in Forest Gate helped build political consensus in support of more resources for Sanders in subsequent decades.

Councillor F.H. Billows called attention to the problem during a February council meeting and proclaimed that there must be "something radically wrong with West Ham to produce such a high zymotic death rate." While Councillor H. Davis called out "Bad houses! Bad drainage!," Billows focused on the growing complaints about "fearful stenches which arose from the gullies in the streets." He suggested that if "the council thought it worthwhile to employ an expert to consider the sanitary condition of the police court, it was also worthwhile doing something to alter the present state of things in the borough generally."[23] In the ensuing debate, members of the newly formed Municipal Alliance and the Labour Group argued over whether they should focus on a flaw in the sewage vents or the poor quality of housing, some of it owned by the Alliance members themselves.[24]

The *Herald* took the middle ground and stated that both poor drainage and substandard housing contributed to high levels of zymotic disease in West Ham. It wrote that "zymotic disease signifies filth disease," even though advances in medical science had established that only some of these diseases were transferred via insanitary conditions. The *Herald* described the foulness of the situation: "The ancient open-drainage system of West Ham has been cut up by blocks of Jerry houses and left in stagnant ponds and blind ditches. It has been superseded by drainpipes, which do not always work properly. Again, our roads are by no means all made-up as in London, whilst we are provided with a special zymotic river, the Channelsea."[25] Clearly, this paper continued to associate disease with filth and argued for improving the urban environment.

Sanders could not fully disprove the widespread association between stenches and diphtheria. He understood that the disease spread through direct contact, but he also acknowledged that living in adverse environmental conditions might sap vitality and make residents more prone to contracting the illness.[26] The idea that smells and filth played a secondary role in infectious disease transmission remained powerful at the end of the century. Medical experts knew that people could be exposed to germs and not become ill, so it seemed reasonable to assume that the environment might make some people predisposed to disease. Doctors used the metaphors of seeds and soil to visualize this combination of environmentalism and germ theory: the seeds (germs) could not grow unless they were in hospitable soil (a body), where the necessary conditions existed.[27]

In July, the borough council addressed the diphtheria epidemic once more, and Councillor W. Godbold pointed to the stenches emanating from sewer gullies. Councillor A. Bishop, dissatisfied with the lack of action, launched a motion to force the Public Health Committee to study the problem of sewer gas and "report the best means of remedying the nuisance."[28] Although some Labour Group members continued to point to overcrowding and poor housing, the council ultimately supported Bishop's motion to study the issue further. In turn, the Public Health Committee instructed Sanders and J.G. Morley, the new borough engineer, to "prepare for their consideration a report with regard to the ventilation of the sewers throughout the Borough, and its connection with the death rate from zymotic disease."[29]

Sanders and Morley presented their reports in September, focusing mostly on the practical challenge of addressing the problem of sewer gas. Much like his predecessor during the Police Court debate, Morley began his report by quoting extensively from the latest scientific findings regarding the absence of any link between sewer gas and disease. These confirmed "that the principal, if not the only, source of micro-organisms in sewer air, is the air without the sewer and not the sewage," and "that there is very little ground for supposing that the micro-organisms of sewage, in the absence of violent splashing, become disseminated in the sewer air."[30] He went on to qualify this claim by admitting it was "quite conceivable, though at present no evidence is forthcoming, that the danger of sewer air causing diseases is an indirect one" and that it "may contain some highly-poisonous chemical substance."[31] Morley placed this evidence at the beginning of his report and probably hoped to convince council that sewer gas was at worst a secondary cause of illness.

Sanders took a more diplomatic approach than his new colleague, acknowledging from the beginning that sewer gas was a considerable problem: "The complaints are legitimate; the foul smells at times are nauseating in the extreme, and cannot but be detrimental to the public health."[32] He then provided some context, explaining that gas was an issue in most large towns and cities, and that it was no worse in West Ham than in other places. Nonetheless, the widespread nature of the problem "does not affect the question of injury to health from the inhalation of sewer air, as it is highly probable that odourless air passing out of a sewer may cause damage as well as noxious vapours."[33] Sanders had seen the correlation between bad smells, filth, and disease, and did not fully understand the degree to which poor environmental conditions made people vulnerable to infectious illnesses such as diphtheria. He noted that Bristol, the only large city with an unvented sewer system, had significantly lower rates of zymotic disease throughout the 1890s than all the other cities that had sewer gas problems. He suggested that the West Ham sewer vents be closed wherever possible, that shafts be installed to carry gas up to "safe heights," and that the sewers and streets be flushed more regularly.[34]

As the two experts had prepared their reports, diphtheria remained in the news, and large numbers of children continued to fall ill. On August 19, the *Herald* stated that the prevalence of diphtheria resulted from a "defective system of sewer ventilation from gullies in the public thoroughfares" and added that it "must be bad to permit sewer gas to escape into the roadways where children play."[35] A few weeks later, the *Herald* published letters from a Forest Gate resident named Charles Matthew and the Forest Gate councillor, Bishop, which claimed that council's inaction in addressing the smells from the sewers was responsible for the continued high rates of diphtheria and the resulting deaths. Bishop's letter suggested that all "council has been doing for 13 or 14 years is to make [the sewers] worse."[36] Although the paper noted that it rarely agreed with Bishop, it supported both his demand for action and his contention that the gas caused diphtheria.[37] Matthew, Bishop, and the *Herald* expressed a wider public concern with the link between sewer gas and the continued cases of diphtheria. Bishop's ally on council, Billows, hinted at the newspaper's role in shaping the public mood when he said he "was glad that the council were at last waking up to the fact that the increase of the zymotic death rate was in part due to the present method of sewer ventilation" and that "now that the public press had taken the matter up, they had got it taken up properly by the council."[38] The Labour Group accused Bishop of "politicking," as he was up for election in little over a month, and he knew full well that the Public Health Committee was already working on the issue.[39]

The Forest Gate resident, Charles Matthew, had also addressed his letter to the Local Government Board (LGB). Early in October, Noel Kershaw, assistant secretary at the LGB, wrote to the West Ham council, asking that it respond to a number of accusations levelled by Matthew.[40] Arguing that West Ham was significantly less healthy than London, Matthew had focused on diphtheria:

(3) Diphtheria causes a large proportion of the deaths from zymotic disease and the existing fever hospital accommodation is inadequate to receive all cases; an extension of the hospital is now in hand.

(4) Diphtheria is most prevalent and most fatal at Forest Gate (including Forest Gate, Park, and Upton Wards), although this is a new district with good roads, gardens, and house drainage almost entirely carried out under the supervision of the Town Council's Inspectors. Upon the occurrence of disease the house drains are almost uniformly found to be in good order.

(5) With such general conditions as tend to check disease some special cause of such disease must exist.

(6) Such cause is to be found in the offensive stench from the sewer gratings in the parts of the district suffering most from diphtheria.

(7) The nuisance recurs annually and its return is always attended by increased diphtheria and other zymotic disease.

(8) Complaints have been made to the Town Council, but nothing is done beyond occasional flushing and use of disinfectants, which do not lessen the nuisance and danger to health.[41]

He concluded that "a great amount of preventable infectious disease in the Borough of West Ham is the direct result of a defective system of sewerage," and he accused council of failing "to take immediate action to prevent further sickness and death."[42] In reaction to this letter, Kershaw requested that the borough council "instruct the Medical Officer of Health to prepare a report as to the circumstances under which the epidemic prevalence is maintained and as to the measures of prevention recently taken by the Medical Officer of Health or the Town Council."[43] Sanders duly prepared a document to address the accusations of Matthew, to explain his analysis of the outbreak, and to summarize the actions needed to reduce the disease in future.

Sanders again approached his task with care, clarifying the many junctures at which he disagreed with Matthew but avoiding a direct confrontation with the popular environmental understanding of the causes of disease. He pointed out that many other towns and cities were then experiencing high levels of diphtheria, which meant that a general cause was at work, not merely local conditions. He used a wide range of statistical evidence to show that West Ham was healthier than Matthew had suggested and that rapid growth created a population where lower death rates, but higher infectious disease rates, were to be expected, as many such diseases mostly affected infants and children. He demonstrated that while Forest Gate had the highest rate of infections of the four wards, Stratford had the highest death rate from diphtheria during the first nine months of 1899, countering Matthew's claim that the disease was predominantly located in Forest Gate. Sanders rejected the suggestion that Forest Gate had no drainage or housing problems, citing its pockets of low-quality housing to prove his point.[44]

He admitted that sewer gas might make individuals more susceptible to diphtheria, spreading the "disease indirectly by inducing a condition of low vitality, often associated with sore throat, a condition rendering the sufferer intensely susceptible to fall prey on exposure to infection."[45] However, he made it clear that sewer gas itself did not spread diphtheria and therefore could not be its primary cause. Although the public often believed that "foul-smelling sewers and drainage defects" were its source, "no such direct relationship can be traced."[46] To reinforce this theme, he noted that "houses of the worst sanitary type sometimes remain free of the disease, while others in which diphtheria is prevalent, present a few insignificant or even no drainage defects."[47] Without resorting to long quotes from scientific experts, Sanders weakened the environmental explanation for the dissemination of diphtheria and introduced a number of theories based on person-to-person transmission.

He stated that schools played a major part in the spread of the disease and suggested that more attention should be focused on them:

Looking over the attacks throughout the past, one seems able to detect waves of diphtheria passing over first one school, which for a time forms the chief centre of the attack in the Borough, and then moving on to a second school whence, after a more or less determined assault, followed, it might be, by a temporary truce, a fresh campaign opens at a third.[48]

Sanders used statistics to support this theory; he pointed to a number of tables in his report to show that almost three-quarters of West Ham's diphtheria fatalities were school-aged children between three and fifteen years old. He noted how easily the disease spread through schools, and though he did not refer to germs, he described their transmission:

> The reasons for this result are clearly apparent when one views the necessarily close gathering of the children in class rooms, the limited floor area that can be allowed each scholar, the possibilities of indirect contagion through the medium of drinking cups, the liability of children in a feverish condition during the early stages of sore throat to use such drinking vessels more frequently than their healthier schoolmates.[49]

Sanders pointed to crowding as the second major factor in the spread of diphtheria, observing that most West Ham residents lived in "two-storeyed, double-family, six-roomed" homes.[50] When public health officials were notified about a case of infectious disease, an inspector visited the house and instructed the family to isolate the patient. In crowded dwellings, this was not practical, and the healthy children continued to associate with the sick person, not only contracting the disease themselves but potentially passing it on to other families through their attendance at school. Sanders suggested that more hospital spaces, not improved sewers, were the best means to control diphtheria, as they would enable health officials to ensure isolation, while providing better nursing and effective therapy using the new anti-toxin.[51]

Sanders and J.G. Morley, both aware of the latest scientific bacteriological theories, worked in a social context that remained deeply influenced by the older understandings of disease. In addition, their geographical context provided ample evidence for a strong connection between a degraded environment and disease. They were not sure that foul-smelling gases were harmless, but they knew that they were not the primary cause of disease, which put them at odds with members of the public and local councillors, who wanted to concentrate attention and resources on solving the sewer gas problem. These tensions complicated Sanders's efforts to improve public health in West Ham. He needed to continue dealing with the environmental problems that accompanied poor drainage and inadequate sewers, but at the same time he tried to allocate more resources to isolate the carriers of infectious diseases, such as diphtheria. In the case of diphtheria, the public focus on sewer gas simply distracted attention from the true cause of the illness, but ameliorating insanitary conditions did help to diminish the prevalence of other diseases. Thus, a dual approach was adopted, one that cleaned the environment and removed people to hospitals. In the years that followed, this would prove successful at reducing deaths from infectious diseases.

COUNTING AND MAPPING DEATHS IN A CRISIS

Born in the late 1850s, Charles Sanders came to West Ham in 1887 as its new medical officer of health, and from the start he struggled to manage and improve its troubling health conditions. He had trained at St. Bartholomew's Hospital and worked briefly at a number of hospitals and at the docks in London. He remained in West Ham until 1924, when he retired at the age of sixty-five.[52] During his early years in West Ham, the borough struggled to build schools, sewers, parks, and other public amenities to service its growing population. The Public Health Committee and Sanders lacked the resources and legal power to improve housing or to properly deal with outbreaks of infectious disease. The health of residents suffered accordingly.[53] West Ham did not operate its first hospital until 1896, and even then it was too small to accommodate the expanding number of sick people.[54] In his 1895–96 annual report, Sanders acknowledged that the rising rates of zymotic disease were a "matter calling for serious attention," but he also pointed to the insufficient resources available, as even with the new hospital "our accommodation is very much below requisite."[55] During his first decade in West Ham, Sanders enumerated an increasingly unhealthy district in his annual reports, while he worked hard to build an adequate public health infrastructure for its residents.

Alongside diphtheria, deaths from typhoid and diarrhea in West Ham climbed to alarming rates during the 1890s. The unhealthy decade culminated with a number of particularly deadly years around the turn of the century. In 1899, West Ham's infant mortality rate, or deaths per thousand live births, was the sixth worst among the thirty-three largest English towns. The cause of this was diarrhea, and 1899 stands out as West Ham's worst year between 1877 and 1923. Figure 15 shows how the infant mortality rate of West Ham diverged from that of London at the turn of the century. Typhoid deaths also jumped to 330 per million in 1899, which was well above the 1881–90 average of 189 in London (see Figure 16).[56] In 1901, an epidemic that Sanders traced to an ice cream vendor drove the typhoid

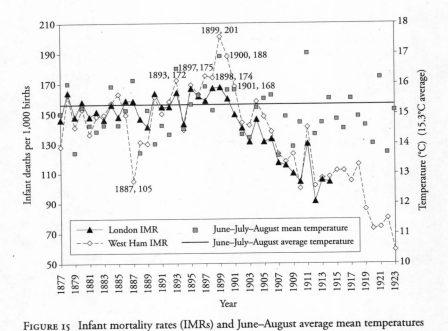

FIGURE 15 Infant mortality rates (IMRs) and June–August average mean temperatures in West Ham and London, 1877–1923.
Sources: County Borough of West Ham, Charles Sanders, *Annual Report of the Medical Officer of Health for 1923*, 40, Newham Archives and Local Studies Library; Temperature data from Tim Legg, "Hadley Centre Central England Temperature (HadCET) Dataset," Met Office Hadley Centre for Climate Change, http://hadobs.metoffice.com/hadcet/; and D.E. Parker, T.P. Legg, and C.K. Folland, "A New Daily Central England Temperature Series, 1792-1991," *International Journal of Climatology* 12, no. 4 (1992): 317-42.

death rate up to 370 per million, but this last spike was an outlier in the first decade of the twentieth century. Both the typhoid and infant mortality rates (IMRs) dropped significantly early in the twentieth century.

Hot summer weather contributed to the high infant mortality and typhoid death rates around the turn of the century. The correlation between fecal-oral diseases and weather helps to explain the growing rate of infant deaths across England during the relatively hot and dry 1890s. However, the correlation was not linear, and cleaner and more affluent districts experienced much smaller IMR spikes in hot, dry years than dirty and impoverished districts. For this reason, hot weather effectively put urban areas to a "sanitary test."[57] West Ham's performance on this test declined during the final two decades of the nineteenth century. During the early 1880s, West Ham's IMRs compared relatively well with similar areas in

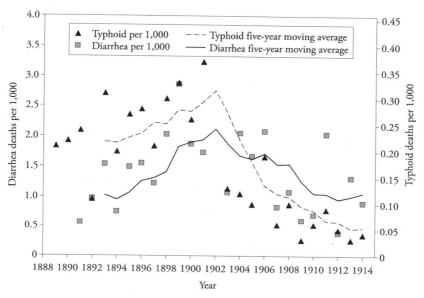

FIGURE 16   Deaths from fecal-oral route diseases in West Ham, 1890–1915.
Sources: Spreadsheet of health statistics compiled from County Borough of West Ham,
Charles Sanders, *Annual Reports of the Medical Officer of Health* (1896-97 to 1901 and 1903
to 1914), Newham Archives and Local Studies Library; along with population estimates
calculated by evenly distributing population growth between the 1891, 1901, and 1911
census years.

Greater London, but it became one of the least healthy districts in the
metropolis by the end of the 1890s.

In the five years from 1880 to 1884, West Ham compared favourably with
other similar regions in London. As Map 17 reveals, its average IMR, at
148.6 per 1,000 throughout these five years, was similar to that of Greenwich (147.4), Poplar (152.9), Lambeth (145.4), and Kensington (146.6), and
better than that of the comparably sized Fulham (159.6) on the western
edge of London. All these rates were significantly higher than that of Hampstead, in the northwest, whose average IMR was 119.1. Map 18 indicates
that from 1896 to 1900, at the height of West Ham's public health crisis,
its IMR ranked among the worst in London. It rose faster than that of
many other districts, confirming that the suburb failed the sanitary test.
Comparing Maps 17 and 18 shows the significant decrease in infant health,
with only a handful of the districts holding steady or improving. With a
rate of 180.2 over the five years, West Ham, along with Polar (177.2),
joined a number of other inner city districts that climbed into the high

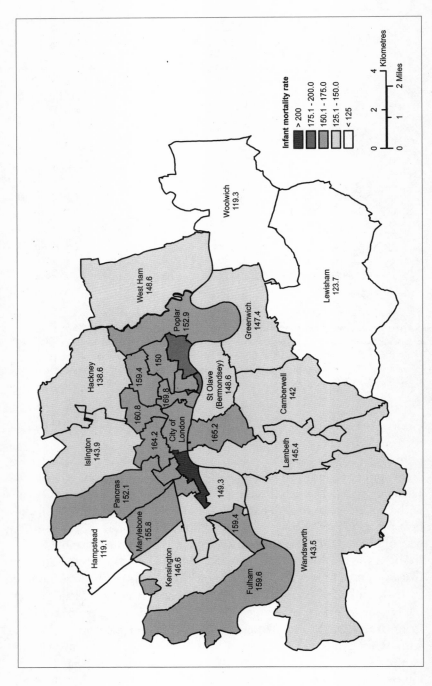

MAP 17   Average infant mortality rates, London and West Ham, 1880–84

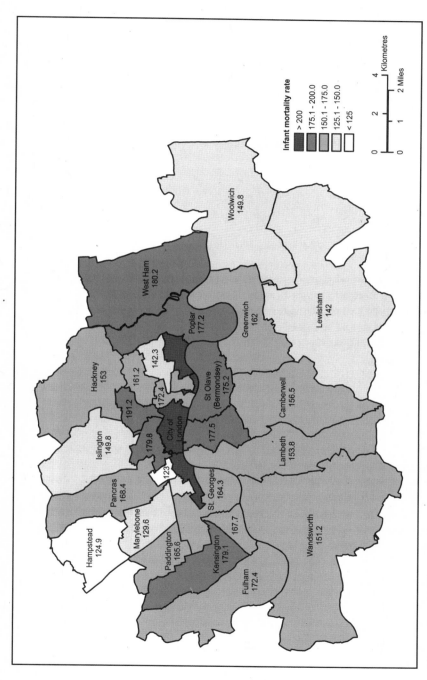

Infant mortality rate

> 200
175.1 - 200.0
150.1 - 175.0
125.1 - 150.0
< 125

Kilometres
2 Miles

Hampstead
124.9

Marylebone
129.6

Pancras
168.4

Islington
149.8

191.2

179.8

123

City of
London
177.5

Hackney
153

161.2

172.4

142.3

West Ham
180.2

Poplar
177.2

St Olave
(Bermondsey)
175.2

Greenwich
162

Woolwich
149.8

Paddington
165.6

Kensington
179.1

St Georges
164.3

Fulham
172.4

Lambeth
153.8

Camberwell
156.5

Lewisham
142

Wandsworth
151.2

MAP 18 Average infant mortality rates, London and West Ham, 1896–1900

170s and 180s. In contrast, outer areas such as Islington (149.8) and Camberwell (156.5) experienced only minor rises in their IMRs during these years with hot and dry summers. The City of London, the Strand, and Stepney (not labelled, but shown in dark grey on the map) appear to have the worst rates, but this is misleading, as all three had hospitals in which many of the children died, a fact that significantly distorted their IMRs.[58]

Sanders acknowledged that West Ham was the fifth worst among the thirty-three largest English cities in 1899 and blamed diarrhea and enteritis as the primary cause of the deaths. The year before, he had referred to the hot weather in August and September to account for the higher rates of diarrhea, but he made no effort to explain why West Ham's IMR climbed significantly higher than that of Camberwell or Fulham. He did try to explain the rising zymotic death rate, which was largely driven by the growing number of infant and childhood fatalities:

> The constant accession of young, good lives, such as young married couples from the Metropolis, which has gone on for many years, side by side with the building boom, while tending to lower the general death-rate has not been sufficient to counteract the evils attending rapidly-built houses, more rapidly inhabited – evils such as dampness of dwelling and fouling of the soil, which render the rising generation more prone to succumb to attacks of zymotic disease than, under happier circumstances, they would be.[59]

When West Ham was compared with more established districts, its younger demographic helped explain its higher zymotic death rate, but it did not account for the mounting crisis over the previous few years or for the district's relative performance against other growing suburbs, particularly as its IMRs were offset by its number of births. Sanders's actions, however, were considerably more nuanced than the excuses in his annual reports. He recognized and studied the regional inequalities in West Ham and developed new approaches to improve environmental and housing conditions in its worst sections.

The problems of poor housing that Sanders interpreted as the cause of high infant mortality were closely associated with social status and income. Most residents of Forest Gate did not generally live in damp homes and did not suffer from high levels of infectious disease. Just as the geography of health differed significantly between Hampstead and Poplar, the death rates in West Ham differed equally significantly between the prosperous northeast and the marginalized southwest. In the late 1890s, Sanders began a study of the significant variations in West Ham's geography of health. He gathered evidence that demonstrated the association between infectious diseases, high mortality rates, crowded low-quality housing, and poor environmental conditions.

In 1897, Sanders selected eight districts within the four West Ham wards to calculate health statistics and show the differing levels of public health problems. In that year, he sent investigators to enumerate the inhabitants of each zone, and he used these base numbers to estimate the population in subsequent years.[60] The Woodgrange district, located south of the railway and north of Romford Road in the east of Forest Gate, was a middle-class commuter suburb.[61] The Stratford Marsh, Bidder Street, and Hallsville districts contained the oldest sections of housing, which dated back to the 1850s and stood on the marshlands.[62] The Croydon Road area was a somewhat newer section of housing in Canning Town.[63] The final districts were the three isolated clusters of housing in Silvertown.[64] Map 19 shows the average total death rates for the eight areas between 1897 and 1899.[65]

The Woodgrange area, located far from the Lower Lea, the marshlands, and the factories, maintained a significantly lower level of mortality than all the other districts. Hallsville and Mid-Silvertown were the worst, both with death rates of 28.33, 10 points above the national average during the 1890s.[66] Bidder Street was not much better, with an average of 26.37. The mortality rate in the remaining districts was above the national average and significantly higher than that of Woodgrange. It was difficult for Sanders to isolate a single factor that had contributed to the high death rates in the seven marshland districts, as all shared crowded, old, and poorly built housing, dirty yards, accumulated sewage resulting from drainage problems, close proximity to heavy industry, and poor social conditions.[67] Nonetheless, his surveys confirmed that poor environmental conditions contributed to the elevated death rate during West Ham's public health crisis.

IMPROVING HEALTH, LOCALLY AND NATIONALLY

In 1909, B.G. Bannington, a sanitary inspector hired by Sanders in 1898, noted that the decline in the zymotic death rate and IMRs since the late 1890s "indicate[d] a considerable saving of life" and a "corresponding increase in general health."[68] Bannington compared these markers of improved health with statistics that chronicled a decade of house-by-house inspections, nuisances found, notices served, drains repaired, and public

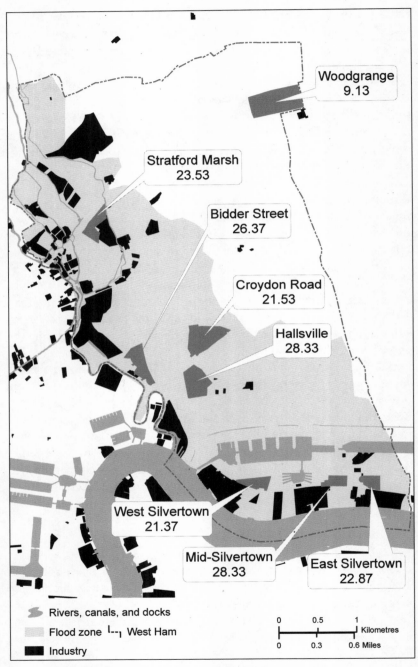

Woodgrange
9.13

Stratford Marsh
23.53

Bidder Street
26.37

Croydon Road
21.53

Hallsville
28.33

West Silvertown
21.37

Mid-Silvertown
28.33

East Silvertown
22.87

Rivers, canals, and docks

Flood zone l--ı West Ham

Industry

0	0.5	1	
			Kilometres
0	0.3	0.6 Miles	

MAP 19 Average deaths per thousand in eight health areas, 1897–99

complaints about sanitary conditions. He explained that the significant increase in sanitary monitoring, the new powers granted to the Corporation of West Ham in 1898 to force property owners to fix sanitary problems, and the growing public awareness that complaints to public health officials were efficacious had all improved the "general sanitary conditions of house property" in the suburb.[69] Bannington confidently linked the upsurge in public health intervention with improved health outcomes.[70]

The dramatic decline of West Ham's IMR, however, corresponded with a similar trend across London and throughout England in the early twentieth century, making it a challenge to tease out local causes from general ones.[71] Summers were cooler after 1899, which was clearly a factor in decreasing the IMR, as was the significant reduction of manure and flies that came with the falling urban horse populations throughout urban England, but it took local government action to decouple hot summers from diarrhea epidemics. In 1907, new legislation required that a father or someone who was present at a birth must immediately register it with the government, which notified public health visitors of all homes with newborns, though as with everything else involving local governments, implementation was uneven in the early years.[72] Differences in local politics and the quality of health officials, along with the limited resources available in areas with low property values, meant that as the general trend improved, considerable local variation remained. In this comparative context, West Ham lost its late-1890s status as one of the worst districts and rejoined Greater London's relatively healthy middling districts when hot weather returned in 1911.

The steep reduction in fecal-oral diseases, as seen in Figure 16, was the most important factor in the declining IMR and lowered zymotic death rate during the early twentieth century. Public health officials contributed significantly to this trend.[73] The micro-organisms that caused diarrhea had not been clearly identified in the early twentieth century, which limited Sanders's ability to deal with a major killer of young children in West Ham. He developed two approaches, including the reforms targeting urban environmental conditions and educational campaigns, which helped bring diarrhea under control. These measures, along with increased hospital care and supervision of the food supply, also helped reduce the number of deaths from typhoid.

Sanders knew that breast-fed infants were significantly freer from diarrhea than those who were bottle-fed. In 1896, he argued that only the direct education of mothers by female inspectors could decrease deaths from diarrhea (along with measles and whooping cough):

It would appear that nothing but a gradual education of the poorer classes as to the danger of these diseases and the best method of treatment, is likely to produce definite and positive results. And it is here, I believe, that the role of the woman inspector, offers the best hope of sanitary salvation, a woman inspector, who, being a trained district nurse could devote herself to teaching the poorer mothers how to rationally rear their bottle-fed infants, and how to avoid the dangers due to an ignorant treatment of the foregoing diseases, the especial assailants of infancy working, it may be, through years of patient routine without any apparent immediate results, but gradually accumulating an educational reserve of immense value to the well-being of the Borough in more ways than that originally intended.[74]

Sanders's propensity to blame ignorant mothers, an attitude shared by many health officials, was highly problematic, as it downplayed the import-ance of poverty and poor housing, shifting the blame away from society to individuals. It also failed to address the malnourishment of the mothers, which commonly resulted in underdeveloped and premature babies.[75]

In 1899, Sanders persuaded council to hire two inspectors. Rosetta Gardiner, who was twenty-two, held certificates in sanitation and first aid nursing, and had experience as a health visitor. Catherine Heaviside was thirty-six, held basic nursing and sanitation certificates, and had been a schoolteacher.[76] They performed educational work while simultaneously furthering the campaign to improve sanitation by reporting the problems they encountered during their visits with new mothers.[77] This dual focus on education and addressing immediate sanitary problems suggests that Sanders and his team were not satisfied with simply blaming the victims. At least by the end of his career, Sanders was well aware of the significant role that poverty played in public health problems, and in 1920 he sup-ported the borough council's policy to supply dried milk powder to nursing mothers and young children.[78] In many cases, sanitary interventions targeted the landlords, not the tenants. Nonetheless, they significantly in-creased government surveillance of private homes, an intrusion that some parents resented.[79]

Assigning the two female inspectors to work among the poor in West Ham, a community that tallied more than twenty-four births a day in 1900, probably did not change the behaviour of mothers quickly enough to explain the dramatic drop in IMRs. However, a number of charities complemented their work, and perhaps the combined efforts contributed to more sanitary feeding practices during the first decade of the century.[80] Nevertheless, this new attention to motherhood had less of an impact on

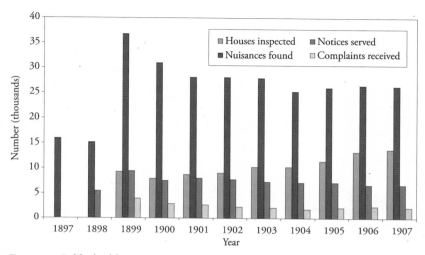

FIGURE 17 Public health interventions, 1897–1907.
Source: B.G. Bannington, "Health, Rates and House Rents," *Public Health* 22 (1909): 370.

declining IMRs than the house-by-house inspections and the resulting improved environmental conditions.

Despite his reluctance to address diarrhea directly, Sanders, in an indirect fashion, led the effort that helped control this disease. The major campaign of house-by-house inspections upgraded conditions throughout the borough. By repairing thousands of drains and many more nuisances in homes and yards, public health interventions significantly contributed to the decline of the diarrhea death rate between 1900 and 1915. Figure 17 records that health interventions greatly increased after 1898.

The increased activity began after council had passed a motion in October 1898 instructing Sanders to begin house-by-house inspections in the borough.[81] During the subsequent decade, his team of inspectors visited thousands of homes each year. In the first year, after Sanders convinced council to increase his staff from ten to twelve inspectors, they managed to visit more than nine thousand homes. They found so many nuisances that they inspected fewer dwellings during the next year, as they were too busy following up on the problems discovered in 1899.[82] Figure 18 demonstrates the tangible results of the new house-by-house inspections, as 2,341 drains were improved or replaced during the first year alone.

B.G. Bannington argued that the nuisances gradually diminished because the general condition of the drains improved remarkably after a decade of enforcement, and there were fewer problems to solve.[83] Drains

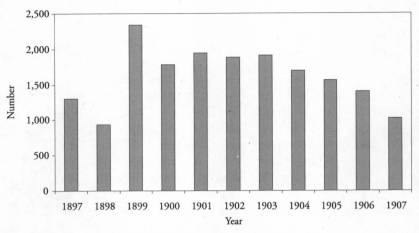

FIGURE 18 Number of drains relaid or repaired, 1897–1907.
Source: B.G. Bannington, "Health, Rates and House Rents," *Public Health* 22 (1909): 370.

were just one factor that health officials dealt with during house inspections. Sanders's regular reports to the Public Health Committee record that his team inspected "drains and soil pipes," water closet "pans or traps," "surface gullies, sinks and sink-pipes," "stack pipes and rain-water gutters," "water fittings and cisterns," "flushing apparatus," and the condition of "yards paving" around the houses. The inspectors made a note of defects in roofs, floors, staircases, windows, doors, fireplaces, walls, and ceilings. They also ensured that the home had a functioning water supply, provided many new garbage bins with lids, forced people to dispose of "offensive accumulations," made sure that animals were properly kept, and disinfected thousands of rooms.[84] Altogether, they found 36,750 nuisances in 1899 and served 9,436 notices to force property owners to remedy the problems.[85] All of Sanders's reports to the Public Health Committee request permission to prosecute anyone who did not comply with a notice, and he was regularly given permission to have the necessary work done at the borough's expense, after which the bill would be passed on to the owner. A decade of this intensive intervention vastly improved living conditions in West Ham and contributed to the substantial drop in the diarrhea and typhoid death rates.

In 1921, Sanders suggested that a reduction in the number of flies had probably helped to lessen diarrhea fatalities.[86] Dr. James Niven, the Manchester MOH, had provided evidence for the direct link between flies and diarrhea in 1910, after a five-year study. Nigel Morgan's case study of Preston shows that the explosive growth of its horse population during the last decades of the nineteenth century corresponded with an increase of infant diarrhea, a pattern that occurred in many British towns at the time.[87] Reducing flies, which spread micro-organisms, also helped to reduce the rates of fecal-oral diseases.[88] A simple improvement in West Ham, where health inspectors ensured that each house had a proper garbage bin with a lid, saved lives.

The decline in typhoid deaths (see Figure 16) resulted from a combination of upgraded environmental conditions and germ-theory-based public health efforts. Cleaner homes, yards, and streets decreased the accumulation of sewage and diminished the prevalence of typhoid. Sanders also became better at linking typhoid outbreaks with certain food retailers – ice cream vendors in 1901 and shellfish sellers in 1906 – knowledge that enhanced his regulation of the food supply.[89] Moreover, in 1899 Sanders started sending typhoid cases to hospital.[90] In ideal circumstances, such patients could be nursed at home, as long as they were kept in a clean room and their excrement was disposed of carefully. However, maintaining this standard of care was difficult in the crowded residences throughout much of West Ham, and Sanders found a high number of secondary cases after the initial outbreak. Removing the sick person from the home contributed to the dramatic decline of typhoid.[91] Improving environmental conditions did not prevent Sanders from developing approaches to reduce the spread of particular germs between individuals in West Ham. Typhoid is the best example of his hybrid approach significantly decreasing deaths from a major infectious disease.

Public health improved in West Ham during the first decade of the twentieth century, but the geography of the suburb continued to produce significant regional variations. Map 20 shows the IMRs for the twelve municipal wards. The bar graphs and chart record the IMRs for 1901, 1904, 1911 (which had a hot summer), and 1914 for each ward. The map confirms the dramatic improvement from 1901, two years after the height of the IMR crisis, through to 1914. It also clearly shows that though progress occurred in all twelve wards, the biggest gains came in the marshland wards. The map confirms Sanders's research and shows that the marshland wards had significantly higher IMRs in the earlier years. Babies born in Forest Gate or Upton in 1901 were almost twice more likely than their counterparts in High Street or Custom House to survive their first year. After more than a decade of house-by-house inspections and better residential conditions, the gap narrowed significantly: in 1914, the IMRs in Tidal Basin (137) and High Street (134) still remained above the averages

Ward	INFANT MORTALITY PER 1,000 BIRTHS			
	1901	1904	1911	1914
New Town	175.9	194	129	111
Forest Gate	106.9	112	152	85
High Street	205.3	202	171	134
Broadway	160.3	207	150	122
Park	122.0	123	122	91
Upton	96.1	105	79	78
West Ham	153.3	140	130	96
Plaistow	190.6	170	120	78
Hudson	155.3	164	150	90
Canning Town	194.3	156	135	109
Tidal Basin	200.6	192	165	137
Custom House	205.7	176	156	123
West Ham Whole	172.9	165	141	108

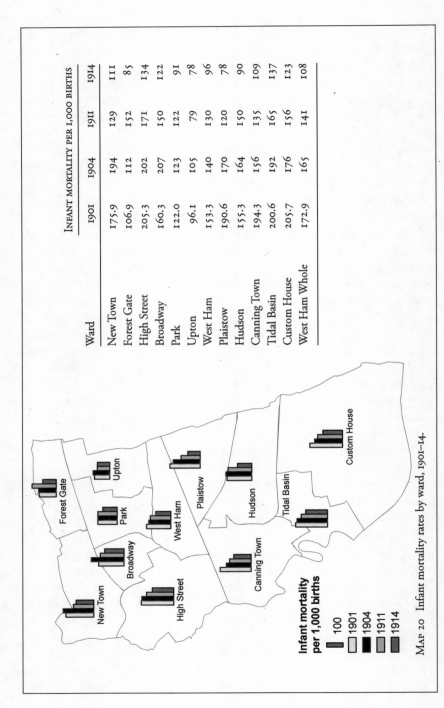

Infant mortality per 1,000 births

100
1901
1904
1911
1914

MAP 20 Infant mortality rates by ward, 1901–14.

for London (104) and West Ham (108), but both had improved by more than 65 infant deaths per 1,000 births since 1901. During the hot summer of 1911, only Forest Gate saw a significant jump in its IMR; the other wards experienced lower rates than in either 1901 or 1904. This suggests that West Ham was significantly more prepared to pass the sanitary test than it had been at the turn of the century.[92]

In the sanitary test of 1911, West Ham rejoined the middle rankings (Map 21). None of the boroughs saw their IMRs jump back to the 180–200 range of 1899, but they did not all perform equally. Many outer boroughs passed the sanitary test, as their IMRs remained near or below 100. Shoreditch lay at the other end of the spectrum, and its rate jumped to 170 from 147 in the previous year. West Ham had a smaller increase: its IMR rose from an average of 120.4 in 1906–10 to 141.0 in 1911. During the next hot summer, that of 1921, West Ham finally passed the sanitary test with confidence, as its IMR remained a very low 74.0 despite the above-average temperatures.

AFTER WEST HAM'S DEATH rates decreased so remarkably, health officials turned their attention to the one cause of disease that still lay well beyond their control: poverty. In 1909, Bannington noted that it impeded further progress: "It is ... being more and more realised that the great 'condition of the people' question, the 'social problem' – poverty and ignorance in the mass – set a limit to the results that might be obtained by health administration."[93] During its initial stages, British public health focused only on a narrow range of sanitary issues and did not address the larger social factors that influenced health.[94] In West Ham, this began to change in the early twentieth century: in 1923, during a lecture given near the end of his career, Sanders argued that health officials needed to deal with social problems, including poverty, ignorance, intemperance, and vice. In the first decades of the twentieth century, West Ham had started to address these problems by paying higher rates of outdoor relief, providing sanitary education, decreasing the number of licensed establishments, and attempting to deal with venereal disease.[95] However, Sanders and his team had little authority to directly improve the standard of living of the casually employed and unemployed in West Ham.

The expanded post-1898 public health interventions were the first successful efforts to deal with the interconnected social, medical, and environmental problems that had afflicted the marshland districts of West Ham since the 1850s. As health improved, and better drains and sewers reduced the amount of human waste, the degradation of the environment eased.

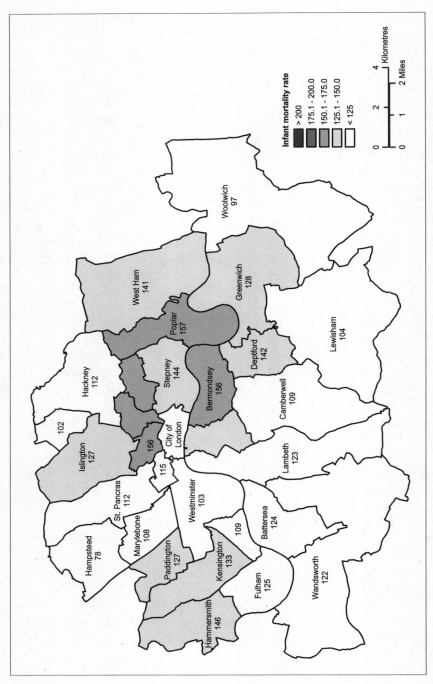

MAP 21 Corrected infant mortality rates in London and West Ham, 1911. The statistics recorded for this year allocated infant deaths to their home borough, not the location of the hospital in which the children died.

Unfortunately, decades of pollution had left the Lea's back rivers in a terrible state, and the upgraded sewers and drains in West Ham were offset by further population growth to the north in Leyton and Walthamstow. The back rivers needed to be cleaned out to create a healthier landscape for the public and to make them more useful for industry. Following Sanders's success in the early twentieth century, J.G. Morley tried to improve both social and environmental conditions in West Ham by proposing a major unemployment relief project in the Lower Lea Valley.

6

Fixing Rivers, Fixing Society

ON JULY 31, 1888, a thunderstorm inundated West Ham with heavy rains. One person died after being struck by lightning, and hundreds of homes and factories in the south of the borough were flooded, as were many more in other parts of Greater London. Early reports from London's *Daily News* and the *Borough of West Ham and Stratford Express* focused on the human tragedies caused by the event. Poor people who lived in the flood-prone communities on the Isle of Dogs in East London or in Canning Town were forced out of their homes and lost property, food, and animals. To make matters worse, the flood spread sewage throughout these impoverished areas, increasing the threat of disease.[1] The hardest-hit victims in London were generally in low-income communities on the marshlands and floodplains in the Thames Estuary and Lea Valley.

The constant threat of flooding in the Thames Estuary exacerbated regional inequality in Greater London. Not only did the residents of the Isle of Dogs, Bermondsey, and Canning Town face regular flooding, but they were also burdened with the costs of drainage and flood defence.[2] This environmental challenge compounded the difficulties created by the local funding of social services through the Poor Law.[3] These expensive requirements created a major fiscal restraint on all other local government activities. These flood-prone districts needed, but did not receive, regional or national funding to properly address the problem.

West Ham was also vulnerable to economic crises during the late nineteenth and early twentieth centuries. A particularly severe economic downturn in 1904 and 1905 led the *Daily News,* the *Daily Telegraph,* and other

London newspapers to focus extensive attention on social problems in West Ham. Looking back a few years later, R.A. Bray, a reviewer for the *Economic Journal,* suggested that the general public had discovered West Ham during the winter of 1904–05: at that point, the "silent and unnoticed" suburb "became articulate, and its voice reached the civilized places of the land."[4] This economic crisis combined with larger trends to decrease West Ham's once significant industrial advantages and end its remarkable expansion. A major jute factory in Stratford shut down, production at the Thames Ironworks shipyard greatly diminished, and the building trade collapsed.[5] The cyclical recession threw thousands out of work in other industries or at least into irregular work. Finally, heavy fogs closed the docks at Christmas 1904, placing even more people temporarily out of work.[6]

The newspaper frenzy and the subsequent formation of the Outer London Inquiry Committee helped frame the expansion of working-class suburbs beyond the jurisdictional boundaries of the London County Council as the new "problem" threatening the social and political stability of the metropolis. The national government responded to this problem by enabling local distress committees to administer farm colonies, emigration programs, and relief works. A new Liberal government expanded this initiative to include some direct national funding from the Exchequer. This funding, which targeted labour-intensive projects that would not otherwise be completed in the private sector, inspired West Ham's engineer, J.G. Morley, to propose a major project in 1908 that would reduce the threat of flooding in the Lower Lea Valley and address the unemployment crisis in the region.

Throughout West Ham's transition from rural marshland to industrial suburb, flooding was an ongoing problem, as much of the land was located below the high tide level of the Thames and Lower Lea Rivers. As discussed in Chapter 1, an 1824 flood sparked conflict between mill owners and upstream landowners and industrialists. In the mid-1850s, Henry Morley noted that flooding regularly occurred during the winter months, and he described the foul result – the spreading of accumulated sewage throughout the landscape and homes of south and western West Ham.[7] Two decades later, Lewis Angell, the West Ham Local Board's engineer, reported on a major flood of November 15, 1875, the second large inundation in twenty months. A heavy gale combined with high tides to breach the flood defences for about forty-five minutes, during which water had poured over the land and overwhelmed the sewers. The sewer pump's steam engine was also extinguished, delaying the removal of the water for a few hours. Angell warned that flooding posed a major threat to life and property in West

Ham, as the suburb occupied large sections of former marshlands. He could see evidence that large sections of West Ham had been submerged in the past and suggested that this could happen again. Although the flood of 1875 had done relatively little damage when the Lea overtopped the earthen river walls, he worried that one of these walls might collapse during a future deluge, sending a crushing rush of water into the suburb. He recommended close monitoring of the walls and an increase in their height. The board responded by forwarding Angell's report to the Dagenham commissioners of sewers and the Local Government Board. Although there is no evidence that floods ever destroyed a river wall in West Ham, they continued to flow over these defences during the decades that followed.[8]

Among West Ham's many environmental problems, flooding was perhaps the most spectacular, as it temporarily returned the landscape to marsh, allowing the river an occasional victory in the long process of suburban and industrial development. The damage was often exacerbated when chemical and other hazardous materials were disseminated by flood waters, as was human waste from the sewer system and privy pits. Moreover, heavy rains regularly caused the massive London Main Drain to dump a mix of storm water and sewage into the Lower Lea at Old Ford. Many houses were contaminated by this polluted water.[9]

Unfortunately for the people and businesses of West Ham, the flooding had three causes. A normal heavy rainfall could simply overwhelm the storm sewer system and cause minor flooding in the lower districts. This transformed the streets into mud, spread pollution from ditches or privy pits, and occasionally entered homes and factories.[10] Second, major or prolonged rainstorms, like the one in 1888, could swell the Lower Lea, which was obstructed by bridges, mills, and pollution, causing it to overflow its banks. Finally, gales in the North Atlantic occasionally sent storm surges up the Thames Estuary, flooding into West Ham from downriver. This was the case in the floods of 1897, 1904, and 1928, each of which resulted in significant destruction across large sections of the borough.[11] Figure 19 shows a stone marker near Three Mills that records the date and height of these three tidal surges (the date on the eroded bottom stone is 29.11.97).[12]

The natural process of flooding in the Lea's marshlands was amplified by human intervention before and during the nineteenth century. The Lee Navigation straightened much of the Middle Lea, speeding the delivery of flood waters down the valley.[13] Agriculture, housing, and industry began to develop in the Lea watershed during the sixteenth century and expanded dramatically during the nineteenth century, decreasing the absorption of

FIGURE 19 Flood levels recorded on a wall near Three Mills. The numbers give the dates of the floods, and the horizontal lines above them show the height of the water. | Newham Archives and Local Studies Library, Newham.

rainwater and speeding its path to the rivers.[14] Major flood defences were finally constructed in the Middle Lea Valley during the early 1890s, north of the Lea Bridge, further rushing storm water down to the Lower Lea.[15] These changes in the upper river were not matched with improvements in the Lower Lea. Bridges, watermills, and accumulated debris in the streams all slowed the passage of flood waters down to the Thames.[16]

Population growth on the marshlands in West Ham and the Lea Valley increased the import of flooding throughout the nineteenth century. The thousands of new homes and hundreds of factories intensified the potential for property damage. The local board of health and later the Borough of West Ham steadily improved the sewer system from the totally inadequate marsh drainage ditches found in 1855, but the ongoing problem of flooding clearly demonstrated the failure to fully address the hazards of suburban development on these unsuitable wetlands.[17]

FLOODING

The flood of July 1888 focused attention on a single issue. A speaker at a public meeting argued that, despite its long list of priorities, the new borough council needed to concentrate on better drainage: "A recreating

ground was a very good thing, and a public library no one would say any-
thing against. A public hall for south West Ham would also be a good thing,
but this matter of drainage was more necessary than either of these."[18]
West Ham's location meant that significant sewer improvements and flood
defences were essential, simply to maintain its built environment. In 1889,
following this public outcry, West Ham gained new powers, which included
taking control over drainage and flood defence from the ill-equipped
Dagenham commissioner of sewers.[19] In 1898, Mayor William Ivey suggested that the high tax rates in West Ham were a result of all the infrastructure work undertaken by the borough and that the 1888 flood in
particular had forced it to spend £120,000 on sewers alone.[20]

The industrialization of West Ham was facilitated by a steady flow of
coal on the rivers. The ongoing problems with flooding and drainage
demonstrate that the residential communities in the south were equally
dependent on this resource. Much of West Ham relied on the continuous
efforts of engineers and machinery to keep the water back and to drain
any water that did accumulate. The south of West Ham was only partially
reclaimed with infill, and thus it depended on large coal-fuelled pumps
to remove the water that naturally collected on this low ground. The reliance on coal and mechanical power was highlighted during the 1875 and
1888 floods, as water extinguished the pumps both times and halted the
drainage. In 1888, a fire engine was needed to drain the pump house.[21]
The borough took control of this constant drainage effort in 1889, which
was among the many factors that kept tax rates high in West Ham.[22]

Entries in the minute book of the Sewers Committee reveal that the
borough engineer monitored the river walls throughout West Ham and
forced landowners to maintain these essential defences. This was an important reminder that later efforts to improve the defences transformed walls
that had been constructed centuries earlier. There is no indication, however,
that the committee addressed problems such as clogged streams, mills, and
old bridges; nor do the minutes discuss how the engineer safeguarded the
pump house against future floods.[23] The Lee Conservancy Board (LCB)
engineer did work on a plan to improve the back rivers north of High Street
in 1890–92, but he eventually dropped it when numerous landowners opposed his scheme.[24] In the following decade, flooding caused further damage, confirming the ineffectiveness of the borough's efforts and the failure
of the various stakeholders to work with the LCB to solve the problem.

Floods in 1897 and 1904 again demonstrated West Ham's vulnerability
to storm surges. Again the poorer communities and the factory grounds
were most affected. The 1897 flood pushed up the back rivers, significantly

damaging many factories and stopping production at others. The *West Ham Guardian* described its consequences in the oldest district of southern West Ham:

> The recent gale had a peculiar effect at Canning Town, especially in that portion known as old Canning Town, which is very low lying and abuts on the banks of Bow Creek and the River Lea. At high tide on Monday afternoon, the latter river overflowed the banks with the result that the wharves and streets flooded, the water in some places being as high as the window ledges of the houses.[25]

The paper also described the destruction at a number of important factories:

> As far as we can ascertain, the most serious damage done in the district was in the yard of the Thames Ironworks where, we are informed, the water caused two boilers to burst, with the result that several men were out of employment for the day ... In some parts of Stratford the roads were for a time four feet under water, and factory girls had to be taken from the workshops in a van.[26]

The storm surge of December 30, 1904, ran over the banks of the Lower Lea network and the River Roding in East Ham. Again it pushed north into the heart of Stratford's industrial zone, with two feet of water flowing down Stratford High Street. The stone marker in Figure 19 shows that this flood was significantly worse than the one in 1897. However, the *Borough of West Ham and South Essex Mail* provided little detail on the extent of the damage.[27] It did report on the water in the High Street and the noteworthy flooding at Howard's lumberyard in Canning Town, which suggests that the inundation must have been widespread in the low-lying portions of the borough.[28] The 1904 flood coincided with a worsening unemployment crisis, so it should come as no surprise that J.G. Morley, the borough engineer, identified flood defences as a major priority for government schemes to use unemployed workers.

UNEMPLOYMENT

Unemployment, like environmental problems, became increasingly associated with West Ham in the 1890s and the early twentieth century. The mixed manufacturing, construction, and transportation industries proved very vulnerable to economic downturns, and large numbers of builders and dockers were thrown out of work during the mid-1890s and in about 1905. During this period, social scientists and economists began to identify the links between regular economic cycles and spikes in unemployment. A spike in unemployment was understood as being more damaging than normal baseline unemployment, as it "reaches further into the social organism, and affects men usually far removed from that fringe which is sensitive to the slightest fluctuations; men who are not in the least accustomed to think of themselves as likely to be disturbed by the ordinary changes of the labour market."[29] Unemployment was increasingly seen as a problem, one that was distinct from pauperism, in the 1880s, 1890s, and the early twentieth century.[30] During these decades, social reformers and social scientists began to quantify poverty in large towns, and the supposed physical deterioration of jobless urbanites emerged as a major national concern.[31] This context is important in understanding the growing willingness to intervene in the labour market and the desire to improve the environmental state of urban spaces. West Ham became the focal point for public discussion of this newfound problem and the site of numerous small and large experiments to diminish distress from unemployment.[32]

Recruitment during the Second Boer War (1899–1902) brought the poor physical condition of Britain's young men to national attention. As many of the enlistees were from the urban working class, inner-city space became of particular concern in the extensive debates over the cause of the perceived decline of Britain's imperial subjects.[33] The theory of degeneration had two variations. Advocates of eugenics believed that deterioration was caused by "faulty heredity and looked to selective breeding as the solution."[34] Environmentalists, in contrast, believed that it sprang from degraded urban conditions. So, though eugenics gained strength at the turn of the century, environmentalists remained prominent and focused on improved sanitation, curtailing coal smoke, and increasing access to fresh air and green spaces.[35] They were more powerful and influential than the fringe eugenicists in shaping public policy. Health officials and sanitary engineers were deeply committed to bettering the environmental state of cities, and they rejected the eugenicist claim that their intervention simply impeded natural selection because it allowed too many weak people to survive and reproduce. As health officials were powerful civil servants, they continued working to improve urban environmental conditions, with significant success, as was the case in West Ham.

Social reformers and politicians began to focus on prolonged unemployment as a third cause of degeneration in Britain. In doing so, they combined the long-standing concern of the Charity Organisation Society (COS), an organization founded in 1869 to prevent recipients of charity from becoming demoralized and losing their motivation to work, with a newer observation that respectable men who had lost their jobs and thus had little to eat would lose the strength and confidence they needed to return to work once trade resumed.[36] This new perspective concentrated on the long-term social consequences of joblessness, contending that once a labourer fell from the category of "deserving" unemployed and joined the "crowd of 'loafers' and general 'hangers-on,'" his productive potential was lost, and he and his dependants would become burdens on society.[37] The high levels of joblessness that began to occur in 1904 provided an opportunity to experiment with new methods of unemployment relief that prevented degeneration, both by enabling men to work and by improving the urban environment. This approach could benefit both the unemployed men and society generally, and it gained pockets of support from individuals throughout the political spectrum.

The economic crisis that began in 1904 was especially severe in West Ham.[38] It worsened to the point where four to five thousand West Ham residents were registered as unemployed, a tally that omitted many jobless skilled unionized workers and most unemployed women.[39] The closing of Ritchie and Son's jute factory and the failure of the Thames Ironworks to secure naval contracts made the circumstances particularly difficult. Many construction workers also lost their jobs, and the reduced work at the Royal Docks transferred many casual labourers into the unemployed category. At the time, however, experts did not see the economic downturn as the main cause of the unemployment crisis.

Leonard Humphries, secretary of the West Ham Distress Committee (WHDC), reported in June 1906 on the many sources of distress in the borough:

> The recognised specific causes for the increasing numbers of the workless are (a) trade depression, (b) seasonal fluctuations, (c) the wide extent in certain districts of dock and casual labour, (d) the shifting of industries, (e) changed and changing industries, (f) the absence, at present, of proper facilities for easy flow of labour from one district to another, (g) the influx from the villages into the towns, (h) the thousands of unskilled general labourers.[40]

Humphries acknowledged that all these factors contributed to the crisis in West Ham, but he largely dismissed the business cycle as a significant cause: "The common belief, too, that 'poor trade' explains the trouble does not, in this Borough at least, meet the case."[41] Like other experts at the time, he focused much of the blame on the large numbers of casual workers in West Ham: "The bane of the whole matter here is, of course, the great mass of casual labour, employed especially in dock districts and in populous industrial centres."[42] Humphries invoked educational reform as the best method of solving this problem, suggesting that academic subjects be given less weight than the acquisition of manual skills. This fixation on the high levels of casual and low-skilled employment in West Ham continued in later years, and the Outer London Inquiry Committee centred a considerable portion of its investigation and report on this topic.[43]

The statistics that Humphries provided in the first WHDC report, however, suggest that the collapse of the building trade was the largest cause of distress in the borough.[44] West Ham's industrial and population growth levelled off in the first decade of the twentieth century, during which the population increased by only 21,672 people, rising from 267,358 to 289,030.[45] In addition, factories stopped expanding and began to close, again decreasing the demand for construction labour. However, officials in West Ham, including the medical officer of health, did not notice that the rapid population growth had ended until the 1911 census revealed it to them.[46] Thus, we should not be surprised that Humphries and others failed to see the significance that 2,622 of the 4,785 registered unemployed were from the "Building and Constructive Trades," whereas only 1,300 came from the large category of "Engineering, Locomotion, Transport and General Metal Works," which presumably included both dockers and laid-off shipbuilders.[47] Because Humphries and other observers were so fixated on casual labour, they dismissed the trade cycle. They also failed to recognize the obvious significance of the end of the decades-long building boom that had accompanied rapid growth in West Ham.

RELIEF FOR THE UNEMPLOYED

Responding to the crisis in the winter of 1904–05, the West Ham Board of Guardians augmented outdoor relief and re-established its labour yard, and the West Ham Borough Council expanded its own relief works.[48] As neither had the financial resources to alleviate all the poverty in West Ham, the *Daily News* and the *Daily Telegraph* set up relief funds, as did a number of other newspapers, and funnelled large amounts of money into the suburb.[49] The *Daily News* raised £11,800 for relief works, food, and fuel, while the *Daily Telegraph* raised £14,835 that it gave to the Salvation Army and clergymen to distribute among the poor.[50] Charity and social reform experts, as well as some newspapers, condemned these acts of "irresponsible" relief and charity.

A January 1905 article in the *Times* launched a particularly vitriolic attack, in which the writer suggested that unemployment was not a pressing problem in West Ham:

> A large proportion [of the people] are engaged in good and regular work which is not dependent on season and is suffering from no appreciable disturbance. The estimate that one-third of the entire population is starving or on the verge of it is obvious nonsense. The fact is that the bulk of the people are going about their business as usual in the daytime and filling the theatres ... at night, to say nothing of the public houses.[51]

He conceded that some distress did exist in West Ham and went on to provide an explanation for it:

> This, however, is not to say that there is no distress. There is always distress in a community of the size of West Ham, and always more in a trading than in an industrial centre. The reason for this fact, which I cannot stop to prove, is probably that trading business suffers from greater irregularity and employs a much larger proportion of the lowest class of labour; it calls for and attracts the unskilled, the casual, and the shiftless labourer, who cannot get work elsewhere ... There is always distress in the borough, and always more in winter than in summer.[52]

The writer expressed skepticism about relief works and direct charity, as both created moral hazards and enticed increasing numbers of lazy people to the district. He claimed that the current unemployment problems demonstrated that the borough's decade of experiments to relieve joblessness had simply failed: "The prevalence of distress and the habit of seeking relief have not been diminished by sundry experiments in 'advanced' or 'progressive' administration."[53]

He was even harsher regarding the charitable efforts of the competing newspapers:

> Why should a man work when he can get money for asking? Money has been poured into the place. I do not know how much, because there are so many funds, no accounts, and no responsibility; but I was told on Wednesday

that about £15,000 had come in, not to be expended on work for the un-employed, but to be given away. I have seen many relief funds distributed ... and the same thing always happens - greed and demoralization among those who receive it, corruption among those who handle it.[54]

He ended with a warning that this charity could potentially spiral out of control, spreading to the many other socially depressed regions of Outer London:

Already some astute person has made the discovery that West Ham does not exhaust the terra incognita of Greater London. There is Edmonton; and why not East Ham and Leyton, and half-a-dozen more, all quite as deserving and quite as distressed? ... The thing is catching, and all the arguments ad-duced on behalf of West Ham apply to the others, perhaps more strongly.[55]

The *Times* article prompted a flurry of letters from those who were engaged in charity work in West Ham, to which the journalist duly replied. The *Daily Telegraph* pointed to the wide range of highly respectable organiza-tions and individuals with which it worked to spread relief, including the Salvation Army and Reverend C. Baumgarten, who was "well known" for his "strong C.O.S. [Charity Organisation Society] views."[56] In response, the *Times* reporter said that he did not doubt the good character or inten-tions of the people involved but reiterated that it was "humanly impos-sible to distribute relief on this scale and with this degree of publicity without causing the evils I have mentioned."[57] The contributions of this writer show that some conservatives remained deeply committed to a non-interventionist approach to social and economic policy.

Some progressive social reformers were also uneasy about the ad hoc nature of the expanding relief efforts. Many experts, following in the tradition of the COS and under the influence of classical liberal econom-ics, believed that careful measures must be taken to avoid demoralization.[58] A report published by a group of Cambridge social scientists raised concerns with the indiscriminate relief and charity in West Ham during the crisis:

In the last week of the old year the situation was one that amazed those who had any experience of winter distress. The Guardians were giving what amounted to indiscriminate out-door relief; the Borough Council yielding to the pressure of those who demanded the right to work on their own terms, had provided relief works; and the other agencies were endeavouring to get rid of the sums of money which poured in from every quarter.[59]

Despite the concerns raised by the *Times* and some social reform experts, the public's attitude to unemployment and poverty was changing. Many people simply ignored the experts and supported the relief funds with donations. These changes were also reflected in government policy, as when Balfour's Conservative government allowed the limited, but still significant Unemployed Workmen Act to pass in 1905.

The bill came about after an effective public campaign by the Social Democratic Federation, the Independent Labour Party, and the Labour Representation Committee during the economic slump of 1904–05. Its passage was also facilitated by the growing acceptance among some members of the political elite that many of the unemployed were good men who were out of work through no fault of their own.[60] For example, Walter Long, the president of the Local Government Board in 1904 and the Conservative cabinet minister who initially proposed the Unemployed Workmen Act, recognized that many of the jobless were not individually responsible for their misfortune. He "became convinced that the majority of unemployed were honestly seeking work, and that it was a 'national crime' to turn such men into paupers by refusing to relieve them until they were on the verge of starvation."[61] Long's views and his proposed solution, which included a London-wide "penny rate" that would have forced wealthier sections of the city to shoulder much of the burden for supporting the unemployed, came under attack from both his Conservative colleagues and his left-wing critics. Within a few months, a cabinet shuffle replaced Long with Gerald Balfour, removing a key advocate for the unemployed from this important position.

During the first half of 1905, protests in the streets across Britain and a political campaign led by Keir Hardie in the House of Commons demanded that unemployment legislation be created. Through to the final week before the bill passed, at the very end of the legislative session, Prime Minister Arthur Balfour, older brother of Gerald, hoped to avoid a final vote so he could let the bill die on the order books. However, a riot in Manchester on August 1 forced the government to act and ensured the bill's third reading a few days later.[62] The bill that ultimately did pass was a hollow shell of what had been proposed earlier in the year. It did not include a local tax to pay for relief works, and it reduced the ten-year experimental period to test out this new form of government intervention to three years. Nonetheless, the bill was a small victory for Labour politicians, as it signalled the growing recognition that some unemployed deserved state support. It empowered municipalities such as West Ham to form distress committees that would register the unemployed, rank them according to whether they were "deserving" or "undeserving," and prioritize them on the basis of gender, age, and status as chief male bread-winners in a family.[63] The committees also had limited authority to raise funds to build farm colonies, sponsor relief works, and support emigration to the colonies, with money collected from the charitable public. Once the committees were formed, they took on a significance of their own, increasing the statistical and practical knowledge of the unemployment problem and lobbying for more power and money to help the many "deserving" unemployed who were registered during the act's first year.[64]

PROTESTS AND LAND GRABBERS

West Ham was already experimenting with relief works before the new law passed in 1905, and the local political and social context forced the borough government to remain at the forefront of unemployment relief. During the crisis of 1904–08, the large minority of labour and socialist politicians on the borough council placed considerable pressure on council to address joblessness. As a result, the Municipal Alliance was compelled to support a variety of efforts to provide relief for the unemployed. Grassroots groups, including the South West Ham Distress Committee (SWHDC), an association for the unemployed that was organized by W.R. Hughes of Mansfield House University Settlement, participated in local rallies and acts of civil disobedience. In May 1906, they demonstrated their strength to the national government by marching through London to Hyde Park.[65]

The SWHDC also pushed council to provide parcels of unused land, owned by the borough, for free allotment gardens.[66] This led to a major clash between the ruling Municipal Alliance and the Labour Group at a July 1906 council meeting. The Alliance was unwilling to let the unemployed use the land for free, though some members supported renting it as allotment gardens. The Labour Group argued that allotment gardens were an easy way to support the unemployed and noted that, as the Bromley Gasworks had supported the SWHDC with a land grant, the borough council could surely do the same. The meeting concluded with shouted insults, in which Councillor Arthur Hayday from the Labour Group told Councillor William Crow, "Your heart is as black as your dirty face ... You black old crow; you black-hearted scoundrel!"[67] Next morning, a vote was taken to use the land for rented allotments, rejecting the request to provide it free of charge to the unemployed. In the aftermath of this defeat for the Labour Group, Ben Cunningham, a socialist borough councillor and a leader of the organized unemployed, led a group of men to occupy the land. They set up the Triangle Camp, pitched a tent, and began cultivation – though their farming efforts were more symbolic than practical as it was already July. Within a few weeks, the police cleared away these gardening protestors, ending the dispute over access to municipal land.[68] The Municipal Alliance was significantly more co-operative in the establishment of a distress committee and the development of public works projects that targeted the unemployed.

A Farm Colony and a Shovel-Ready Lake

The authors of the Unemployed Workmen Act attempted to avoid negative repercussions from government interference in the labour market by stipulating that the work done by the unemployed must be of actual "value" as well as "exceptional to the ordinary work undertaken by public authorities as part of their current obligations."[69] As a result, municipal engineers were often tasked with finding "useful" work for the unemployed. Environmental improvement projects provided low-skilled occupations for large numbers of people, so the jobless were put to work digging drainage ditches and landscaping parks.

The WHDC formed in October 1905, shortly after the Unemployed Workmen Act passed in August. During the winters of 1905–06 and 1906–07, it developed a number of projects. The largest was a labour colony farm, located in South Ockendon, where unemployed men were removed from the community to work on the land for three months at a time, while their wives and children were supported at home. Given the limited amount of relief that it provided, this farm was very expensive, but it fit within the shared vision of the political elite (Labour included) that urban social problems could be solved by repopulating the countryside.[70] The farm would give unemployed city dwellers a taste of the countryside and would teach basic agricultural skills (Figure 20).[71] Liberal, Labour, and socialist politicians envisioned a future in which land monopolies were divided or nationalized and urbanites resettled on small farms. The labour colony farm also provided training for potential emigrants to Canada.

Although the long-term goal of recolonizing the countryside with farm-colony-trained labourers remained incomplete in 1906, the WHDC justi-

FIGURE 20 Hay and pea-bine stacking at the labour colony farm. | County Borough of West Ham Distress Committee, "First Annual Report and Secretary's General Observations, October 5th 1905–June 30th 1906," insert between 16 and 17, Newham Archives and Local Studies Library.

fied the high cost of its agricultural experiment by citing its social gains. The farm itself did not make a profit, but it did allow "the men's powers as workers" to be "maintained, and that lamentable physical and moral deterioration resulting from continued unemployment prevented."[72] Ideologically, it met the goal of supporting the deserving unemployed for a time. The difficulty of housing a few hundred men on an isolated farm with a limited budget led to morale problems by the spring of 1907. On March 22, the *Mail* reported that forty-eight men had been let go after they complained about excessive hours of work, bad food, and their generally poor treatment at the farm.[73]

A second WHDC project focused on improving the drainage of Wanstead Flats, north of Forest Gate (Figure 21). This venture provided 9,430 total days of work in its first winter (1905–06). During the second winter (1906-07), the WHDC took on a bigger scheme to build New Heronry Lake in the same area, which became the largest relief work yet undertaken in Britain, as 2,022 men shared 45,000 days of labour.[74] With

FIGURE 21 Excavating and concreting at New Heronry Lake, part of the Wanstead Flats project. | County Borough of West Ham Distress Committee, "Second Annual Report for the Year Ending June 30th, 1907," insert between 8 and 9, Newham Archives and Local Studies Library.

its high standard of work and reasonable cost, it was a major success. Moreover, the cheapness of materials and the fact that most of the labour was performed with hand tools made it ideal for unemployment relief, as much of the funding went directly to wages for the men.[75]

The environmental benefits of the Wanstead Flats project, which included improved water management and recreational facilities, were decidedly anthropocentric. When the flats were drained to create the lake, a significant amount of water was diverted from West Ham's sewer system. This diminished the burden on the system, reduced the use of coal at the sewage works, and probably decreased the amount of storm water flushing into the River Lea.[76] The lake project also restored a recreational space that had dried up in previous decades, so it had the dual benefit of alleviating poverty for thousands of workers while simultaneously improving the local environment for everyone. That concrete was used to line the muddy lakebed reveals that it was not intended to restore the natural environment.[77] It did, however, demonstrate the ability of unemployed workers to complete a major civil engineering project, and it inspired the borough engineer to contemplate the more ambitious endeavour of improving the Lea back rivers in 1908.

The photographs from the WHDC's first two reports show men stacking hay and excavating a lake (see Figures 20 and 21). The absence of women in these images highlights the failure of these projects to equitably distribute relief funding among the unemployed. Prevailing gender ideologies limited the benefits for women as the new relief efforts overwhelmingly focused on preserving the bodies and characters of men. The wives of men who received relief would benefit indirectly, but they themselves were not allowed to register as unemployed, and they remained beholden to the good graces of their spouses. Moreover, though single and widowed women were permitted to register with the WHDC to benefit from the employment exchange, none worked at the farm or drainage projects. In general, the crafters of the Unemployed Workmen Act and the distress committees seemed willing to leave jobless women to the mercy of the Poor Law.[78] This was because the legislation and the committees concentrated on sustaining "deserving" breadwinners through periods of unemployment and because the work found for the unemployed involved heavy physical labour that was not deemed suitable for women. In the third year (1907–08), the WHDC made a modest attempt to redress this imbalance by employing about twenty women in needlework, making sheets for the farm and clothing for some of the emigrants whom the committee sponsored.[79] The committee's choice to find appropriate "women's work" demonstrates the predominance of gender ideology, as women were certainly capable of working on the farm, a task that they performed on many real farms throughout Britain. The neglect of unemployed women demonstrates that the politicians who created the Unemployed Workmen Act never intended to deal with the whole problem of unemployment and intentionally focused on supporting a small percentage of the jobless, the "deserving" male workers.[80]

Expanding Relief

Large relief works and the farm both cost a great deal of money, more, in fact, than the WHDC, the West Ham Council, or the Board of Guardians could afford. Such projects could not be sustained if the WHDC relied on donations alone, and the efforts of the first year did not meet the demand created by the high levels of unemployment in West Ham. In the first report of the WHDC, Secretary Leonard Humphries argued that the national government should take the lead in creating relief work. It should encourage more people to work the land through small holdings and should engage the unemployed in large national public projects, such as increasing the timber supply through tree planting, reclaiming wastes and marshlands, and improving waterways or building new ones. There was a clear emphasis on using the jobless to "improve" the environment and to decrease the urban population through land reform, mirroring the local projects that the WHDC undertook.[81] The committee also began to push against the limits of the act, and it requested additional funding from the government to help save more of the unemployed from turning to the Poor Law.

After the 1906 national election, the MPs of the vastly expanded and formalized Labour Party again worked in conjunction with the street protests to pressure the new Liberal government to expand the Unemployed Workmen Act and fund the program directly. Many of these MPs represented West Ham or had a long-standing connection to it, including Will Thorne (Labour), Charles Masterman (Liberal), Percy Alden (Liberal), John Bethell (Liberal), and Keir Hardie (Labour).[82] They fought to expand funding for unemployment relief, and some of them backed a Labour Party proposal to guarantee the "right to work" in a revised unemployment act. The pressure they exerted, along with protests in the streets, eventually led to the creation of a £200,000 fund from the Exchequer to support locally managed works for the jobless.[83] This was a significant development, as most forms of social assistance relied entirely on local taxation, and the 1905 act limited the distress committees to operating with charitable donations. The influx of national money allowed J.G. Morley and the WHDC to undertake the large-scale Heronry Lake project in the winter of 1906–07.[84]

However, the allocation of £200,000 did not end the tensions between the Liberal government and those battling on behalf of the unemployed. In March 1907, the *Mail* reported on a disagreement between Will Thorne and his erstwhile socialist ally, John Burns, the new Liberal president of the Local Government Board, over extending relief funding beyond the winter months, as the numbers of unemployed had not significantly declined during the spring of that year.[85] Burns refused to continue the funding, and the WHDC scrambled to find alternative sources of money to complete Heronry Lake. In the end, the Epping Forest local authority funded the remaining work, and the lake was finished with much fanfare in early July 1907. Despite this success, John Bethell, who was still a borough councillor in West Ham and now a Liberal MP for nearby Rumford, worried about the challenges of finding both another project and the necessary capital to support a similar number of unemployed during the following winter.[86] In 1908, the WHDC considered eighteen new projects, but identifying one in or near West Ham that would not displace other employees and still provide a large amount of unskilled work proved problematic. As the committee report noted, the difficulty of finding "suitable Relief Works increases with successive years."[87] Although the committee failed to develop a new major project, J.G. Morley began to consider one that was significantly larger and more important than draining the Wanstead Flats.

FLOOD AND UNEMPLOYMENT RELIEF

In January 1908, Morley developed a plan to address flooding and unemployment with a single public works project. He contacted Charles Tween, the Lee Conservancy Board (LCB) engineer, and suggested a partnership to use the national funds and workers available from the WHDC as a unique opportunity to finally improve the deplorable condition of the Stratford back rivers. Tween agreed to work with Morley if it were made clear that the LCB was not responsible for funding West Ham's drainage or flood defence.[88] On a more enthusiastic note, Tween reported to the LCB in February: "It appears to me that the time has now arrived when something should be done to properly cleanse, canalize and maintain these back waters."[89] He proposed that the LCB should call for a conference between itself, West Ham, and the London County Council, with the intent of collectively tabling a bill in Parliament to canalize the rivers. Throughout 1908, Morley and Tween worked with the West Ham Council, the LCB, and the WHDC to develop an ambitious flood defence and canalization scheme. Tween's engineering reports and the LCB minute books show that LCB officials became keen supporters of the initiative once they realized that the Local Government Board might fund it with unemployment relief money.[90]

Between January and April 1908, Morley and Tween proposed a complete re-engineering of the Stratford back rivers, from Lea Bridge down to Bow Creek (excluding the Channelsea River and Abbey Creek). Encouraged by the promise of significant funding, they created a wish list of improvements to reduce the threat of flooding and facilitate transportation on these damaged streams. Tween started with a plan, commissioned by his predecessor in 1892, in which four of the northernmost back rivers would be transformed into canals.[91] These would be standardized at six feet below the overshot level at Bow Lock and would range from forty to sixty feet in width.[92] Tween suggested a significantly more comprehensive plan to canalize all the Stratford back rivers, proposing to extend them down to Bow Lock in the south and including the Bow Back River, the Three Mills Back River, and the Three Mills Wall River. A number of locks would be added to make the new canals fully navigable. As many back rivers were navigable only during bimonthly spring tides, this would constitute a significant improvement.[93] Meanwhile, Morley negotiated with Hackney, Leyton, and Walthamstow to pool their unemployment relief funds and upgrade the flood defences all the way from Lea Bridge, a few miles north of West Ham, down to Bow Lock. This was particularly important, as the Middle Lea, north of the Lea Bridge, already had flood defence improvements that hurried water south, but no work had been done in the Lower Lea, resulting in an increased problem of flooding.[94]

The proposed project would have transformed the riverscape of the Lower Lea Valley, cleaning out the years of accumulated sewage, garbage, and pollution that clogged the riverbeds and transforming the back rivers into navigable canals. This would have enhanced the river's economic utility by making transportation possible throughout the tidal cycles and by reducing the environmental hazards brought on by flooding. Tween believed that his proposal would help spur economic development in the area, and he told Morley in February 1908 about the "great benefit which would accrue to the Borough if all the Back Streams at Stratford were canalized and made properly Navigable by opening up the land on either side for factories."[95]

Tween's plan – to improve the river's usefulness for humans and to reduce the health threats posed by the stagnant pollution and flooding – reflected the perspectives of early-twentieth-century civil engineering. It did not entail environmental remediation, as might be undertaken today. No thought was given to re-naturalization, reed beds, or marshland preservation, but most Edwardians would have commended it. In a world of significant and debilitating environmental degradation, introducing simple improvements and orderly management was a big step for both the rivers and the local population. For centuries, humans had built walls along the Lea and drained its marshlands, so this infringement into its natural agency simply furthered its transformation into an engineered and natural hybrid. In contrast, removing some of the pollution from the riverbeds could have improved the health of the streams, allowing more life to return and reinstating water flow down the Pudding Mill River. The benefits to the rivers, however, would have been detrimental to the nearby land, as the engineers planned simply to dump the polluted sludge on adjacent properties.[96]

In the end, the ambitious scheme of Morley and Tween was scuttled by the complexities of using unemployed workers, the determined resistance of some land and water rights owners, and cost. The only reason they had embarked on its planning was because the WHDC was searching for large projects that might correspond to Local Government Board (LGB) guidelines and thus receive national funding. The Heronry Lake project was the biggest British relief work of its day, and the WHDC hoped to find another large venture to attract more funding from the national government. Canal construction, however, was more complicated than lake construction. Normally, a dredger would be used to deepen and widen streams into canals. Replacing the dredger with unemployed workers would require that dams be built and the water pumped away so that large numbers of men with hand tools could dig out the riverbeds. During this time, factories and mills would lose access to water, and a flash flood could cause extensive damage if one of the streams were unavailable to carry the water downriver. Tween worried that West Ham, the WHDC, and the LCB might not have the legal authority "to stop these streams for any lengthy period when it can be shown that all the work of deepening and widening the same can be done by dredging without in any way interfering with the flow of the water."[97] He and Morley also recognized that the WHDC, which had no regular funding, could not take on the liability for any lawsuits that might arise.[98] Moreover, the owners of the large Three Mills site were very reluctant to accept the loss of their mills to improve flood defences for the rest of the community.[99] Mills at these locations dated back nearly a thousand years, and their claim on the rivers predated any of the nineteenth-century urban-industrial development. Despite these drawbacks, Tween's October 30 report remained optimistic that the money was available and that the legal and practical challenges could be overcome:

> It appears to me that it all resolves itself into a question of responsibility and negotiations and mutual consents and to carry these successfully through the West Ham Corporation and the Conservancy should work hand in hand. It appears there is money to be had, and the unemployed want work, and there is work to be done which will make a general improvement, but there are difficulties in the way. If these cannot be overcome in an amicable man-

ner the Lee Conservancy Board and West Ham Corporation should jointly go to Parliament to obtain the necessary powers required to attain that which both bodies appear to desire.[100]

This optimism did not persist, and by the end of November West Ham and the LCB began negotiating a significantly reduced scheme to clean the stagnant Pudding Mill River.[101]

The canal project was doomed because the WHDC lacked the sustained funding that was necessary to support relief works of this scale. Each project needed approval from the LGB, and all had to fit within the very limited guidelines of the 1905 act. This meant that the distress committee spent considerable time planning numerous projects in the hopes that one or two might be accepted. Moreover, it could not plan multi-year relief works, as funding was approved one year at a time.[102] During the early months of 1908, the Labour Party and some Liberals fought to pass new unemployment legislation that would guarantee the right to work.[103] Under this proposal, distress committees would be responsible for either finding employment for the jobless through labour exchanges and relief works or providing direct outdoor relief payments.[104] Major cabinet ministers, including Winston Churchill and Lloyd George, pushed for an aggressive Liberal alternative to the Labour Party's right-to-work proposal.[105] This political activity provided some hope that regular and sustained funding might be available for local distress committees through an expanded grant from the Exchequer supplemented by a local rate. However, LGB president John Burns opposed both the Labour Party bill and the idea of sustained funding through a local rate. With the passion of a convert, the socialist-turned-Liberal identified the moral hazard of the state guaranteeing employment and refused even to put forward a moderate government alternative to amend and renew the Unemployed Workmen Act during the spring of 1908.[106] By late 1908, public pressure had forced the government to reach a compromise. However, Burns remained powerful, and though the compromise increased the amount of central funding for grants and provided some limited amendments to the 1905 act, it did not include continuous funding or the ability to rely on a local rate.[107] The shift from the large-scale canalization plan to the more limited Pudding Mill cleanup coincided with the failure of Thorne and other local politicians to secure an improved funding model for the distress committees.[108]

In an attempt to save a small part of the back rivers project, Tween pointed out that the Pudding Mill River was so congested that little water flowed down it, even during floods, and he suggested the LCB, the WHDC, and the borough council could still partner to improve one river during the winter of 1908–09. This led to a second conflict, as West Ham wanted Tween to manage the Pudding Mill River cleanup, but the LCB was unwilling to take sole responsibility for the project. Tween's final report on the unsuccessful project complained that Morley and the borough council had failed to provide enough support for a scheme that would have helped elevate social and environmental problems in West Ham:

> I have done all I can to forward this proposal. I have prepared plans, sections and estimates, and, at Mr. Morley's request endeavoured to find sites for depositing the spoil. It rather appears to me that the Corporation wish to throw all the responsibility and liability (if any) upon our Board, and I must say I do not think the Corporation are reciprocating the honest endeavour of our Board to find work for their unemployed.[109]

This final disagreement led to the end of negotiations and left the back rivers unimproved. The WHDC eventually gave up on finding a project in West Ham and settled on sending the unemployed to clean the Ornamental Waters at Wanstead Park.[110]

FLOODING AND RELIEF

A decade after the 1909 collapse of the WHDC canal project, the condition of the back rivers and the threat of flooding drew attention once again. In 1919, P.M. Crosthwaite, another engineer, was commissioned to write a report on recent flooding in the Lea and Stort Valleys. He too identified the problem of the obstructed and polluted condition of the Lower Lea, which, combined with the the extensive improvements of the Middle Lea and the suburban development in the watershed and marshlands, created an ongoing threat of flooding.[111] There is no indication that Crosthwaite's report led to immediate action, and obstacles remained a problem in the Lower Lea in 1920. The floodgates on the City Mill and Waterworks Rivers, which were still owned by the Corporation of the City of London, were in a state of disrepair. Local businesses demanded action, and this created a conflict between the LCB, West Ham, and the the City of London. The Ministry of Transport intervened to try to find a resolution. The LCB records show that the board remained steadfast in its refusal to accept responsibility for the back rivers and insisted that the City Corporation was liable for maintaining the floodgates because it owned the mills and adjacent land. The City, which had long ago leased the land to various businesses, refused to pay the cost of fixing river navigation in West Ham. After months of conferences, officials in the Ministry of Transport failed to broker a compromise and realized they had no legal jurisdiction to force a solution. The issue ended in a stalemate once the ministry disengaged from the process.[112]

The successive failures to act had consequences. During the early hours of January 7, 1928, a storm surge collided with the Thames, itself swollen by heavy rains, and drove a great volume of water up the estuary, inundating large sections of London. As Figure 19 shows, in the Lower Lea Valley, the 1928 flood was considerably worse than those of 1897 and 1904. The water rose so quickly that it killed a number of Westminster residents who were sleeping in basements. In West Ham, it spread throughout the low-lying districts, from Canning Town up to Stratford High Street. The local paper reported,

> Floods in West Ham have been known before when there have been abnormally high tides, but never has there been one which assumed the proportions of that which devastated the areas mentioned during the weekend. Thousands of houses and scores of factories and wharves adjacent to the waterways, and remote from them, were flooded to the depth of several feet, roads were made impassable for vehicular and pedestrian traffic and the workings of the L.N.E.R. on the line to North Woolwich and the dock area were stopped.[113]

This flood, even more devastating than the three major floods since 1888, once again emphasized the need for a new system of defences in the Lower Lea network.

A year later, the global economy collapsed, creating another unemployment crisis. Officials in West Ham quickly saw this as an opportunity to finally address the problem of the back rivers. Fortunately, the national government was now willing to help finance major work creation projects, and a bill was passed in 1930 to that end. With the funding secured, a Joint Committee made up of the LCB and the West Ham Borough Council worked to transform the riverscape of the Lower Lea, while employing large numbers of jobless men.[114] Instead of simply digging out the existing stream network and adding canal walls, as proposed in 1908, the engineers reorganized the back rivers, expanded the High Street, and built new bridges. The Pudding Mill and Three Mills Rivers were filled in, and the

Bow Back and Waterworks Rivers were moved. At the same time, the City Mills, Pudding Mills, and Waterworks Mill were destroyed to accommodate the widening of the High Street. Three Mills survived, and a new flood diversion canal, called the Prescott Canal, was added to avoid conflict with its owners. The project was a success, providing work for the unemployed and improving the urban landscape, but it could not halt the negative economic trend in West Ham. The borough continued to deteriorate through the middle of the twentieth century, joining other inner suburbs of Greater London with high rates of unemployment and social distress.[115]

THE HISTORY OF FLOODING in West Ham made evident the deep interconnections between social and environmental problems in the borough. These difficulties dated from the early years of suburban development, as Alfred Dickens and Henry Morley reported in detail during the mid-1850s (see Chapter 3). The sewers were improved over time, but the condition of the Lower Lea declined significantly throughout the second half of the nineteenth century, and development on the marshlands increased the threat of flooding. In 1888, 1897, 1904, and 1928, the poorest residents of West Ham, who lived in its oldest riverside neighbourhoods, suffered as water rushed into their homes. Each event reinforced the need for better flood defences, something that Angell called for as early as 1875.

This situation highlighted a major geographical inequality in Greater London. The long-standing convention that those who benefitted from flood defence and drainage infrastructure must pay the costs created significant additional pressures on taxation rates in marshland and floodplain districts. This was a major tension in the County of London, where wealthy areas, most of which were located on hills, resisted paying for drainage in East and South London.[116] As an independent borough, West Ham was responsible for funding its own drainage, flood defence, and any other measure to improve the flow of the back rivers while at the same time paying for health, education, recreation, public buildings, roads, and all other municipal services. The fiscal constraints of relying on local property taxes limited the effectiveness of its flood defences and explains the continued threat from the 1850s through to the 1930s.

The frequency of flooding was matched by the regularity of economic crises in West Ham. The downturn that gained national attention in the winter of 1904–05 was not the first period of high unemployment, but it was particularly severe and sustained, as it marked the end of rapid economic growth in the suburb. In this context, J.G. Morley and Charles

Tween hoped to address the problem of the back rivers with an ambitious scheme to reduce flooding and improve navigation. They argued that money targets for unemployment relief could have major knock-on effects, stimulating economic recovery among Lower Lea industry, but their plan failed, and West Ham's industrial economy declined throughout the twentieth century.

Conclusion

EARLY-TWENTIETH-CENTURY West Ham was an enigma. It was a vital part of London, the industrial heart of the metropolis, but it was not among the twenty-eight boroughs that were consolidated under the County of London in 1900.[1] West Ham had as many people as the northern city of Bradford, and it ranked seventh among English county boroughs, but it was not as well known as other major industrial cities located outside the capital. It had significantly more people per acre (61.7) than Liverpool (44.9), Birmingham (39.0), and Manchester (33.0).[2] It was also much larger than the industrial suburbs of cities beyond London. It had 100,000 more residents than Manchester's Salford and more than twice the population of Newcastle's Gateshead.

West Ham's population and importance were officially recognized by its status as an independent county borough. Only Croydon shared this designation in Outer London. West Ham was also the fourth most populous local government district in Greater London, though most of the smaller core metropolitan boroughs maintained significantly higher population densities.[3] There were other densely inhabited boroughs along the Thames Estuary that contained large docks or concentrations of industry, including Poplar and Bermondsey. But because West Ham lay beyond the orbit of the Metropolitan Board of Works or the London County Council to co-ordinate large-scale infrastructure projects, it struggled with the intense challenges posed by rapid growth, high concentrations of economically marginalized people, and the ongoing environmental instability that resulted from urban development on marshlands.[4] Independence limited the resources that were available to the borough council, but it also opened up opportunities. West Ham was free to experiment with new forms of government intervention. The Labour Group's political victories were more significant in autonomous West Ham than they were in neighbouring Poplar, a second-tier metropolitan borough.

Overlapping social and environmental problems came to a head during the 1890s, and the voting public responded by demanding that the government address them. West Ham's place at the forefront of social democratic politics in Britain was marked by the success of Keir Hardie, Will Thorne, and the Labour Group's 1898 victory. But the borough trailed other progressive jurisdictions in relying on local government intervention and the public ownership of utilities to improve urban conditions.[5] Within Greater London, the newly formed London County Council pursued a progressive agenda from 1889 onward, creating a notable contrast to the West Ham Borough Council in the subsequent decade.

The cost of building, operating, and maintaining the schools, sewers, and other public utilities of a city with a quarter of a million residents was enormous. The property owners and politicians of West Ham became fixated on keeping local taxes down. This created an opening for socialist and labour politicians, whose constituents did not pay rates directly. The Labour Group focused public attention on the social and environmental consequences of political inaction by demanding that union wages be paid for municipal work and that steps be taken to alleviate unemployment. It pursued progressive policies, such as assuming control of the water supply and increasing the resources for the medical officer of health to regulate rental housing.

The 1898 election demonstrates the importance of environmental instability in driving political change in nineteenth-century urban Britain. Deleterious conditions amplified social concerns and facilitated the emergence of new urban politics. On its own, West Ham's high concentration of casual labourers, dockers, and factory workers does not account for the early triumph of labour politics and socialism, as these voters were significantly disadvantaged in the franchise system of the 1890s. The Labour Group successfully associated infrastructure issues with wider geographic inequality and promised expanded government intervention as a solution to West Ham's many problems.

Labour fell from power after two years, as its opponents embraced some social democratic policies and campaigned on a number of wedge issues, including the Labour Group's alleged support for its union friends, apparent support for atheism, and the class-based antagonism of socialists.[6] A new coalition of Conservatives and Liberals, known as the Municipal Alliance, took power in 1900. It retained control until 1910 and then again after 1912 through to 1919, when the Labour Party won and remained in office until West Ham was dissolved in 1965.

The 1900 defeat of the Labour Group curtailed the development of municipal social democracy in West Ham.[7] During its first decade in power, the Municipal Alliance launched just one major publicly controlled project, a tram network.[8] But it is important to remember that the Alliance maintained many of the interventionist programs that dated from the late 1890s. Although it dismantled the unionized works department, it backed the expanded public health department and supported the formation of the distress committee in 1905, even as it fought bitterly with the Labour Group about how to respond to unemployment. Its ongoing support for government intervention reveals a canny understanding of some of the mistakes that led to the 1898 defeat and a keen appreciation of the public's desire for better local conditions and enhanced economic and environmental stability.[9]

Government experts played an increasingly important role in developing and implementing policy during the late nineteenth and early twentieth centuries.[10] Politicians relied on these men to improve the environmental state of West Ham. Experts such as Charles Sanders, Lewis Angell, and J.G. Morley became responsible for fixing the dysfunctional landscape and bettering the human habitat. Morley also became directly involved with schemes run by the distress committee, in which unemployed workers were used to improve the parks in and around West Ham.

Concerns about environmental problems played a role in the creation of powerful municipal experts, as the complexity of the issues necessitated more authority for local officials. Medical Officer of Health Charles Sanders and his team gained the power to regulate both the borough's interior and exterior environments. By the early twentieth century, they had the right to enter homes and force owners to improve their sanitation. They also monitored industry, restricted the location of noxious trades, supervised working conditions, watched for excessive smoke, and inspected food sellers. The engineers could compel the owners of private property to improve river walls as they planned longer-term solutions to the threat of flooding. As increasing numbers of tasks were assigned to the medical officer of health, the public health department expanded from a handful of employees in the 1880s to more than a thousand in the 1930s.[11] The borough's experts became indispensable, as the complexity of the challenges posed by disease and unpredictable rivers demanded difficult and technical solutions.

WEST HAM'S LONG DECLINE

The 1920s saw the beginning of a long decline in West Ham as new rings of development spread Greater London residents farther afield. The population of the borough, which increased slightly to 300,860 between 1911 and 1921, started to drop, slowly at first, to 294,278 in 1931 and then more quickly to 201,024 in 1939 and to 170,993 in 1951. Bombing raids during the Second World War destroyed thousands of houses and numerous factories. However, the longer trend of population collapse from 1931 to 1961 came from a reduction in the numbers of families that crowded into West Ham's dwellings and from a declining birth rate.[12]

In 1965, West Ham, East Ham, and North Woolwich amalgamated to form the London Borough of Newham. This was a part of the larger consolidation of municipal governments throughout Greater London, passed by Harold Macmillan's Conservative government two years earlier. In 1971, Newham was among fourteen of London's thirty-two boroughs that had a population of between 200,000 and 250,000. By 1991, its population had bottomed out at 200,678, slightly fewer than West Ham's population in 1891, and the borough languished with significant social, economic, and environmental challenges.

The economic dynamism of West Ham ended in the early twentieth century. During that period, few homes and factories were built on the open marshlands of the Lower Lea and the Thames Estuary, as electricity and improved over-ground transportation allowed industry to locate away from rivers. New factories were generally located in the upper reaches of the Lea Valley and northwest of Greater London.[13] Factory closures in the early twentieth century initiated a protracted process of deindustrialization that persists today. Mergers and acquisitions saw larger corporations take control of many West Ham firms and downsize or close many of these locations.[14] Still, numerous factories remained in the Lower Lea Valley until 2006, when the government started to expropriate the land for the Olympic Park in advance of the 2012 Olympics. Today, there are a few large factories in Silvertown, though it too is transitioning away from industry.

The 2012 Olympics

The 2012 Summer Olympics, which coincided with the opening of the Westfield Stratford City shopping mall and new housing developments, significantly increased the prominence of the Lower Lea Valley. On the day that London learned it would host the games, Jack Straw, secretary of state for foreign and Commonwealth affairs, stood up in the House of Commons and highlighted their transformative potential:

> London's bid was built on a special Olympic vision. That vision is of an Olympic games that will be not only a celebration of sport but a force for regeneration. The games will transform one of the poorest and most deprived areas of London. They will create thousands of new jobs and homes. They will offer new opportunities for business in the immediate area and throughout London.[15]

The bid also promised to ameliorate the environmental state of the Lower Lea Valley. Throughout the twentieth century, the Lea had remained one of the most polluted rivers in England, and many of its factory sites and former landfills were extremely contaminated.[16] Newham also had some of the most challenging social problems in the country, with high levels of unemployment and poverty.[17]

The Olympics and the wider efforts to revitalize the Lower Lea Valley obscured the region's past. The enormous costs of cleaning the toxic soil and the ongoing concern about the resulting social dislocation hinted at its complicated social and environmental histories, but there was little effort to celebrate its important role in the industrialization of Greater London or the development of social democracy.[18] A promotional webpage from 2006 labelled the valley as "one of the capital's most underdeveloped areas" and added that it had "outstanding potential," which would be transformed by the Olympic Games.[19] News stories and websites publicized archaeological discoveries, highlighting a four-thousand-year-old axe and Roman artifacts found in the area while bulldozers flattened nineteenth-century industrial buildings and a century-old allotment garden.[20] The pleasant eighteenth-century House Mills were preserved, but few of the chemical factories or engineering works remain. The Olympic Delivery Authority and political leaders showed little interest in the industrial history of the region as they focused on promoting an optimistic post-industrial future for the Lea Valley.

Their hopeful vision in some ways paralleled an earlier prophecy for the area, one penned by William Morris in his utopian novel, *News from Nowhere* (1890). A socialist born in the Lea Valley, Morris (1834–96) anticipated the closure of its factories, but he could not have foreseen the patchwork of brownfields, light industry, and rundown housing that evolved during the twentieth century or the carefully engineered Queen Elizabeth Park, legacy Olympic sporting venues, shopping malls, and housing developments that dominate the region today. In the imagined future of *News from Nowhere*, West Ham had reverted to the pastoral marshlands of his youth:

> The houses are scattered wide about the meadows there, which are very beautiful, especially when you get on to the lovely river Lea (where old Isaak [sic] Walton used to fish, you know) about the places called Stratford and Old Ford, names which of course you will not have heard of, though the Romans were busy there once upon a time ... Past the Docks eastward and landward it is all flat pasture, once marsh, except for a few gardens, and there are very few permanent dwellings there: scarcely anything but a few sheds, and cots for the men who come to look after the great herds of cattle pasturing there ... There is a place called Canning's Town, and further out, Silvertown, where the pleasant meadows are at their pleasantest: doubtless they were once slums, and wretched enough.[21]

This passage hints at the "wretched" conditions in West Ham, but it also portrays a future in which industrial development has been rejected and the destruction wrought during the nineteenth century has been repaired. By the mid-twentieth century, market forces, new technology, and lack of regulation were effective in diminishing West Ham's industry, but they did not pay for its environmental remediation. After decades of steady decline, the rehabilitation of the Lower Lea Valley became the utopian vision of a new generation, this time expressed by planners and property developers.

In 2006, Olympic promoters promised a future that was more in tune with Tony Blair's New Labour than with the socialism of William Morris, but they nonetheless saw major landscape transformation and environmental remediation as the means to address the long-standing socioeconomic challenges of the region. As a promotional website explained,

> The Olympic Park will lie at the heart of the Lower Lea Valley, just four miles from Tower Bridge. Currently one of the capital's most underdeveloped

areas, the Lea Valley is an area of outstanding potential which will be transformed by the Olympic Games and Paralympic Games. The Games legacy will transform this area into one of the largest urban parks created in Europe for more than 150 years, stretching 20 miles from the Hertfordshire countryside to the tidal estuary of the River Thames. A network of footpaths, cycleways and canal towpaths will link the communities on either side of the valley. Riverside housing, shops, restaurants and cafes will provide new amenities for the local community. New playing fields will sit alongside the world-class sport facilities that will be adapted for community use. The natural river system of the valley will be restored, canals would be dredged and waterways widened. Birdwatchers and ecologists will be able to enjoy three hectares of new wetland habitat. And the park will be planted with native species, including oak, ash, birch, hazel, holly, blackthorn and hawthorn, providing a home for wildlife in the middle of the city. The rehabilitation of the Lower Lea Valley lies at the heart of the Olympic legacy to east London, restoring an eco-system and revitalising an entire community.[22]

This glowing vision of urban regeneration was part of a marketing campaign to sell the Olympics to the British public. The project's backers had the political and economic clout to transform the region with the Olympic Park, an enormous retail mall, high-speed rail hubs, and a major residential development. The revitalization of the Lower Lea had further knock-on effects, and there are now plans for a third business centre in Silvertown to complement the City of London and Canary Wharf. The legacy of the industrial economy – polluted brownfields and rivers – had long been a major hindrance to redevelopment, but the Olympics allowed the government to spend billions of pounds on resolving the problem. Although the reality of the redevelopment schemes failed to live up to the utopian promises of social and environmental harmony, Newham is currently re-emerging as an economically dynamic and densely populated part of Greater London, a century after West Ham began its dramatic decline.

The remarkable redevelopment of the Lower Lea and Newham is occurring at a pace that rivals the first boom period of the nineteenth century. The population of Newham grew by more than 100,000 between 1991 and 2011, reaching 308,000.[23] The former wetlands of the Lower Lea and Thames Estuary now feature major convention centres, sporting venues, shopping malls, office towers, and riverside housing for the affluent. With this trend, the environmental conditions are improving. Toxic waste is removed from the soil, and reed beds add to the biodiversity of the back rivers. And though the Queen Elizabeth Olympic Park is a far cry from

Morris's utopian vision of restored rivers and marshlands, the urban environment is now in significantly better shape than it was during the early twentieth century.[24]

The social transformations are more concerning. Iain Sinclair, a leading critic of gentrification and the Olympics, argues that rising rents and demolitions are displacing the people of West Ham and Hackney.[25] The history of this area demonstrates a long-standing and ongoing correlation between social and environmental conditions. As the Olympic organizers and other developers succeeded in cleaning the environment, the socially marginalized residents of nearby housing faced eviction to make way for further redevelopment.[26] Away from the gentrified Lower Lea Valley, Royal Docks, and River Thames, the rest of Newham continues to struggle with major social problems. A 2013 report ranked Newham as the worst local government district in the country for overcrowding, and it remained among the bottom three districts in London for child poverty, unemployment, and the low-paid work of its population.[27] There are also some positive signs that the government is showing a real commitment to improving social problems as part of the Olympic legacy, and the local government has been innovative in developing successful schemes to place residents in the jobs that are being created in the region.[28] West Ham and the Lower Lea Valley are again emerging as a driver of Greater London's economic development, but the extent to which this trend will be darkened by the endemic social challenges that have plagued West Ham since the mid-nineteenth century remains unclear.

During the second half of the nineteenth century, market forces transformed the marshlands of the Lower Lea Valley and Thames Estuary into a productive industrial zone. As observers recognized from the start, this incurred major environmental and human costs. Pollution from sewage and industry damaged the rivers and reduced biodiversity. Floods regularly inundated factories and homes. Children and adults died by the thousands from infectious diseases caused by the insanitary state of the crowded streets near the rivers. Some of the environmental and human damage was an unavoidable cost that accompanied industrial and population growth. It was not possible to preserve the marshlands while simultaneously building the factories. However, solutions were available in many other cases. The means to provide adequate sewers, functional drains, a reliable water network, decent housing, and flood defences were all available by the late nineteenth century. Politicians, landlords, industrialists, and middle-class voters chose to focus on rapid economic growth and low tax rates instead of fixing the environmental, health, and social problems of West Ham.

Making matters worse, local politicians had limited resources, and the national governments declined to shoulder responsibility. The voters of West Ham finally supported a new political direction at the end of the nineteenth century. They embraced government intervention and regulation to limit the damage done by the unfettered market, but by that time the damage was done. Although public health improved, the economy faltered, poverty persisted, and the Lea remained one of the most polluted rivers in England.

Historical GIS

HISTORICAL GEOGRAPHIC INFORMATION Systems methods adapt software and approaches designed for environmental management and urban planning to examine spatial history.[1] The digitization of most nineteenth-century Ordnance Survey maps of London and numerous other historical maps makes it possible to explore urbanization at a very large scale. Digitized historical boundaries and related statistical data from the census and other sources expand this capacity further.

The original Ordnance Survey maps are large and cumbersome, as they provide a highly detailed representation of the urban landscape. The 1893–95 revision of the London, Five Feet to the Mile, Ordnance Survey Maps, consists of 759 sheets, each measuring 74 by 105 centimetres.[2] Obviously, examining each one to identify all the factories and other features of interest in London and West Ham would be exceptionally difficult. It would be more difficult still to gather that information together into a single map without using GIS. Digital mapping software provides the now familiar pan and zoom functions that are available through Internet mapping services. Readers who wish to appreciate the scale of this source material can view an online version of the 1893–95 maps, which are available through a partnership between the National Library of Scotland and the David Rumsey Historical Map Collection.[3] This book relies on a different version of these maps, provided by Edina's Historic Digimap website; this allows researchers to download Ordnance Survey maps, which have already been scanned, trimmed, and georeferenced.[4]

The HGIS database for this project relies on the First Series and First Revisions of the Ordnance Survey City Plans for all of London. The database also includes numerous archival maps from the London Metropolitan Archives and other published maps for West Ham, dating from the early nineteenth century through to the early twentieth century.[5] These maps were georeferenced by finding appropriate control points on modern maps, making it possible to layer them with the maps from the Digimap collection. The database also relied on boundaries and statistical data from the Great Britain Historical Geographic Information Systems project and statistical data found in primary source documents.

Once the primary source maps are digitized and georeferenced, the next step in the HGIS methodology involves creating points, lines, and polygons to represent historical land use patterns. This entailed identifying factories, docks, and waterways across London. In some cases, such as the River Thames, we started with modern Open Ordnance Survey polygons and edited them to better match the river as depicted on the nineteenth-century maps. The GIS polygon data for the factories and docks across London and the railways and roads in West Ham were all created new for this project. It was then possible to combine these layers to create maps such as the ones found throughout this book.

The process of producing these digital layers provides a new systematic way to read historical maps. Carefully locating hundreds of polygons to represent the factories found on the Ordnance Survey maps makes it possible to see concentrations of factories and sections of land that remained open or undeveloped throughout the boom period. Creating the database helps researchers better understand spatial change over time.

Developing an HGIS database also involves linking the points, lines, and polygons with tables of data of various kinds. For the industiral polygon data, our small team of students created a table with the factory name as it appeared on the maps and the category of industry. We also recorded whether the factory appeared on both sets of maps or only on the first series or first revision. This makes it possible to distinguish engineering works from food-processing factories or leather tanneries, and to query the database to create maps for different points in time. The tabular data also include statistics that enabled us to map the geography of disease and infant mortality in West Ham and Greater London. Developing the HGIS database shaped the direction of this book and made it possible to explore the relationship between the changing environmental conditions in and around West Ham and the social and political development of the suburb.

The resulting HGIS database and maps are not an exact representation of the actual historical landscape.[6] The result of large government projects, the Ordnance Survey maps were not simple objective reproductions of reality. They attempted to capture a dynamic landscape at a single moment in time, and they probably made errors as they mapped what was then the largest city in the world. Moreover, the maps are opaque and it is not always clear where one property starts and another one stops. Creating the individual polygons for each factory involved a certain amount of estimation, and the research team employed a quality control process to make the approximations as consistent as possible. Even so, the database is not reliable enough for precise queries, such as the total number of hectares or percentage of land used for industry. The Ordnance Survey maps did not usually label individual buildings, and what labels do exist range from detailed to vague. This makes the digitization process error-prone. It is easier to identify factories that stand along rivers and canals than those in the middle of the city. The small team of students and the author worked to find all of the industry in both the first series and the first revisions but probably missed some factories. The evidence found on the maps was supplemented with other sources, including the Victoria County Histories and the Survey of London (both available through British History Online) and Andrew Tweedie's Grace's Guide website, which hosts extensive resources on British industrial history.[7] Although it is important to acknowledge their limitations, HGIS methods nonetheless give researchers an unparalleled tool that significantly increases our ability to explore London's spatial history. The database remains in development as part of a new project, and it is available to researchers upon request.

Notes

FOREWORD

1 Friedrich Engels, *The Condition of the Working Class in England in 1844* [in German] (Leipzig: Otto Wigand, 1845; English edition consulted, London: Swan Sonnenschein, 1892), 49–50.

2 Richard Lawton, "An Age of Great Cities," *Town Planning Review*, 43, 3 (1972), 199–224; quotation on 199. Most of the data in the remainder of this paragraph are also derived from this source, but see also for final estimates: A Vision of Britain through Time, "Population of Urban Districts, grouped by the numbers of their populations, 1911," http://www.visionofbritain.org.uk/census/table_page.jsp?tab_id=EW1911GEN_M7&show=.

3 Estimates of the number of cities with populations of more than 100,000 vary because of the difficulties of determining the functional spatial limits of towns and the frequency with which boundaries were adjusted.

4 Asa Briggs, *Victorian Cities* (London: Odhams Press, 1963), 16.

5 Briggs, *Victorian Cities*, 176 (Queen Victoria at the opening of the City Hall), 164, 160 (civic leader Dr. J.D. Heaton), 165 (chorus).

6 *Chambers' Edinburgh Journal*, 1858, cited by Briggs, *Victorian Cities*, 83.

7 Benjamin Love, *Manchester As It Is: Or, Notices of the Institutions, Manufactures, Commerce, Railways etc.* (Manchester: Love and Barton, 1839), 10.

8 Arthur Sherwell, *Life in West London: A Study and a Contrast* (London: Methuen, 1901), cited by Briggs, *Victorian Cities*, 324.

9 Briggs, *Victorian Cities*, 140; Asa Briggs, *The Age of Improvement* (London: Longman, 1959); Gertrude Himmelfarb, *Victorian Minds* (New York: Knopf, 1968); Peter J. Bowler, *The Invention of Progress: Victorians and the Past* (Oxford, New York: B. Blackwell, 1989).

10 Alfred, Lord Tennyson, "Locksley Hall," written 1835 and published in *Poems* (Boston: W.D. Ticknor, 1842), available at: https://www.poetryfoundation.org/poems-and-poets/poems/detail/45362.

11 Ibid.

12 "Cold, wet, shelterless midnight streets" is from Charles Dickens, "Preface," in *Oliver Twist* (London: Richard Bentley, 1838) [Illustrated by George Cruikshank]. The "landscape of Hell" phrase is from W.G. Hoskins, *The Making of the English Landscape* (London: Hodder and Stoughton, 1955), 171, cited by Martin Daunton, "Introduction," in Martin Daunton, ed., *The Cambridge Urban History of Britain*, vol. 3, *1840–1950* (Cambridge: Cambridge University Press, 2000), 5.

13 *Manchester Guardian*, February 17, 1849.

14 *Report on the Sanitary Condition of the Labouring Population of Great Britain* (1842) cited by Briggs, *Victorian Cities*, 98.

15 Simon Szreter and Graham Mooney, "Urbanization, Mortality and the Standard of Living Debate: New Estimates of the Expectation of Life at Birth in Nineteenth-Century British Cities," *Economic History Review*, 51, 1 (1998), 84–112.

16 Simon Szreter, "Economic Growth, Disruption, Deprivation, Disease and Death: On the Importance of the Politics of Public Health for Development," *Population and Development Review*, 23, 4 (1997), 693–728, quoted in Daunton, "Introduction," 22; and Simon Szreter and Anne Hardy, "Urban Fertility and Mortality Patterns," in Daunton, *Cambridge Urban History*, 3: 629–72.

17 Daunton, "Introduction," 11 and 1 (for "rotten, stagnant ..."). The manure estimate is from Henry Mayhew, "Of the Horse-Dung of the Streets of London," in *London Labour and the London Poor: A Cyclopaedia of the Conditions and Earnings of Those That Will Work, Those That Cannot Work, and Those That Will Not Work*, vol. 2 (London: Griffin, Bohn and Company, 1861), 196. Mayhew considered this a low estimate, acknowledging that the Board of Health, put "the amount of animal manure deposited in the streets of London at no less than 200,000 tons per annum ... Between the Quadrant in Regent-street and Oxford-street," says the first Report on the Supply of Water to the Metropolis, "a distance of a third of a mile, three loads, on the average, of dirt, almost all horse-dung, are removed daily." This amounted to approximately 1,000 tons per annum. See also Appendix 3a of "The Charmed Circle" in Peter Atkins, ed., *Animal Cities: Beastly Urban Histories* (Burlington, Ashgate, 2012), 72, for Manchester estimate below.

18 Briggs, *Victorian Cities*, 98.

19 "Sketches Among the Poor," *Blackwood's Edinburgh Magazine*, 41 (January 1837), 48–50.

20 Elizabeth Gaskell, *Mary Barton: A Tale of Manchester Life* (London: Chapman and Hall, 1848), Preface.

21 Engels, *The Condition*, 63.

22 Michael Rawson, "The March of Bricks and Mortar," *Environmental History*, 17, 4 (2012), 844–51, quotation on 848 suggests the allegory without referencing Engels.

23 Katy Layton-Jones, "The Synthesis of Town and Trade: Visualizing Provincial Urban Identity, 1800–1858," *Urban History*, 35, 1 (2008), 72–95, quotation on 75.

24 Izaak Walton and Charles Cotton, *The Compleat Angler, or the Contemplative Man's Recreation* (London: Richard Marriott, 1653).

25 Briggs, *Victorian Cities*, 80, 85.

26 "The Incorporation of West Ham," *The Times* (London), November 1, 1886.

27 *West Ham Guardian*, January 7, 1899, cited in Jim Clifford, "The Urban Periphery and the Rural Fringe: West Ham's Hybrid Landscape," *Left History*, 13, 1 (2008), 129–42, quotation on 137; and in this book (p. 66).

28 William Cobbett, *Rural Rides* (London: T. Nelson and Sons, 1830), first published in *Cobbett's Weekly Register*, January 5, 1822.

29 See Phillip F. Kelly, *Landscapes of Globalization: Human Geographies of Economic Change in the Philippines* (London and New York: Routledge, 2000), i.

INTRODUCTION

1 [Henry Morley], "Londoners over the Border," *Household Words,* September 12, 1857. Dickens Journals Online, http://www.djo.org.uk/household-words/volume-xvi/page -241.html.

2 Ibid.

3 Using the census to count the population of cities is notoriously difficult because census boundaries rarely include the full population. By 1911, West Ham was the seventh largest county borough in England and Wales. It had a smaller population than Bristol, but was slightly larger than Bradford. The County of London continued to dwarf the largest county boroughs, including Liverpool, Manchester, and Birmingham; three of the twenty-eight metropolitan boroughs that together formed the County of London, Islington, Wandsworth, and Lambeth, had larger populations than West Ham. This still meant that West Ham ranked fourth among the local government districts in the Greater London region.

  I wrote a web-scraping program to collect data from the census reports compiled by Great Britain Historical GIS at the University of Portsmouth and available online at A Vision of Britain through Time, http://www.visionofbritain.org.uk/census/. The 1911 population data are compiled from the reports of 1,835 local government districts. The West Ham population data for 1851 and 1901 come from the parish level boundaries: "West Ham CP/AP through Time: Census tables with data for the parish-level unit, 1801-1961," A Vision of Britain through Time, http://www.visionofbritain.org.uk/unit/10241388/cube/ TOT_POP.

4 R.A. Bray, Review of *West Ham: A Study in Social and Industrial Problems, Being the Report of the Outer London Inquiry Committee,* by Edward G. Howarth and Mona Wilson, *Economic Journal* 18, no. 69 (March 1908): 60.

5 The 1893–95 revision of the Ordnance Survey London Plans identified 105 factories in West Ham.

6 Louise Raw, *Striking a Light: The Bryant and May Matchwomen and Their Place in History* (New York: Bloomsbury Academic, 2011); John Tully, *Silvertown: The Lost Story of a Strike That Shook London and Helped Launch the Modern Labor Movement* (New York: Monthly Review Press, 2014).

7 James Hanley identifies the major inequality between London regions that needed to drain levels and those located on higher ground away from the Thames during the mid-nineteenth century. James G. Hanley, "Public Health, London's Levels and the Politics of Taxation, 1840–1860," *Social History of Medicine* 20, no. 1 (April 1, 2007): 21–38.

8 This was a common issue in industrial cities, where ratepayers dominated the franchise. The Second Reform Act in 1868 started a transition in which local politicians, such as Joseph Chamberlin, could rely on working-class voters to support higher rates and increased government intervention. Simon Szreter, *Health and Wealth: Studies in History and Policy* (Rochester, NY: University of Rochester Press, 2005), 1–20.

9 Ibid., 9–12, 356–59.

10 Frank Mort and Miles Ogborn, "Transforming Metropolitan London, 1750–1960," *Journal of British Studies* 43, no. 1 (January 1, 2004): 1–14; Alan G. Crosby, "Urban History in Lancashire and Cheshire," *Northern History* 42, no. 1 (March 2005): 75–89.

11 David Harvey provides a good theoretical foundation for an approach to urban history that remains attentive to the material conditions of city life and how they shape social and cultural consciousness. David Harvey, *The Urban Experience* (Baltimore, MD: Johns Hopkins University Press, 1989), 230.

12 Stephen Mosley, "Common Ground: Integrating Social and Environmental History," *Journal of Social History* 39, no. 3 (2006): 915–33; Bill Luckin, "At the Margin: Continuing Crisis in British Environmental History?" *Endeavour* 28, no. 3 (September 2004): 97–100; William Cronon, "Modes of Prophecy and Production: Placing Nature in History," *Journal of American History* 76, no. 4 (March 1990): 1122–31.

13 Arthur F. McEvoy, "Working Environments: An Ecological Approach to Industrial Health and Safety," *Technology and Culture* 36, no. 2 (April 1995): S145–73; Gregg Mitman, "In Search of Health: Landscape and Disease in American Environmental History," *Environmental History* 10, no. 2 (2005): 184–210.

14 Anthony S. Wohl, *Endangered Lives: Public Health in Victorian Britain* (London: Dent and Sons, 1983); Anne Hardy, *The Epidemic Streets: Infectious Disease and the Rise of Preventive Medicine, 1856–1900* (Oxford: Clarendon Press, 1993); Bill Luckin, *Pollution and Control: A Social History of the Thames in the Nineteenth Century* (Boston: A. Hilger, 1986).

15 Andrew C. Isenberg, ed., *The Nature of Cities* (Rochester, NY: University of Rochester Press, 2006); Christine Rosen and Joel Tarr, "The Importance of an Urban Perspective in Environmental History," *Journal of Urban History* 20, no. 3 (May 1, 1994): 299–310.

16 For urban environmental histories of London and Manchester, see Peter Thorsheim, *Inventing Pollution: Coal, Smoke, and Culture in Britain since 1800* (Athens: Ohio University Press, 2006); and Stephen Mosley, *The Chimney of the World: A History of Smoke Pollution in Victorian and Edwardian Manchester* (Cambridge: White Horse Press, 2001).

17 Richard Dennis, "Modern London," in *The Cambridge Urban History of Britain*, ed. Martin Daunton (Cambridge: Cambridge University Press, 2001), 3:95–132; Jerry White, *London in the Nineteenth Century* (London: Jonathan Cape, 2007); James Belich, *Replenishing the Earth: The Settler Revolution and the Rise of the Angloworld, 1783–1939* (Oxford: Oxford University Press, 2009), 1–20, 437–55.

18 Martin Daunton, "Introduction," in Daunton, *The Cambridge Urban History of Britain*, 3:1–58; Simon Szreter and Anne Hardy, "Urban Fertility and Mortality Patterns," in Daunton, *The Cambridge Urban History of Britain*, 3:629–72; Bill Luckin, *Death and Survival in Urban Britain: Disease, Pollution and Environment, 1850–1950* (London: I.B. Tauris, 2015), 69–89.

19 Thorsheim, *Inventing Pollution;* Mosley, *The Chimney of the World.*

20 For a survey of the literature on social segregation in nineteenth-century cities and London in particular, see Michael Savage and Andrew Miles, *The Remaking of the British Working Class, 1840–1940* (London: Routledge, 1994), 57–72.

21 Mort and Ogborn, "Transforming Metropolitan London"; Dennis, "Modern London"; Clive Emsley, Tim Hitchcock, and Robert Shoemaker, "Bibliography: London and Its Hinterlands," *Old Bailey Proceedings Online*, Version 7.0, December 2016.

22 Notable exceptions include Harold James Dyos, *Urbanity and Suburbanity: An Inaugural Lecture Delivered in the City of Leicester, May 1973* (Leicester: Leicester University Press, 1973); Harold James Dyos, *Victorian Suburb: A Study of the Growth of Camberwell* (Leicester: Leicester University Press, 1961); Nick Draper, "Across the Bridges: Representations of Victorian South London," *London Journal* 29, no. 1 (2004): 25–43; and Timothy Cooper, "The Politics of the Working-Class Suburb: Walthamstow, 1870–1914," in *Urban Politics*

and Space in the Nineteenth and Twentieth Centuries: Regional Perspectives, ed. Barry M. Doyle (Newcastle upon Tyne: Cambridge Scholars, 2007), 160–72.

23 J.L. Hammond, "The Industrial Revolution and Discontent," *New Statesman* (London), March 21, 1925, quoted in John Marriott, "Smokestack: The Industrial History of the Thames Gateway," in *London's Turning: Thames Gateway – Prospects and Legacy*, ed. Philip Cohen and Michael J. Rustin (London: Ashgate, 2008), 17.

24 Gareth Stedman Jones, *Outcast London: A Study in the Relationship between Classes in Victorian Society* (Harmondsworth, UK: Penguin, 1976), 152–55; Marriott, "Smokestack," 17–18.

25 Michael Ball and David T. Sunderland, *An Economic History of London, 1800–1914* (London: Routledge, 2002); Marriott, "Smokestack."

26 Archer Philip Crouch, *Silvertown and Neighbourhood (Including East and West Ham)* (London: T. Burleigh, 1900); John Marriott, "West Ham: London's Industrial Centre and Gateway to the World I: Industrialization, 1840–1910," *London Journal* 13, no. 2 (1987): 121–42 (hereafter Marriott, "West Ham: Industrialization").

27 Stéphane Castonguay and Matthew Evenden, eds., *Urban Rivers: Remaking Rivers, Cities, and Space in Europe and North America* (Pittsburgh: University of Pittsburgh Press, 2012).

28 Dale H. Porter, *The Thames Embankment: Environment, Technology, and Society in Victorian London* (Akron, OH: University of Akron Press, 1998).

29 Alwyne C. Wheeler, *The Tidal Thames: The History of a River and Its Fishes* (Boston: Routledge and Kegan Paul, 1979).

30 Ibid.; Luckin, *Pollution and Control;* Porter, *The Thames Embankment;* Peter Ackroyd, *Thames: The Biography* (New York: Nan A. Talese, 2008); Gavin Weightman, *London's Thames: The River That Shaped a City and Its History* (New York: St. Martins Press, 2005). For a popular account of the River Lea, see Jim Lewis, *Water and Waste: Four Hundred Years of Health Improvements in the Lea Valley* (London: Libri, 2009).

31 Mitman, "In Search of Health."

CHAPTER 1: THE RIVER LEA AND INDUSTRIALIZATION IN WEST HAM

1 Porter, *The Thames Embankment.*

2 A similar pattern of industrial development occurred on Long Island and in New Jersey, which lay beyond the jurisdiction of New York City, in the late nineteenth century. See Andrew Hurley, "Creating Ecological Wastelands: 'Oil Pollution in New York City, 1870–1900," *Journal of Urban History* 20, no. 3 (May 1994): 340–65.

3 Stedman Jones, *Outcast London*, 152–55; Marriott, "Smokestack," 17–18.

4 John Marriott, "West Ham: London's Industrial Centre and Gateway to the World II: Stabilization and Decline 1910–1939," *London Journal* 14, no. 1 (1989): 43–58 (hereafter Marriott, "West Ham: Stabilization and Decline").

5 W.R. Powell, ed., "West Ham: Industries," in *A History of the County of Essex*, 6:79–89, Victoria County History, British History Online, Institute of Historical Research, University of London, 1973.

6 The East London Waterworks Company, which supplied the region with piped water, relied on the Lea, wells, and a pipe that transported water from the Thames west of London.

7 There are a number of very good sources on the industrial history of West Ham. See Marriott, "West Ham: Industrialization," 121–42; Marriott, "West Ham: Stabilization and Decline," 43–58; Edward Goldie Howarth and Mona Wilson, *West Ham: A Study in Social*

and Industrial Problems: Being the Report of the Outer London Inquiry Committee (London: J.M. Dent, 1907); Powell, "West Ham: Industries"; and Marriott, "Smokestack," 17–30.

8 United Kingdom, House of Commons, "Report from the Select Committee on Rivers Pollution (River Lee); Together with the Proceedings of the Committee, Minutes of Evidence, and Appendix," *Nineteenth Century House of Commons Sessional Papers*, 1886, Proquest U.K. Parliamentary Papers (1886-062337), 1–4 (hereafter, United Kingdom, House of Commons, "Report from the Select Committee on Rivers Pollution (River Lee)"); Frederic Johnson, *Weldon's Guide to the River Lea, from London to Hertford* (London: Weldon, 1880), 6–7.

9 On the 1805 map (Map 2), there are only three back rivers shown north of the high street; it is not clear whether this is an error on the map or if a new leat was dug during the early nineteenth century.

10 According to legend, King Alfred the Great of Wessex diverted the Lea in the ninth century to trap the Viking fleet and created the multiple streams, either in the Lower Lea or perhaps in the Upper Lea. There is no indication that the story is true, but it does demonstrate a long historical consciousness that the Lea changed its course. W.R. Powell, ed., "West Ham: Rivers, Bridges, Wharfs and Docks," in *A History of the County of Essex*, 6:57–61.

11 W.R. Powell, ed., "West Ham: Ancient Mills," in *A History of the County of Essex*, 6:89–93.

12 Ibid.; Robin Wroe-Brown et al., "Saynes Mill: Excavation of a Tide Mill on the River Lea, London," *Post-medieval Archaeology* 48, no. 2 (November 1, 2014): 357–87.

13 The conflicts between millers and upstream communities discussed below confirm that disagreement existed regarding the limited energy resources on the Lower Lea. On the energy limits of an organic economy, see E.A. Wrigley, *Energy and the English Industrial Revolution* (Cambridge: Cambridge University Press, 2010); and Kenneth Pomeranz, *The Great Divergence: China, Europe, and the Making of the Modern World Economy*, rev. ed. (Princeton, NJ: Princeton University Press, 2001).

14 Powell, "West Ham: Industries."

15 Ibid.

16 Committee of the Floods of the Lea, *A Brief Statement of a Case, Involving Not Only the Rights, Privileges, and Property of the City of London, but the Due Administration of Justice* (London: Maurice, 1830), British Library; Committee of the Floods of the Lea and George Hart, *Second Report of the Committee of the Floods of the Lea* (London: Robson, Brooks, 1825), British Library; Committee of the Floods of the Lea and George Hart, *New Tumbling Bay Statement of the Case of the King versus the Commissioners of Sewers* (London, 1824), British Library.

17 W.R. Powell, ed., "West Ham: Agriculture," in *A History of the County of Essex*, 6:74–76.

18 W.R. Powell, ed., "West Ham: Introduction," in *A History of the County of Essex*, 6:43–50.

19 Mary Dobson, *Contours of Death and Disease in Early Modern England* (Cambridge: Cambridge University Press, 2003), 71.

20 This increase from 1,747 to 2,369 acres somewhat exaggerates the amount of land reclaimed, as it includes uplands that were brought under the control of the court to improve drainage of the whole area. Nonetheless, it shows that thousands of acres were slowly drained during the centuries before industrial development began in West Ham, creating the land on which many of the factories and homes were later built. See W.R. Powell, ed., "West Ham: Markets and Fairs, Marshes and Forest," in *A History of the County of Essex*, 6:93–96.

21 James A. Galloway, "Storms, Economics and Environmental Change in an English Coastal Wetland: The Thames Estuary c. 1250–1550," in *Landscapes or Seascapes? The History of the Coastal Environment in the North Sea Area Reconsidered,* ed. E. Thoen et al. (Turnhout: Brepols, 2013), 379–96.

22 Alfred Dickens, *Report to the General Board of Health on a Preliminary Inquiry into the Sewerage, Drainage, and Supply of Water, and the Sanitary Condition of the Inhabitants of the Parish of West Ham, in the County* (London: Eyre and Spottiswoode for H.M.S.O., 1855), 44–46, and the GIS database show the close correlation between ditches and the later street pattern.

23 Committee of the Floods of the Lea, *A Brief Statement;* Committee of the Floods of the Lea and Hart, *Second Report;* Committee of the Floods of the Lea and Hart, *New Tumbling Bay.*

24 Committee of the Floods of the Lea, *A Brief Statement,* 4.

25 Committee of the Floods of the Lea and Hart, *New Tumbling Bay,* Appendix 1.

26 Charles Mackay, *The Thames and Its Tributaries* (London: R. Bentley, 1840), 164.

27 James Thorne, *Rambles by Rivers* (London: Charles Knight, 1844), 199.

28 James Winter, *Secure from Rash Assault* (Berkeley: University of California Press, 2002), 8–9, 143–45.

29 The eastern section of the dock, later named the Albert Dock, was not opened until 1880.

30 Powell, "West Ham: Rivers, Bridges, Wharfs and Docks."

31 Powell, "West Ham: Introduction."

32 Marriott, "West Ham: Industrialization"; Marriott, "Smokestack," 22.

33 Crouch, *Silvertown,* 64.

34 Ibid., 64–65.

35 Ibid., 64; Marriott, "West Ham: Industrialization," 130–33; Marriott, "Smokestack," 22.

36 Marriott, "West Ham: Industrialization," 130–33, 137–38.

37 The 1863–73 and 1893–95 maps (Maps 1, 6–9, and 14–15) rely on a significantly more ac-curate and detailed survey of London than the industry maps for earlier decades. Readers can explore digital versions of the 1863–73 maps (Maps 6, 7, and 14), which are similar to those used to create the HGIS database: "Ordnance Survey, 1st Edition Map of London 1863–80 (1:2500)," Locating London's Past, http://www.locatinglondon.org/static/OS.html.

38 H.E. Malden, ed., "Parishes: Bermondsey," in *A History of the County of Surrey,* 4:17–24, http://www.british-history.ac.uk/vch/surrey/vol4/pp17-24.

39 W.A. Parks, "The Development of the Heavy Chemical Industry of West Ham and District" (master's thesis, University of London, 1949); Powell, "West Ham: Industries."

40 Howarth and Wilson, *West Ham,* 145–47.

41 Marriott, "West Ham: Industrialization," 124–26. Christopher Otter discusses the move-ment of unpleasant industries to Greenwich, directly across the Thames from the Lea's mouth but within the boundaries of London. See Christopher Otter, "Cleansing and Clarifying: Technology and Perception in Nineteenth-Century London," *Journal of British Studies* 43, no. 1 (January 1, 2004): 40–64.

42 J. Andorn (pseud.) and A.W. Barnett, *Industrial Explorings in and around London* (London: J. Clarke, 1895), 136.

43 Stirling Everard, *The History of the Gas Light and Coke Company, 1812–1949* (London: Benn, 1949), 237, 246, 253–54, 289.

44 Ibid., 247.

45 Ibid., 254, 289, 316.

46 Ibid., 287, 301.

47 Marriott, "Smokestack," 29.

48 "Reports on Navigation – Signed Copies Lea Navigation/Stort Navigation, 1908" (January 10, February 7, April 24, and October 26, 1908), Engineer's Reports, Lee Conservancy Board Engineer Office Records, ACC/2423/011, London Metropolitan Archive (hereafter, "Engineer's Reports on Lee Navigation, 1908"); "Minutes, 1908" (January 24, October 30, and November 27, 1908), Lee Conservancy Board, RAIL 845/35, British National Archives (hereafter, "Lee Conservancy Board Minutes, 1908"); "The Channelsea Nuisance," *West Ham Herald,* September 17, 1898; United Kingdom, House of Commons, "Report from the Select Committee on Rivers Pollution (River Lee)," 21, 60–62.

49 B.B. Marston, "Letters to the Editor: State of the River Lea below Tottenham," *The Times,* August 1, 1884; "The Channelsea Nuisance," *West Ham Herald,* September 17, 1898.

50 Editorial, *West Ham Guardian,* January 14, 1899.

51 West Ham Corporation, "Public Health Committee Minutes, 1898–1899" (June 7, July 5, September 6, and September 19, 1899), Newham Archives and Local Studies Library (hereafter, "Public Health Committee Minutes, 1898–1899").

52 D.L. Snook and P.G. Whitehead, "Water Quality and Ecology of the River Lee: Mass Balance and a Review of Temporal and Spatial Data," *Hydrology and Earth System Sciences Discussions* 8, no. 4 (2004): 636–50; Environmental Agency, "Case Study – Water Quality in the Lower Lee Catchment," *Environment Agency,* 2010; Leo Hickman, "Journey along the River Lee," *The Guardian,* October 9, 2009, https://www.theguardian.com/environment/2009/oct/09/river-lee-polluted-source; Environmental Agency, "Fact Sheet – Newham Borough: Environmental Summary, 2009."

53 "Lee Conservancy Board Minutes, 1908" (February 7, 1908), 29.

54 "Engineer's Reports on Lee Navigation, 1908" (January 27, 1908).

55 "The Channelsea Nuisance," *West Ham Herald,* September 17, 1898.

56 "Engineer's Reports on Lee Navigation, 1908," (January 10 and February 7, 1908).

57 "Lee Conservancy Board Minutes, 1908," (October 30 and November 27, 1908).

58 The 1914 Ordnance Survey maps show that some of the marshland had been developed but also that a large portion remained untouched. Ordnance Survey London Town Plans, *Sheet 66: Canning Town and Custom House 1914* (facsimile of original 25-inch to the mile Ordnance Survey maps with reduced scale of approximately 14 inches to the mile) (Leadgate, UK: Alan Godfrey Maps, 1994); Ordnance Survey London Town Plans, *Sheet 53: Bow, Bromley and West Ham 1914* (facsimile of original 25-inch to the mile Ordnance Survey maps with reduced scale of approximately 14 inches to the mile) (Leadgate, UK: Alan Godfrey Maps, 1992).

59 Marriott, "West Ham: Stabilization and Decline," 43–57; Marriott, "Smokestack," 23.

CHAPTER 2: POPULATION GROWTH

This chapter is a revised version of "The River Lea in West Ham: A River's Role in Shaping Industrialization on the Eastern Edge of Nineteenth-Century London" in *Urban Rivers: Remaking Rivers, Cities, and Space in Europe and North America,* edited by Stéphane Castonguay and Matthew Evenden © 2012. Used by permission of the University of Pittsburgh Press.

1 The City of London is the original incorporated city that remained a city within a metropolis, as the conurbation expanded well beyond its borders.

2   Greater London, which became a statistical category in 1870, used the same boundaries as the Metropolitan Police District. The statistical boundary of London expanded in the 1851 census and was used for both the Metropolitan Board of Works and its replacement, the London County Council. Jürgen Osterhammel, *The Transformation of the World: A Global History of the Nineteenth Century,* trans. Patrick Camiller (Princeton: Princeton University Press, 2014), 251. Government statistics continue to use the categories of Inner and Outer London, but their boundaries were reorganized during the twentieth century.

3   Nicholas Goddard and John Sheail, "Victorian Sanitary Reform: Where Were the Innovators?" in *Environmental Problems in European Cities in the 19th and 20th Centuries,* ed. Christoph Bernhardt (New York/Munich: Waxmann Verlag Gmbh, 2004), 87–103; Nicholas Goddard, "Sanitate Crescamus: Water Supply, Sewage Disposal and Environmental Values in a Victorian Suburb," in *Resources of the City: Contributions to an Environmental History of Modern Europe,* ed. Dieter Schott, Bill Luckin, and Genevieve Massard-Guilbaud (Aldershot, UK: Ashgate, 2005), 132–48; Nicholas Goddard, "'A Mine of Wealth'? The Victorians and the Agricultural Value of Sewage," *Journal of Historical Geography* 22, no. 3 (July 1996): 274–90.

4   Goddard, "Sanitate Crescamus."

5   Sewage presented a major environmental and public health challenge in many of Britain's urban rivers. See Luckin, *Pollution and Control;* Jamie Benidickson, *The Culture of Flushing: A Social and Legal History of Sewage* (Vancouver: UBC Press, 2007), 128–53; Goddard and Sheail, "Victorian Sanitary Reform"; Goddard, "Sanitate Crescamus"; and Lawrence E. Breeze, *The British Experience with River Pollution, 1865–1876* (New York: P. Lang, 1993).

6   Luckin, *Pollution and Control,* 52–64; Christopher Hamlin, *A Science of Impurity: Water Analysis in Nineteenth Century Britain* (Berkeley: University of California Press, 1990).

7   Londoners were confronted with river pollution in the centre of the city, as the Thames devolved into a state of crisis between the 1820s and the 1860s. Luckin, *Pollution and Control,* 11–30; Porter, *The Thames Embankment,* 23–76.

8   Dickens, *Report to the General Board,* 57; [Morley], "Londoners over the Border."

9   Hamlin, *A Science of Impurity,* 130–31; Thorsheim, *Inventing Pollution,* 10–18; Dickens, *Report to the General Board,* 57.

10 The zymotic theory blamed microscopic ferments, similar to the yeasts that caused fermentation, as the cause of decay and disease in humans. Like germs, ferments were thought to pass through a water network into bodies and thus cause disease. This theory was a break from the miasmic theories that looked to local environmental problems, such as poor drainage and accumulations of food waste. Hamlin, *A Science of Impurity,* 129–33.

11 Ibid., 190–204; Luckin, *Pollution and Control,* 52–68.

12 As we will see below, Dr. Charles Tidy testified that the sewage effluent of the town of Hertford did not threaten the downstream population; he used chemical analysis to "prove" that the Lea was safe. Also see Hamlin, *A Science of Impurity,* 197.

13 Luckin, *Pollution and Control,* 81.

14 United Kingdom, House of Commons, "East London Waterworks Company. Copy of Report by Captain Tyler to the Board of Trade on the Quantity and Quality of the Water Supplied by the East London Waterworks Company, and of the Memorial from Certain Inhabitant Householders of the East of London upon Which the Inquiry Was Made," *Nineteenth Century House of Commons Sessional Papers,* 1867, Proquest U.K. Parliamentary Papers (1867-043632) (hereafter, United Kingdom, House of Commons, "East London Waterworks Company Report by Captain Tyler, 1867"); United Kingdom, House of

Commons, "Second Report of the Commissioners Appointed to Inquire into the Best Means of Preventing the Pollution of Rivers (River Lee) Vol. I. Report and map, *Nineteenth Century House of Commons Sessional Papers*, 1867, Proquest U.K. Parliamentary Papers (1867-043182).

15 United Kingdom, House of Commons, "East London Waterworks Company Report by Captain Tyler, 1867," 4–5, 8, 15, 17–20. Also see Luckin, *Pollution and Control*, 86–87, 91–92.

16 Luckin, *Pollution and Control*, 91–92.

17 United Kingdom, House of Commons, "Second Report of the Commissioners Appointed to Inquire into the Best Means of Preventing the Pollution of Rivers (River Lee)," x.

18 Ibid., xiii.

19 Ibid.

20 London's sewage led to similar problems in the Thames during the 1850s and prompted similar discussions about the river as an open sewer and a threat to public health. See Luckin, *Pollution and Control*, 17.

21 United Kingdom, House of Commons, "Second Report of the Commissioners Appointed to Inquire into the Best Means of Preventing the Pollution of Rivers (River Lee)," xiv.

22 *The Lee Conservancy Act, 1868, 31 & 32. Vict., c154.*

23 Ibid.

24 United Kingdom, House of Commons, "Report from the Select Committee on Rivers Pollution (River Lee)," 12, 307–11.

25 Hamlin, *A Science of Impurity*, 131; Luckin, *Pollution and Control*, 16–21.

26 B.B. Marston, "Letters to the Editor: State of the River Lea below Tottenham," *The Times*, August 1, 1884. This remark is reminiscent of one made by the Duke of Newcastle in July 1857: he called the Thames a "vast sewer." Quoted in Luckin, *Pollution and Control*, 17.

27 Marston, "Letters to the Editor: State of the River Lea below Tottenham."

28 Ibid.

29 Thomas Francis, "Letters to the Editor: The River Lea," *The Times*, August 21, 1884.

30 Ibid.

31 Ibid.

32 George Singer, "Letters to the Editor: The River Lea," *The Times*, August 25, 1884.

33 United Kingdom, House of Commons, "Report from the Select Committee on Rivers Pollution (River Lee)," 11, 27, 55–59, 307–11.

34 Singer, "Letters to the Editor: The River Lea."

35 George Corble, "Letters to the Editor: The River Lea," *The Times*, August 27, 1884.

36 Ibid.

37 Ibid.

38 C.E. Longmore, "Letters to the Editor: The River Lea," *The Times*, September 3, 1884.

39 Ibid.

40 United Kingdom, House of Commons, "Report from the Select Committee on Rivers Pollution (River Lee)," 9, 39–40.

41 Lamorock Flower, sanitary engineer for the LCB, and Edward Frankland were among the leaders of this new paradigm. Ibid., 30, 32, 39, 47; Hamlin, *A Science of Impurity*, 152–211.

42 Luckin, *Pollution and Control*, 60–61; Hamlin, *A Science of Impurity*, 174–208.

43 Hamlin, *A Science of Impurity*, 197.

44 United Kingdom, House of Commons, "Report from the Select Committee on Rivers Pollution (River Lee)," 64–65.

45 R. Willis, "Letter to the Editor," *The Times*, August 27, 1884.
46 United Kingdom, House of Commons, "Report from the Select Committee on Rivers Pollution (River Lee)," 11, 27, 32, 39, 42, 47–59, 307–11.
47 J.W. Bazalgette, "Letters to the Editor: The River Lea," *The Times*, September 1, 1885.
48 Ibid.
49 Ibid.
50 Lamorock Flower, "Letters to the Editor: The River Lea," *The Times*, September 30, 1885.
51 "The Pollution of the River Lea," *The Times*, October 18, 1886; "Letters to the Editor: The River Lea," *The Times*, October 19, 1886.
52 "Channelsea River" (Hansard, July 8, 1898), vol. 61 cc320–21, http://hansard.millbank systems.com/commons/1898/jul/08/channelsea-river; "The Channelsea Nuisance," *West Ham Herald*, September 17, 1898.
53 "The Lee Valley: Sewage Farms," *British Medical Journal* 1, no. 2051 (April 21, 1900): 987–88.
54 John Sheail, "New Towns, Sewerage and the Allocation of Financial Responsibility: The Post-war UK Experience," *Town Planning Review* 66, no. 4 (October 1, 1995): 386–87.

Chapter 3: Living in West Ham

1 Richard White, "From Wilderness to Hybrid Landscapes: The Cultural Turn in Environmental History," *Historian* 66, no. 3 (2004): 557–65.
2 Dickens, *Report to the General Board*, 5; Christopher Hamlin, *Public Health and Social Justice in the Age of Chadwick* (Cambridge: Cambridge University Press, 1998), 266–74.
3 [Morley], "Londoners over the Border."
4 Powerful smells were closely associated with illness during the mid-nineteenth century. The prevailing understanding blamed miasmic gases, caused by rotting organic matter, as the source of disease. See Hamlin, *Public Health and Social Justice*, 4–6; and Wohl, *Endangered Lives*, 1–9.
5 Dickens, *Report to the General Board*, 42.
6 Ibid., 43.
7 Ibid., 44.
8 Ibid., 45.
9 W.R. Powell, ed., "West Ham: Local Government and Public Services," in *A History of the County of Essex*, 6: 96–112.
10 [Morley], "Londoners over the Border."
11 Hanley, "Public Health, London's Levels," 21–38.
12 [Morley], "Londoners over the Border."
13 Ibid.
14 The word "ague" applied to fevers generally and particularly to malarial-type fevers, which remained associated with marshlands in the mid-nineteenth century. See Mary Dobson's "Malaria in England: A Geographical and Historical Perspective," *Parassitologia* 36, nos. 1–2 (1994): 35; and Dobson, *Contours of Death*.
15 [Morley], "Londoners over the Border."
16 Ibid.
17 Ibid.
18 Dobson, *Contours of Death*, 1–7, 27–28.
19 [Morley], "Londoners over the Border."

20 Dobson, "Malaria in England"; Dobson, *Contours of Death,* 1–7, 27–28.

21 "Havering Level Commission of Sewers Rate Survey," 1881, Newham Archives and Local Studies Library.

22 Owner John Gurney agreed to sell Ham House estate for less than market value to create a park, if the people of West Ham could find the money. Local ratepayers rejected the plan, feeling that their taxes would rise too much. After a long process, the money was found, with large contributions from the Gurney family and the Corporation of the City of London. Donald McDougall, *Fifty Years a Borough, 1886–1936: The Story of West Ham* (West Ham: Curwen Press, 1936), 210–16.

23 Howarth and Wilson, *West Ham,* 58.

24 J.J. Terrett, *"Municipal Socialism" in West Ham: A Reply to "the Times," and Others* (London: Twentieth Century Press, 1902), 5.

25 Howarth and Wilson, *West Ham,* 36–41.

26 "Minute Book and Papers, 1905–1907," Outer London Inquiry Collection, London School of Economics Archive. Charles Booth led a survey of London, published in seventeen volumes between 1886 and 1903. The survey was completed through house-by-house visits and enabled the creation of detailed maps on the social conditions in every street. "What Was the Inquiry?," Charles Booth's London: Poverty Maps and Police Notebooks, https://booth.lse.ac.uk/learn-more/what-was-the-inquiry.

27 John Marriott used "The New Survey of London Life and Labour" of 1929 to confirm that the social divisions in West Ham remained intact two decades later. John Marriott, *The Culture of Labourism: The East End between the Wars* (Edinburgh: Edinburgh University Press, 1991), 19.

28 Howarth and Wilson, *West Ham,* 56.

29 Ibid., 52.

30 Ibid., 20–29, 32–59.

31 Ibid., 41–42.

32 Ibid., 23.

33 The Ordnance Survey maps from 1915 show a significant increase in allotment gardens. The relative abundance of open space set West Ham apart from the older East End. For a discussion of the problems of density in the East End and the clearing of graveyards to create small pockets of green space, see Peter Thorsheim, "The Corpse in the Garden: Burial, Health, and the Environment in Nineteenth-Century London," *Environmental History* 16, no. 1 (2011): 38–68; Ordnance Survey, *London Sheet L (Includes: Barking; East Ham; West Ham),* 1920, National Library of Scotland, http://maps.nls.uk/view/102345870.

34 County Borough of West Ham, Charles Sanders, *Annual Report of the Medical Officer of Health for 1905,* map inserted between 18 and 19, Newham Archives and Local Studies Library.

35 "Public Health Committee Minutes, 1898–1899," (April 19, 1899), 683–85.

36 Ibid., (November 16 and December 7, 1898, January 4, January 18, and March 8, 1899), 40, 108, 191, 281, 485.

37 Thorsheim, "The Corpse in the Garden," 38–68.

38 Terrett, *"Municipal Socialism,"* 4.

39 Ibid., 5.

40 Ibid.

41 The view south from this bridge also appears in Figures 3 and 4, the photos of the Channelsea River, which show the chemical factories, gasworks, and sewage-pumping station. It is still

possible to walk or bike on the Northern Outfall and to enjoy its great view of the Abbey Mills Pumping Station, the Channelsea, a few remaining factory buildings, and gasometers in the distance.

42 Terrett, *"Municipal Socialism,"* 5.

43 *West Ham Guardian,* January 7, 1899.

44 *West Ham Guardian,* December 7, 1898.

45 As will be discussed further in Chapter 6, one school of social reform focused on urban environmental conditions to explain both moral and physical degeneration.

46 *West Ham Guardian,* December 7, 1898.

47 Anne Hardy, *Health and Medicine in Britain since 1860* (Houndmills, UK: Palgrave, 2001), 19–21, 283–85; Christopher Otter, *The Victorian Eye: A Political History of Light and Vision in Britain, 1800–1910* (Chicago: University of Chicago Press, 2008), 64–67.

48 During the water famine in 1898, a special correspondent for the *Times* reported that local angling clubs approached the East London Waterworks Company, asking to net the depleted reservoirs to harvest the fish before they died due to lack of water. This was north of West Ham, but Figure 11 shows that children continued to fish in the heart of the suburb. "The East-End Water Supply," *The Times,* August 26, 1898.

49 "Interview 105," 14–15, "Interview 331," 18, "Interview 216," 8, in P. Thompson and T. Lummis, *Family Life and Work Experience before 1918, 1870–1973* [PDF scans of oral history transcripts], 5th ed. (April 2005), Colchester, Essex, UK Data Service [distributor], SN: 2000, http://doi.org/10.5255/UKDA-SN-2000-1.

50 "Interview 70," 8, 18, 44, in Thompson and Lummis, *Family Life and Work Experience.*

51 "Interview 302," 14, in Thompson and Lummis, *Family Life and Work Experience.*

52 Ibid., 48.

53 "Interview 332," 14, 40, 44, "Interview 70," 16, "Interview 331," 36–37, 43, "Interview 105," 29, "Interview 216," 20, in Thompson and Lummis, *Family Life and Work Experience.*

54 "Interview, 331," 39–41, "Interview 105," 26–27, Thompson and Lummis, *Family Life and Work Experience*; Emily Cannon, "We Slept Three in a Bed" (unpublished memoir), 4, Newham Archives and Local Studies Library.

CHAPTER 4: THE LABOUR GROUP AND THE WATER QUESTION

1 *West Ham Guardian,* November 5, 1898.

2 The left wing of the Liberal Party consisted of Radicals and Progressives. Radicals espoused liberalism's long-time opposition to aristocratic corruption but did not necessarily concern themselves with social issues and urban conditions. Progressives, along with Fabians and labour allies, dominated the London County Council during much of its early history and were committed to using the government to improve social and environmental conditions in the city. In West Ham, a liberal newspaper called the *Herald* promoted a progressive agenda. West Ham also had a strong independent labour political movement by the end of the century. This movement was spearheaded by union leaders who were divided internally between those who remained politically Liberal and those who belonged to the socialist Social Democratic Federation or the Independent Labour Party. On the distinctions between liberals, Radicals, independent labour, and socialists in London and West Ham's municipal politics, see Paul Richard Thompson, *Socialists, Liberals and Labour* (London: Routledge and Kegan Paul, 1967); Leon Fink, "The Forward March of Labour Started? Building a Politicized Class Culture in West Ham, 1898–1900," in *Protest and Survival:*

Essays for E.P. Thompson, ed. John Rule and Robert Malcolmson (New York: Merlin Press, 1993), 279–321; and Pat Thane, "Labour and Local Politics: Radicalism, Democracy and Social Reform, 1880–1914," in *Currents of Radicalism*, ed. Eugenio F. Biagini and Alastair J. Reid (Cambridge: Cambridge University Press, 1991), 244–70. On the prolonged struggle over London's water supply, see John Broich, *London: Water and the Making of the Modern City* (Pittsburgh: University of Pittsburgh Press, 2013).

3   In his brief discussion of how the water question contributed to the Labour Group victory, Leon Fink largely dismisses it as a causal factor, concentrating instead upon New Unionism and class formation to argue that unique economic and social conditions, and skilled coalition building, allowed for the Group's success. He also highlights that the timing of the engineers' strike played an important role in convincing some members of this skilled workers' union to shift their allegiance from the Liberals. Fink, "The Forward March," 292–301. Fink's brief mention of the water shortage inspired the present chapter. Also see John Marriott, "London over the Border: A Study of West Ham during Rapid Growth, 1870-1910," (PhD diss., University of Cambridge, 1983), 151–67.

4   As discussed more fully below, significantly more voters supported Conservative candidates in the 1895 and 1900 parliamentary elections than turned out to support moderate candidates in the 1898 municipal election.

5   Focusing on the history of public health, Simon Szreter develops an important argument on the significance of high rates of infectious disease in English cities in spurring collectivist government intervention during the final three decades of the nineteenth century. Szreter, *Health and Wealth*. Vanessa Taylor and Frank Trentmann make a similar argument about the role of water consumers in the development of a new sense of entitlement to a stable urban environment and the importance of water issues in the rise of social democracy. Vanessa Taylor and Frank Trentmann, "Liquid Politics: Water and the Politics of Everyday Life in the Modern City," *Past and Present* 211, no. 1 (May 2011): 199–241. David Howell also briefly discusses the importance of "municipal preoccupations," including housing, health, and unemployment, which functioned as an important "meeting ground" for trade unionists and socialist activists from the Independent Labour Party. David Howell, *British Workers and the Independent Labour Party, 1888-1906* (Manchester: Manchester University Press, 1984), 280.

6   Sewage disposal in the Lea Valley had a similar record of failure. Whether a municipal water system would have responded better than the ELWC to the demands created by population growth is not clear. See Chapter 3.

7   United Kingdom, House of Commons, "East London Waterworks Company Report by Captain Tyler, 1867," 20–35.

8   Joseph Hillier argues that constant water was not necessarily better than an intermittent supply. Joseph Hillier, "The Rise of Constant Water in Nineteenth-Century London," *London Journal* 36, no. 1 (March 2011): 37–53.

9   "The East London Water Supply," *The Times*, August 29, 1898; "Editorial: The So-Called 'Water Famine' in East London," *The Times*, September 2, 1898.

10 José Harris, *Private Lives, Public Spirit* (Oxford: Oxford University Press, 1993), 33.

11 Ibid.

12 Ibid.

13 United Kingdom, House of Commons, "First Report of Her Majesty's Commissioners Appointed to Inquire into the Subject of the Water Supply within the Limits of the Metropolitan Water Companies," *Nineteenth Century House of Commons Sessional Papers*, 1899, Proquest U.K. Parliamentary Papers (1899-077054), 8.

14 Ibid.

15 Ibid., 7–10.

16 Ibid.

17 William Bryan, "Engineer Reports, 1898," August 25, East London Waterworks Company Corporate Records, ACC/2558/EL/A, London Metropolitan Archive; William Bryan to I.A. Crookenden, August 15, 17, 18, and 19, 1898, in Drought 1898, in Files on Droughts, East London Waterworks Company Corporate Records, ACC/2558/EL/A/16/015, London Metropolitan Archive (hereafter, Drought 1898, Files on Droughts, ELWC, LMA).

18 United Kingdom, House of Commons, "First Report of Her Majesty's Commissioners," 1899, 7–10.

19 Bryan to Crookenden, August 18, 1898, in Dought 1898, Files on Droughts, ELWC, LMA.

20 For a full analysis of the politics of London's water, see Broich, *London*.

21 Broich, *London*, 124–26.

22 George Shaw-Lefevre, "The London Water Supply," *Nineteenth Century*, December 1898, 988.

23 See Broich, *London*, 1–30; and Christopher Armstrong and H.V. Nelles, *Monopoly's Moment: The Organization and Regulation of Canadian Utilities, 1830–1930* (Philadelphia: Temple University Press, 1986), 32.

24 Thane, "Labour and Local Politics," 246–47; Martin Daunton, "The Material Politics of Natural Monopoly: Consuming Gas in Victorian Britain," in *The Politics of Consumption*, ed. M.J. Daunton and M. Hilton (Oxford: Berg, 2001), 88; Broich, *London*, 65–81.

25 Broich, *London*, 82–120.

26 W.F. Gray and H.C.G. Matthew, "Bruce, Alexander Hugh, Sixth Lord Balfour of Burleigh (1849–1921)," in *Oxford Dictionary of National Biography*, online ed. (Oxford: Oxford University Press, 2008), http://dx.doi.org/10.1093/ref:odnb/32129.

27 United Kingdom, House of Commons, "Royal Commission on Metropolitan Water Supply. Report of the Royal Commission Appointed to Inquire into the Water Supply of the Metropolis," *Nineteenth Century House of Commons Sessional Papers*, 1893–94, Proquest U.K. Parliamentary Papers (1893-070339), 72.

28 Broich, *London*, 90–98, 124–26.

29 "The Water Scandal: Our Annual Famine," *West Ham Guardian*, August 24, 1898. The *Guardian* clearly endorsed moderate and Conservative politicians and clubs. The *History of the County of Essex* confirms that it was the main conservative paper in West Ham in 1898. W.R. Powell, ed., "West Ham: Worthies, Entertainments, Sports and Pastimes," in *A History of the County of Essex*, vol. 6:64–67.

30 "The Annual Water Famine," *West Ham Herald*, August 27, 1898. Despite its Radical and temperance stance, the *Herald* increasingly supported the Labour Group in 1898, as the liberal and Radical faction on West Ham's borough council failed to address the significant social problems plaguing West Ham. Fink, "The Forward March," 287–88.

31 "The Annual Water Famine."

32 "Ivey's Letter," *West Ham Herald*, September 3, 1898.

33 "By the Way," *West Ham Herald*, September 3, 1898.

34 Proletaire, "Our Socialist and Labour Column," *West Ham Herald*, August 27, 1898.

35 Special Correspondent, "The East London Water Supply," *The Times*, August 29, 1898.

36 Special Correspondent, "The East London Water Supply," *The Times*, August 30, 1898.

37 "Editorial: The So-Called 'Water Famine' in East London," *The Times*, September 1, 1898.

38 Ibid.

39 "The Water Scandal: Our Annual Famine," *Guardian*, August 24, 1898.

40 During a meeting with Henry Chaplin, the president of the Local Government Board, delegates questioned the drought argument by pointing to the seven water companies that maintained constant service. "Mr. Chaplin on the London Water Question," *The Times*, September 26, 1898.

41 "The East London Water Supply," *The Times*, September 2, 1898.

42 Taylor and Trentmann, "Liquid Politics," 200.

43 "The East London Water Supply," *The Times*, August 29, 1898.

44 "Mr. Chaplin on the London Water Question."

45 "The Secretary to the General Superintendent, Memorandum" (November 23, 1898), Correspondence with Local Authorities and Other Affected Bodies, in Files on Droughts, East London Waterworks Company Corporate Records, ACC/2558/EL/A/16/014, London Metropolitan Archive (hereafter, Correspondence with Local Authorities, Files on Droughts, ELWC, LMA).

46 "By the Way," *West Ham Herald*, September 10, 1898.

47 Drought 1898: Letters from Consumers Concerning Reduction of Rates, in Files on Droughts, East London Waterworks Company Corporate Records, ACC/2558/EL/A/16/018, London Metropolitan Archive.

48 Gladstonian, "Our Liberal and Radical Column," *West Ham Herald*, September 10, 1898.

49 "The East End London Water Supply," *The Times*, September 7, 1898.

50 "The Water Famine," *West Ham Herald*, September 17, 1898.

51 "Mr. Chaplin on the London Water Question." The SDF sent this same resolution to the ELWC before the mass meeting in Trafalgar Square, with a note dated September 15. The resolution is in Correspondence with Local Authorities, Files on Droughts, ELWC, LMA.

52 "Mr. Chaplin on the London Water Question," 3.

53 Ibid.

54 The Conservative government decided to nationalize the water supply to prevent the LCC from leading the initiative. Broich, *London*, 121–46.

55 A number of labour leaders won seats before 1892 with support from the Trade Unions Congress, but they accepted the Liberal whip and were referred to as Lib-Lab MPs. Hardie was the first independent labour MP, and his victory predates the formation of the Independent Labour Party the following year.

56 Banes won again in 1900, defeating Will Thorne. Thorne finally regained the seat for Labour in 1906, after which the area remained a Labour stronghold.

57 Fred W.S. Craig, *British Parliamentary Election Results, 1885–1918* (London: Parliamentary Research Services, 1989), 206–7; W.R. Powell, ed., "Metropolitan Essex since 1850: Population Growth and the Built-Up Area," in *A History of the County of Essex*, 5:2–9.

58 Registration numbers come from the national election in 1900. The 25 percent figure was attained by dividing the number of registered voters by the estimated adult population (over age twenty) in 1901, using the ratio of adults to children in West Ham, as recorded in the 1911 census. Craig, *British Parliamentary Election*, 206–7; Powell, "Metropolitan Essex since 1850."

59 In West Ham, 20,800 individuals, or 59 percent of registered voters, cast a ballot in the 1900 national election, which is about 14 percent of the suburb's adult population. It appears that even fewer voted in the 1898 municipal election, though the inclusion of female householders would have increased the number of eligible voters. Determining the exact number of voters in 1898 is not possible by simply counting the final votes: each voter had three votes, but there were not always three individuals from the various factions running

in all the wards, so some people probably did not use all three votes. Craig, *British Parliamentary Election*, 206–7; "Total Population, West Ham CP/AP," A Vision of Britain through Time, http://www.visionofbritain.org.uk/unit/10241388/cube/TOT_POP.

60 The Third Reform Bill, of 1884, did not expand the franchise for urban voters; it extended the 1867 reforms to the countryside.

61 J. Davis and D. Tanner, "The Borough Franchise after 1867," *Historical Research* (Oxford) 69, no. 170 (1996): 317, 320, 326–27.

62 Marc Brodie, *The Politics of the Poor: The East End of London, 1885–1914* (Oxford: Clarendon Press, 2004), 44–74; M. Childs, "Labour Grows Up: The Electoral System, Political Generations, and British Politics 1890–1929," *Twentieth Century British History* 6, no. 2 (1995): 123–44.

63 Brodie describes the lodger franchise as the "agents' franchise" because it was very complicated for heads of subletting families to maintain their names on election rolls, and they were usually added only if party agents helped them with the process. In 1911, 13.5 percent of the voters in London were from the lodgers franchise. Brodie concludes that this did not significantly increase the representation of poorer or younger voters. Brodie, *The Politics of the Poor*, 66–68.

64 Ibid., 59–63; Childs, "Labour Grows Up."

65 Howarth and Wilson, *West Ham*, 29–59.

66 Fink, "The Forward March," 308–9.

67 Howarth and Wilson, *West Ham*, 29–59.

68 For a sample of the debate on the politics of the working classes and their relationship with socialism, see Gareth Stedman Jones, "Working-Class Culture and Working-Class Politics in London, 1870–1900: Notes on the Remaking of a Working Class," in *Languages of Class: Studies in English Working Class History* (Cambridge: Cambridge University Press, 1983): 179–238; Ross McKibbin, "Why Was There No Marxism in Great Britain?" *English Historical Review* 99, no. 391 (April 1984): 297–331; Fink, "The Forward March"; Thompson, *Socialists, Liberals and Labour*; and Brodie, *The Politics of the Poor*.

69 This builds on Fink's argument in "The Forward March," 295–301.

70 Thompson, *Socialists, Liberals and Labour*, 132.

71 John Bethell was a Liberal banker and politician who nonetheless allied with the Labour Group at the end of the 1890s in West Ham municipal politics.

72 "Candidates' Election Addresses," *West Ham Herald*, October 29, 1898. The *Herald* did not cover every candidate. Seventeen of the twenty-three supported some action to solve the water problem; the paper did not discuss the position of the remaining six.

73 "Candidates' Election Addresses." As reported in the October 15 issue of the *Herald*, Athey's speeches focused on improving housing for the working classes and using direct unionized labour for municipal works. "Athey at the G.R.E. Works," *West Ham Herald*, October 15, 1898.

74 "Alderman Bethell," *West Ham Herald*, October 15, 1898.

75 "Candidates' Election Addresses."

76 Ibid.

77 Ibid.

78 "Editorial: Next Tuesday's Opportunity," *West Ham Herald*, October 29, 1898.

79 "Candidates' Election Addresses."

80 The Liberal Party struggled in parliamentary elections, electing just one MP in West Ham's two constituencies for a single term between 1886 and 1905. This was Archibald Grove, who represented West Ham North from 1892 to 1895.

81 "Editorial: The Municipal Elections," *West Ham Herald,* October 22, 1898.

82 "Editorial: Next Tuesday's Opportunity."

83 Although the rainfall had returned, the supply restrictions continued through early December because the ELWC wanted to build up a large enough reserve to get it through the winter frosts.

84 Municipal elections were held annually, with a third of the seats contested each year, so the 1898 sweep resulted in only a slim majority. "Let 'Em All Come," *West Ham Herald,* November 5, 1898; "The Bye-Elections," *West Ham Herald,* November 26, 1898.

85 Had the 10,385 Conservative voters from the two parliamentary ridings in 1895 supported the moderate and centrist liberal candidates in the 1898 elections, the Labour Group would have won fewer municipal seats. This is particularly true in the north, where 5,635 people voted Conservative in the 1895 election and 6,613 did so in 1900. In 1898, Stratford's third-place candidate, Spittle, who was the highest-polling moderate, received 1,028 votes. The third-place candidate in Forest Gate, Kettle, a Unionist endorsed by the Conservative Association, received 1,965 votes, suggesting that the moderates brought out only 2,993 of their voters. The three Labour Group candidates in the north – Scott, Terrett, and Athey – all held relatively small margins of victory over the candidates whom the Conservative Association had endorsed: In Stratford, Scott and Terrett received 1,246 and 1,142 votes respectively, beating Reed, a moderate who was awarded 1,012 votes, and Rippin, a Liberal who won 979 votes. In Forest Gate, Athey received 2,284 votes, whereas a Liberal named Spratt took 1,954. "Municipal Elections," *West Ham Herald,* November 5, 1898; Craig, *British Parliamentary Election,* 206–7.

86 *West Ham Guardian,* November 5, 1898.

87 *West Ham Guardian,* November 12, 1898.

88 For a discussion of contested terrain, see Chapter 3 of Judith R. Walkowitz, *City of Dreadful Delight* (Chicago: University of Chicago Press, 1992), 41–80. For the importance of social experience in shaping discourses, see Raymond Williams, *Marxism and Literature* (Oxford: Oxford University Press, 1977), 37–38.

89 Taylor and Trentmann, "Liquid Politics"; Frank Trentmann and Vanessa Taylor, "From Users to Consumers: Water Politics in Nineteenth-Century London," in *The Making of the Consumer,* ed. Frank Trentmann (Oxford: Berg, 2006), 53–79.

90 Taylor and Trentmann, "Liquid Politics," 203–4.

91 Thorsheim, *Inventing Pollution,* 41–67; Szreter, *Health and Wealth.*

92 "By the Way," *West Ham Herald,* December 3, 1898.

93 Ibid.

Chapter 5: Environment and Health

1 Bill Luckin, "Perspectives on the Mortality Decline in London, 1860–1920," *London Journal* 22, no. 2 (November 1, 1997): 128.

2 Szreter and Hardy, "Urban Fertility and Mortality," 632; Szreter, *Health and Wealth,* 203–41.

3 Baggallay to Ivey, November 4, 1898, in Appendix to "Public Health Committee Minutes, 1898-1899" (November 16, 1898), 45.

4 For limited biographical information about Baggallay, see John Venn and John Archibald Venn, eds., "Baggallay or Bagallay, Ernest," in *Alumni Cantabrigienses: A Biographical List of All Known Students, Graduates and Holders of Office at the University of Cambridge,*

from the Earliest Times to 1900, Vol. 2, part 1 (Cambridge: University of Cambridge Press, 1940), 113.

5 Reporting on a Board of Guardians meeting of November 12, the *Herald* noted the elevated rate of typhoid in West Ham. "West Ham Board of Guardians," *West Ham Herald*, November 12, 1898. Baggallay's case and a summary of Sanders and Angell's reports appeared in the paper's December 3 issue. "The Public Health Committee Report," *West Ham Herald*, December 3, 1898.

6 John Thresh, "Appendix: Report on the Sanitary Condition of the Police Court, West Ham" in "Public Health Committee Minutes, 1898–1899" (February 8, 1899), 348.

7 Lewis Angell, "Remarks on the Sanitary Conditions of the West Ham Police Court" (February 3, 1899) appended to ibid, 257.

8 Michael Worboys, *Spreading Germs: Disease Theories and Medical Practice in Britain, 1865–1900* (Cambridge: Cambridge University Press, 2000), 243.

9 "The Condition of the Police Court," *West Ham Herald*, February 18, 1899.

10 Hamlin, *Public Health and Social Justice*, 6.

11 Hardy, *The Epidemic Streets*, 268.

12 Ibid.

13 Thomas McKeown and R.G. Record, "Reasons for the Decline of Mortality in England and Wales during the Nineteenth Century," *Population Studies* 16, no. 2 (November 1962): 94–122.

14 Luckin, "Perspectives on the Mortality Decline."

15 Szreter and Hardy, "Urban Fertility and Mortality," 634.

16 Ibid., 635.

17 James G. Hanley, "The Metropolitan Commissioners of Sewers and the Law, 1812–1847," *Urban History* 33, no. 3 (December 2006): 350–68. Also see John Davis, *Reforming London: The London Government Problem, 1855–1900* (Oxford: Oxford University Press, 1988).

18 Luckin, "Perspectives on the Mortality Decline," 132.

19 County Borough of West Ham, Charles Sanders, *Annual Report of the Medical Officer of Health* (1895–1896, 1897, 1898, 1899, 1900), Newham Archives and Local Studies Library.

20 The diphtheria anti-toxin was one of the first curative therapies that arose from the bacteriological discoveries of the 1880s and 1890s. Sanders convinced the Public Health Committee to permit its use in hospitals. Thus, for the first time, hospitals became locales in which patients recovered instead of simply places to isolate disease. Worboys, *Spreading Germs*, 237. Historians continue to debate the effectiveness of the anti-toxin, and Anne Hardy assigns a more important role to autonomous transformations in the disease, which led to lowered morbidity. Hardy, *The Epidemic Streets*, 102–9.

21 The *Herald* reported that the death rate in West Ham was 3.0 per 1,000, whereas in London it was 1.7 for the same two weeks. "West Ham Town Council," *West Ham Herald*, March 4, 1899.

22 "Local Sayings and Doings," *West Ham Herald*, February 25, 1899.

23 Ibid.

24 Formed in the wake of the Labour Group's 1898 election victory, the Municipal Alliance was a political coalition whose purpose was to unite the opposition.

25 "By the Way," *West Ham Herald*, March 4, 1899.

26 Charles Sanders, "Appendix: Report by the Medical Officer of Helath on the Zymotic Death-Rate and the Prevalence of Diphtheria in the Borough," in West Ham Corporation, "Public Health Committee Minutes, 1899–1900" (January 3, 1900), Newham Archives

and Local Studies Library (hereafter, Sanders, "Report on Diphtheria"); Hardy, *The Epidemic Streets*, 87–88; Worboys, *Spreading Germs*, 255.

27 Worboys, *Spreading Germs*, 6–7, 15, 119, 130, 143, 149, 263, 285.

28 "West Ham Town Council," *West Ham Herald*, July 15, 1899.

29 John G. Morley, "Appendix: Report as to Ventilation of Sewers" in "Public Health Committee Minutes, 1898–1899" (October 17, 1899), 1367.

30 Ibid., 1368.

31 Ibid.

32 Ibid.

33 Ibid., 1373.

34 Ibid., 1374.

35 "Local Notes," *West Ham Herald*, August 19, 1899.

36 "Those Awful Smells," *West Ham Herald*, September 9, 1899.

37 "Leader," *West Ham Herald*, September 9, 1899.

38 "West Ham Town Council," *West Ham Herald*, September 30, 1899.

39 Ibid.

40 "West Ham Town Council," *West Ham Herald*, October 14, 1899.

41 Sanders, "Report on Diphtheria," 204–5.

42 Ibid., 205.

43 Ibid., 204.

44 Ibid., 206–13.

45 Ibid., 214.

46 Ibid.

47 Ibid., 214–15.

48 Ibid., 214.

49 Ibid.

50 Ibid., 215.

51 Sanders also focused on the insufficient disinfection infrastructure in West Ham, which made it difficult for public health officials to properly clean the bedding and clothes of individuals who were nursed at home. Ibid., 214–15.

52 E.H.S., "Obituary: Charles Sanders, M.B. M.R.C.S. Late Medical Officer of Health, West Ham," *British Medical Journal* 1, no. 4017 (January 1, 1938): 49–50.

53 B.G. Bannington points to the combination of house-by-house inspections and the West Ham Corporation Act of 1898 as the turning point in improving public health in the suburb. Before this time, Sanders did not have enough authority to deal with poor-quality housing, and tenants could be evicted if they complained to health officials. B.G. Bannington, "Health, Rates and House Rents," *Public Health* 22 (1909): 370–72. The Outer London Inquiry Committee suggested that there were numerous problems with the suburb's jerry-built housing, including that which stood on dust heaps (garbage dumps), and that town officials were unable to properly enforce building regulations in the 1880s. Howarth and Wilson, *West Ham*, 10–15, 17–18.

54 In 1896, West Ham took control of Bromley's Fever Hospital, which was located in Plaistow. McDougall, *Fifty Years a Borough*, 102.

55 Sanders, *Annual Report* (1895–1896), 9, Newham Archives and Local Studies Library.

56 Sanders, *Annual Report* (1899), 19, Newham Archives and Local Studies Library. The figure of 330 typhoid deaths per million was calculated using an estimated population in 1899, determined by evenly distributing population growth between the 1891 and 1901 census

years. For London's 1881–90 average, see Luckin, "Perspectives on the Mortality Decline,"
128.

57 Graham Mooney established the connection between hot, dry summer weather and elevated
deaths from diarrhea. Graham Mooney, "Did London Pass the 'Sanitary Test'? Seasonal
Infant Mortality in London, 1870–1914," *Journal of Historical Geography* 20, no. 2 (April
1994): 161. Naomi Williams and Mooney argue that hot, dry weather "emphasized the
worst aspects of towns and cities." Naomi Williams and Graham Mooney, "Infant Mortality
in an 'Age of Great Cities': London and the English Provincial Cities Compared, c.
1840–1910," *Continuity and Change* 9, no. 2 (August 1994): 207.

58 Infant deaths in these hospitals were officially included in the mortality figures for the
district in which the hospital was located, not the district where the children lived and
where in many cases they had been born. These statistics were not regularly corrected until
1912, though some MOHs, including Sanders, made an earlier effort in their annual reports
to include in their statistics local residents who had died elsewhere. Thus, using the reported
deaths to map health statistics is fraught with difficulty. Maps 17 and 18 use the uncorrected
numbers for all of the London districts and the corrected numbers from Sanders's 1923
annual report for West Ham, making direct comparisons a little inaccurate. The corrected
rate in Bromley for 1907 was 124.0, compared with the crude rate of 116.5. For the purposes
of Maps 17 and 18, the relatively small difference in IMR when a borough with over five
thousand births did not record fifty deaths locally does not significantly alter the geographic
trends, aside from incorrectly emphasizing the central districts with large hospitals. Graham
Mooney, Bill Luckin, and Andrea Tanner, "Patient Pathways: Solving the Problem of
Institutional Mortality in London during the Later Nineteenth Century," *Social History
of Medicine* 12, no. 2 (August 1, 1999): 227–69; Mooney, "Did London Pass"; Sanders,
Annual Report (1895–1896), 5, Newham Archives and Local Studies Library; Sanders, *Annual
Report* (1911, 1923), Newham Archives and Local Studies Library; Metropolitan Borough
of Poplar, and Fredk. Wm. Alexander, *Annual Report for the Year 1907, on the Sanitary
Condition and Vital Statistics of the Metropolitan Borough of Poplar*, 12.

59 Sanders, "Report on Diphtheria", 208. Before 1904–10, when the link between flies and
the spread of bacteria was discovered, there was speculation that soil temperature and
quality might contribute to infectious disease. This explained the correlation between warm
weather and high rates of diarrhea. Sanders also mentioned soil temperature. Sanders,
Annual Report (1898), 10–11, Newham Archives and Local Studies Library.

60 The streets included in each area were listed in the 1897 report. Sanders, *Annual Report*
(1897), 7–11, Newham Archives and Local Studies Library.

61 In 1907, the Outer London Inquiry Committee reported that Woodgrange Road had a
number of "good class shops" and that "practically the whole population of the ward
[Upton] belongs to the middle class, and a large proportion has some unearned income."
Quoted in Howarth and Wilson, *West Ham*, 43–44.

62 The Outer London Inquiry Committee described the Stratford Marsh area: "In the angle
made by the High Street and the Channelsea River are a few old and small houses, chiefly
inhabited by costers and unskilled workers of a low grade. The Channelsea School, one of
the oldest and smallest in the borough, contains ... some of the poorest children in the
north of the borough." And the Bidder Street area: "Old Canning Town contains some
wharves along the river Lea ... and an area of old houses inhabited by the very poor." The
committee report also mentioned the Hallsville area: "A group of streets in the northwest of the ward, which is the oldest part and farthest removed from any open space, are

inhabited mainly by casual or unemployed labourers. Some years ago the Town Council contemplated closing one of the streets in this area, but refrained because the agents made an effort to improve it. Some of the houses were in a state of extreme dilapidation, the floors, window frames, and doors having been used as firewood by the tenants, and the stoves sold for old iron." Quoted in ibid., 33–34, 49, 55–56.

63   The report had this to say about the Croydon Road area: "The other half of Hudson's Ward, north of the Barking Road, consists mainly of four- and six-roomed houses of the older type, which were not designed for two families. They are inhabited chiefly by dockers and casual labourers." Quoted in ibid., 52.

64   The report also described the limited housing south of the docks: "Silvertown is divided into east and west by a part of the Great Eastern Railway. East Silvertown dates from fifty years ago, and came into existence to supply accommodation for the workers in three large factories ... West Silvertown was built to house labourers in the docks and newer factories. The character of the accommodation varies much ... West Silvertown contains some very small and badly built houses, with small yards." Quoted in ibid., 58.

65   The data in this map come directly from Sanders's reports and have not been corrected or checked against census data. Because Sanders focused on small sections of West Ham, his data should be fairly accurate.

66   The average death rate in England and Wales during the 1890s was 18.2. Hardy, *The Epidemic Streets*, 269.

67   Sanders, *Annual Report* (1897), 7–12, Newham Archives and Local Studies Library; Sanders, *Annual Report* (1898), 6–7, Newham Archives and Local Studies Library; Sanders, *Annual Report* (1899), 6, Newham Archives and Local Studies Library; Sanders, *Annual Report* (1900), 10–11, Newham Archives and Local Studies Library.

68   Bannington, "Health, Rates and House Rents," 372.

69   Ibid., 371.

70   Ibid., 372.

71   Williams and Mooney, "Infant Mortality," 186.

72   Mooney, "Did London Pass," 168.

73   Anne Hardy demonstrates that the decline in some of the other major infectious diseases during the late nineteenth century was not primarily driven by public health intervention. In the case of scarlet fever, diphtheria, and whooping cough, autonomous transformations in the diseases themselves lowered morbidity and contributed to the diminishing death rates. Hardy, *The Epidemic Streets*.

74   Sanders, *Annual Report* (1895–1896), 13, Newham Archives and Local Studies Library.

75   Carol Dyhouse, "Working-Class Mothers and Infant Mortality in England, 1895–1914," *Journal of Social History* 12, no. 2 (Winter 1978): 253–59.

76   West Ham Corporation, "Public Health Committee Minutes, 1899–1900" (March 7, 1900), 472, Newham Archives and Local Studies Library.

77   Sanders, *Annual Report* (1899), 8–9, Newham Archives and Local Studies Library.

78   Charles Sanders, "Sanitary Advantages of Social Amenities. An Address Delivered before the Metropolitan Counties Branch," *British Medical Journal* 2, no. 3287 (December 29, 1923): 1249; McDougall, *Fifty Years a Borough*, 110.

79   D. Porter, "'Enemies of the Race': Biologism, Environmentalism, and Public Health in Edwardian England," *Victorian Studies* 34, no. 2 (1991): 159–78; Ellen Ross, *Love and Toil: Motherhood in Outcast London, 1870–1918* (New York: Oxford University Press, 1993), 202–9.

80 Sanders, *Annual Report* (1901), 11–12, 218, Newham Archives and Local Studies Library.
81 "The West Ham Council," *West Ham Herald,* October 29, 1898.
82 Bannington, "Health, Rates and House Rents," 371.
83 Ibid.
84 People did keep livestock in their yards. Oral history interviews suggest that keeping hens for eggs was fairly common. There were also a number of piggeries throughout suburban West Ham and probably some small dairies as well. "Public Health Committee Minutes, 1898–1899" (November 16 and December 7, 1898, January 4, January 18, and March 8, 1899), 40, 108, 191, 281, 485.
85 Bannington, "Health, Rates and House Rents," 370.
86 Sanders, *Annual Report* (1920–1921), 7–8, Newham Archives and Local Studies Library.
87 Nigel Morgan, "Infant Mortality, Flies and Horses in Later-Nineteenth-Century Towns: A Case Study of Preston," *Continuity and Change* 17, no. 1 (2002): 98–101, 121–27.
88 Hardy, *The Epidemic Streets,* 183–87.
89 Sanders, *Annual Report* (1901), 197–219, Newham Archives and Local Studies Library; Sanders, *Annual Report* (1906), 14–20, Newham Archives and Local Studies Library.
90 Sanders, *Annual Report* (1901), 218–19, Newham Archives and Local Studies Library.
91 Hardy, *The Epidemic Streets,* 184, 188; Sanders, *Annual Report* (1901), 11, 218, Newham Archives and Local Studies Library; Sanders, *Annual Report* (1899), 19–20, Newham Archives and Local Studies Library.
92 Mooney, "Did London Pass."
93 Bannington, "Health, Rates and House Rents," 372.
94 Hamlin, *Public Health and Social Justice,* 2, 12–14.
95 Sanders, "Sanitary Advantages of Social Amenities."

CHAPTER 6: FIXING RIVERS, FIXING SOCIETY

1 "The Great Flood in the Isle of Dogs," *London Daily News* (August 1, 1888); "Storm in West Ham," *Borough of West Ham and Stratford Express,* August 4, 1888.
2 By the mid-nineteenth century, people commonly paid only for urban infrastructure that directly benefitted their property, a practice that was firmly entrenched in English law. It created regular conflicts throughout the rest of the century. Hanley, "Public Health, London's Levels"; Hanley, "The Metropolitan Commissioners."
3 The issue of poor relief is well developed in the literature. See John Davis, "London Government 1850–1920: The Metropolitan Board of Works and the London County Council," *London Journal,* 26, no. 1 (May 1, 2001): 47–56.
4 Bray, Review of *West Ham: A Study in Social,* 60.
5 Powell, "West Ham: Industries," 79–89.
6 Bray, Review of *West Ham: A Study in Social,* 60. For a detailed discussion of the "discovery" of South London, see Draper, "Across the Bridges."
7 [Morley], "Londoners over the Border."
8 Lewis Angell, "Engineer Report," West Ham Local Board Minutes (West Ham, November 23, 1875), 282–83, Newham Archives and Local Studies Library.
9 A local newspaper described the damage done to Hemingway and Company Dry Colour works as a 1928 flood spread through its factory and destroyed large amounts of its chemical stocks. Presumably, this was a regular problem for the many chemical works in the flood zone. "The Great Flood," *Borough of West Ham, East Ham and Stratford Express,* January 11, 1928.

10 For example, a heavy rainfall caused flooding on October 29, 1898. *Courier and Borough of West Ham News,* November 4, 1898.

11 After another major flood in 1953, this problem was finally addressed with the construction of the Thames Barrier in 1982–84.

12 "Overflow of the Thames and Lea," *West Ham Guardian and Essex Courier,* December 4, 1897; "Floods in the District," *Borough of West Ham and South Essex Mail,* January 7, 1905; "The Great Flood," *Borough of West Ham, East Ham and Stratford Express,* January 11, 1928.

13 United Kingdom, House of Commons, "Report from the Select Committee on Rivers Pollution (River Lee)," 1–4.

14 Local Government Board, P.M. Crosthwaite, "Rivers Lee and Stort Flooding" (London, 1920), identifier: 001111178, British Library.

15 "Engineer's Reports on Lee Navigation, 1908" (April 24, 1908).

16 Crosthwaite, "Rivers Lee and Stort Flooding."

17 Dickens, *Report to the General Board,* 44–46; Powell, "West Ham: Markets and Fairs"; Powell, "West Ham: Agriculture."

18 "Storm in West Ham," *Borough of West Ham and Stratford Express,* August 4, 1888.

19 Thirty years earlier, Alfred Dickens had asserted that this commission was not intended to manage a suburban sewer system, but it took a major flood to finally transfer its powers to the new borough council. Dickens, *Report to the General Board,* 8–9, 57–59.

20 "Past, Present and Future, a History of West Ham by the Mayor, a Lecture Delivered at Finsbury," *West Ham Herald,* October 29, 1898.

21 "Storm in West Ham," *Borough of West Ham and Stratford Express,* August 4, 1888; Angell, "Engineer Report," 280–81.

22 West Ham's borough council was continually attacked for the high level of local taxation, and some blamed the municipal socialism pushed by progressives and labour politicians. However, the borough had a more basic problem, as massive population growth in the late nineteenth century forced it to expand the public infrastructure in a very short time, and most of its inhabitants were poor, meaning that even high rates of property tax did not deliver a great deal of revenue. Times, *Municipal Socialism: A Series of Articles Reprinted from the Times* (London: G.E. Wright, Times Office, 1902); Terrett, *"Municipal Socialism";* "Past, Present and Future, a History of West Ham."

23 County Borough of West Ham, "Minute Book, West Ham Sewers, 1890–1903," Newham Archives and Local Studies Library.

24 The plan is described in "Reports on Navigation – Signed Copies Lea Navigation/Stort Navigation, 1890–93" (June 17, 1892), Engineer's Reports, Lee Conservancy Board Engineer Office Records, ACC/2423/004, London Metropolitan Archive (hereafter, "Engineer's Reports on Lee Navigation, 1890–93") and the reason for its failure is recalled in "Engineer's Reports on Lee Navigation, 1908" (January 27, March 11, 1908). The Engineer's Report from March 11, 1908, suggests that the planning and negotiations began in 1880, not 1890, and continued through to 1892. I believe that "1880" is a typo.

25 "Overflow of the Thames and Lea," *West Ham Guardian and Essex Courier,* December 4, 1897.

26 Ibid.

27 The quality of local reporting declined in the early twentieth century after the *Guardian* stopped publishing and the *West Ham Herald* came under new ownership in 1899. In 1902, the *Herald* changed its name to the *Borough of West Ham and South Essex Mail.* Fink, "The Forward March," 309.

28 "Floods in the District," *Borough of West Ham and South Essex Mail,* January 7, 1905.
29 Geoffrey Christie Miller, Gerard Collier, and Edward Goldie Howarth, *Report of a Temporary Colony at Garden City for Unemployed Workmen Mainly from West Ham during February, March and April 1905* (London: P.S. King and Son, 1905), 3.
30 José Harris, *Unemployment and Politics: A Study in English Social Policy, 1886–1914* (Oxford: Clarendon Press, 1972), 4, 10–11; John Atkinson Hobson, *The Problem of the Unemployed: An Enquiry and Economic Policy* (London: Methuen, 1896).
31 Stedman Jones, *Outcast London,* 281–314, 320–21; Harris, *Unemployment and Politics,* 47–50; Harris, *Private Lives,* 237–44; George R. Boyer, "The Evolution of Unemployment Relief in Great Britain," *Journal of Interdisciplinary History* 34, no. 3 (2004): 420–21; Hobson, *The Problem of the Unemployed.*
32 Percy Alden, a leading figure among the social scientists who "discovered" unemployment, gained much of his knowledge of the problem as the warden of Mansfield House, a university settlement in West Ham, and as a councillor and deputy mayor of the borough council.
33 Richard Soloway, "Counting the Degenerates: The Statistics of Race Deterioration in Edwardian England," *Journal of Contemporary History* 17, no. 1 (January 1982): 137–64; Porter, "'Enemies of the Race,'" 159–78; Thorsheim, *Inventing Pollution.*
34 Thorsheim, *Inventing Pollution,* 69.
35 Thorsheim, *Inventing Pollution,* 71–73; Hardy, *The Epidemic Streets,* 19–21, 283–85.
36 For a detailed discussion of concerns with charity and the demoralization of the poor, see Stedman Jones, *Outcast London,* 262–314. In West Ham, the newly formed Distress Committee remained concerned about poorly implemented charity leading to demoralization, and it worked with the COS to investigate all the unemployed people who were registered during the first year. But it was also concerned with allowing good workers to maintain their strength and good character. County Borough of West Ham Distress Committee, "First Annual Report and Secretary's General Observations, October 5th 1905–June 30th 1906," Newham Archives and Local Studies Library (hereafter Distress Committee, "First Report"), 24–25.
37 Distress Committee, "First Report," 25.
38 The *Daily News* published a series of articles on the human consequences of the unemployment crisis in West Ham during the winter of 1904–05. Many were included in Arthur Copping and A.G. Gardiner, *Pictures of Poverty. Being Studies of Distress in West Ham with An Account of the Origin and Administration of "The Daily News" Relief Fund* (London: Daily News, 1905).
39 The distress committee reports provide some indication of the levels of unemployment in 1905–06 and 1906–07. During the first year, 4,785 individuals had registered by May 1906, and in the second year there were 2,310 re-registrations and 2,515 first-time applications. In both years, the committee believed that these figures were too low, as skilled and unionized workers were reluctant to register, and women recognized that registration had limited benefits. The committee had some evidence from a survey carried out by West Ham in 1902, before the economic downturn, that unemployment was probably significantly higher: "In accordance with a decision of the Town Council on the 28th November, 1902, a 'house-to-house' census of the whole Borough (other than certain districts unlikely to be much affected) was carried out the following month. The results showed a total of 5,382 men unemployed in the Southern Wards, and 833 in the Northern Division, or gross

total of 6,215, excluding 495 casual workers doing a day or two's turn at date of such census. Several circumstances, since operative, would, it is feared, have produced a still bigger total had such form of Registration been adopted under the Act." Distress Committee, "First Report," 7; County Borough of West Ham Distress Committee, "Second Annual Report for the Year Ending June 30th, 1907," Newham Archives and Local Studies Library (hereafter Distress Committee, "Second Report"), 7.

40 Distress Committee, "First Report," 26.

41 Ibid., 25.

42 Ibid., 27.

43 Howarth and Wilson, *West Ham,* 399–409.

44 Distress Committee, "First Report," 34–35.

45 This increase of 21,672 was significantly lower than those of 1891–1901 (62,455) and 1881–91 (75,950).

46 Medical Officer of Health Charles Sanders continued to use estimates based on the rapid growth that he had encountered since starting his job in 1887, and this caused incorrect death rate estimates for 1905–10. For an example, see Sanders, *Annual Report* (1909), Newham Archives and Local Studies Library.

47 Distress Committee, "First Report," 34–35. In the third report, the committee revised statistics from the first three years using new categories, creating a new category of "General Labour" with 2,489 registered unemployed in 1905–06; this contributed to the reduction in "Building and Constructive Trades" to 277 labourers and 687 skilled workers. This does not provide much more clarity and does not explain why these individuals were placed in the "Building and Constructive Trades" in the first report. County Borough of West Ham Distress Committee, "Third Annual Report and Secretary's General Review 1905–1908" (hereafter Distress Committee, "Third Report"), 81, Newham Archives and Local Studies Library.

48 The West Ham Board of Guardians, which administered the Poor Law, and the Borough of West Ham were separate entities in the early twentieth century. Their geographic areas of jurisdiction overlapped but were not entirely coterminous, as the board of guardians administered a significantly larger area than council did. However, the members of both board and council were elected, which meant that some of them directly represented the working poor and the unemployed.

49 Distress Committee, "First Report," 34–35; "The Daily Telegraph Shilling Fund for the Starving Poor of West Ham," *The Times,* January 3, 1905.

50 Boyer, "The Evolution of Unemployment Relief," 422.

51 Special Correspondent, "The Unemployed. West Ham," *The Times,* January 2, 1905.

52 Ibid.

53 Ibid.

54 Ibid.

55 Ibid.

56 This coded language was meant to reassure the public that they were not engaged in irresponsible giving, as the Charity Organisation Society led a movement in the 1860s to prevent demoralization through direct charity. "The Daily Telegraph Shilling Fund"; Stedman Jones, *Outcast London,* 256–70.

57 Special Correspondent, "The Unemployed. West Ham."

58 "The Daily Telegraph Shilling Fund."

59 Miller, Collier, and Howarth, *Report of a Temporary Colony,* 5. One of the authors of the report, Howarth, went on to work with the West Ham Distress Committee and the Outer London Inquiry Committee.

60 Kenneth D. Brown, "Conflict in Early British Welfare Policy: The Case of the Unemployed Workmen's Bill of 1905," *Journal of Modern History* 43, no. 4 (December 1971): 616–19, 626–27; Harris, *Unemployment and Politics,* 153, 158–62.

61 Harris, *Unemployment and Politics,* 153.

62 Brown, "Conflict in Early British Welfare," 616.

63 Distress Committee, "First Report," 8–9; Harris, *Unemployment and Politics,* 168–69; Boyer, "The Evolution of Unemployment Relief," 424–26.

64 The first report from the West Ham Distress Committee included a detailed report from the secretary on the scale of the unemployment problem, its causes, difficulties with the act, and proposed solutions. He had a year's worth of data and experience to draw upon, which enabled him to show that the unemployment problem did exist, as thousands of "deserving" unemployed men had been registered, and that the act could not resolve the crisis. Distress Committee, "First Report," 25–30.

65 *Borough of West Ham and South Essex Mail,* May 19, 1906; *Borough of West Ham and South Essex Mail,* July 7, 1906.

66 *Borough of West Ham and South Essex Mail,* July 14, 1906.

67 Ibid.

68 Ibid.; *Borough of West Ham and South Essex Mail,* July 21, 1906; *Borough of West Ham and South Essex Mail,* July 28, 1906; Powell, "West Ham: Local Government."

69 "Engineer's Reports on Lee Navigation, 1908," (October 2, 1908).

70 This was the main "unemployment" policy that the Liberals, then led by Henry Campbell-Bannerman, put forward in the 1906 general election campaign. See Kenneth D. Brown, "The Labour Party and the Unemployment Question, 1906–1910," *Historical Journal* (Cambridge) 14, no. 3 (September 1971): 599.

71 The Distress Committee was aware that the vast majority of the registered unemployed in West Ham had grown up in the city and therefore had little experience of work on the land. Distress Committee, "First Report," 26–27.

72 Distress Committee, "First Report," 15.

73 *Borough of West Ham and South Essex Mail,* March 22, 1907.

74 Distress Committee, "First Report," 12; Distress Committee, "Second Report," 35; *Borough of West Ham and South Essex Mail,* July 12, 1907.

75 *Borough of West Ham and South Essex Mail,* July 12, 1907; *Stratford Express* article reprinted in Distress Committee, "Second Report," 12.

76 Distress Committee, "Second Report," 9–10. The engineer's report explained that the reduction in the volume of water decreased the demands on the pump house; I have speculated that the pump house would consume less coal as a result.

77 Distress Committee, "Second Report," 9–10.

78 Distress Committee, "First Report," 22; Distress Committee, "Second Report," 19–20; Distress Committee, "Third Report," 23, 45–47.

79 Distress Committee, "Third Report," 23.

80 Harris explains that the legislation instructed distress committees to concentrate on the most deserving unemployed who had a background of being regularly in work, but that most committees chose to support men with the most dependants and highest level of

needs. In West Ham, priority was given to married men, based on their age, level of distress, and number of dependants. Those under fifty were generally sent to the farm, whereas those over fifty were mostly sent to the local relief works. Harris, *Unemployment and Politics*, 172–73; Distress Committee, "First Report," 11, 13.

81 Distress Committee, "First Report," 28.

82 Will Thorne and Charles Masterman were the MPs for West Ham; Percy Alden and John Henry Bethell represented nearby constituencies, but both had been councillors in West Ham; and Keir Hardie, the leader of the new Labour Party, was from Scotland and represented a Welsh riding, but had been the Labour MP for West Ham South in 1893.

83 Brown, "The Labour Party," 600–2, 606–7.

84 Distress Committee, "Second Report," 9–10.

85 *Borough of West Ham and South Essex Mail,* March 22, 1907.

86 *Borough of West Ham and South Essex Mail,* July 12, 1907.

87 Distress Committee, "Third Report," 15.

88 "Engineer's Reports on Lee Navigation, 1908" (January 10, 1908).

89 "Engineer's Reports on Lee Navigation, 1908" (February 7, 1908).

90 There are no equivalent records for the West Ham engineer.

91 "Engineer's Reports on Lee Navigation, 1908" (March 11, 1908).

92 "Engineer's Reports on Lee Navigation, 1890–93" (June 17, 1892).

93 "Engineer's Reports on Lee Navigation, 1908" (March 11, 1908).

94 "Engineer's Reports on Lee Navigation, 1908" (April 24, 1908).

95 "Engineer's Reports on Lee Navigation, 1908" (February 7, 1908).

96 "Engineer's Reports on Lee Navigation, 1908" (October 2, December 11, 1908).

97 "Engineer's Reports on Lee Navigation, 1908" (October 30, 1908).

98 Ibid.

99 "Engineer's Reports on Lee Navigation, 1908" (October 2, 1908).

100 "Engineer's Reports on Lee Navigation, 1908" (October 30, 1908).

101 "Engineer's Reports on Lee Navigation, 1908" (December 11, 1908); "Copy of Letter: Fred E. Hilleary (Representing the West Ham Corporation) to Lee Conservancy Board," reprinted in the "Lee Conservancy Board Minutes, 1908" (November 27, 1908), 288.

102 Distress Committee, "Second Report," 14; Distress Committee, "Third Report," 15–17.

103 These included Keir Hardie and Will Thorne in the Labour Party and Percy Alden, John Bethell, and Charles Masterman in the Liberal Party. These individuals figure prominently in Brown's "The Labour Party," but he does not identify their shared background in West Ham politics.

104 Outdoor relief involved direct payments or either cash or food and fuel, and was much preferred to indoor relief in a poorhouse.

105 Brown, "The Labour Party," 605–6, 609–11.

106 Ibid., 602–7, 611.

107 A local rate could have provided distress committees with sustained funding, though this would have been a limited victory in West Ham, as the predominantly working-class suburb had little potential for wealth redistribution. Ibid., 611.

108 Burns won on October 19, 1907, which prevented a local rate to support relief works. Between late October and early December, Tween downgraded his plan to address the Pudding Mill River alone. Brown, "The Labour Party," 610–11; "Engineer's Reports on Lee Navigation, 1908" (October 30, December 11, 1908).

109 "Reports on Navigation – Signed Copies Lea Navigation/Stort Navigation, 1909" (January 9, 1909), Engineer's Reports, Lee Conservancy Board Engineer Office Records, ACC/2423/012, London Metropolitan Archive.

110 County Borough of West Ham Distress Committee, "Fourth Annual Report Report," 1909, Newham Archives and Local Studies Library, 7 and 12.

111 Crosthwaite, "Rivers Lee and Stort Flooding."

112 "Minutes, 1920" Lee Conservancy Board, RAIL 845/47, British National Archives, 8–9, 24, 48, 84–85, 117, 137–38, 166–67, 177, 195.

113 "The Great Flood," *Borough of West Ham, East Ham and Stratford Express,* January 11, 1928.

114 "Joint Committee Engineer Reports" (March 10, 1931 to June 26, 1938), Newham Archives and Local Studies Library.

115 Marriott, "West Ham: Stabilization and Decline."

116 Hanley, "Public Health, London's Levels"; Hanley, "The Metropolitan Commissioners of Sewers."

CONCLUSION

1 A county borough was an independent city that did not share jurisdiction with the county. The boroughs were a mix of major industrial cities and historically independent cities such as Liverpool, Manchester, York, and Bath. London was a unique case in which, as of 1900, the London County Council shared control with the metropolitan boroughs.

2 To rank West Ham's population, I wrote a web-scraping program to collect data from the census reports compiled by Great Britain Historical GIS at the University of Portsmouth and available online at A Vision of Britain through Time, http://www.visionofbritain.org.uk/census/. The 1911 population data is compiled from the reports of 1,835 local government districts; the acreage was collected by visiting the Vision of Britain webpages of the most populated local government districts.

3 Southwark had 169.5 people per acre, and Stepney had 158.4. Hackney's density (67.7) was closer to that of West Ham. Ibid.

4 Dennis, "Modern London," 101–4, 114–16.

5 Taylor and Trentmann, "Liquid Politics," 199–241; Szreter, *Health and Wealth.*

6 Fink, "The Forward March," 306–11.

7 Powell, "West Ham: Local Government."

8 Ibid.

9 Fink, "The Forward March," 310–12.

10 Roy M. MacLeod, ed., *Government and Expertise: Specialists, Administrators, and Professionals, 1860–1919* (Cambridge: Cambridge University Press, 1988).

11 McDougall, *Fifty Years a Borough,* 100.

12 The average size of households in West Ham steadily diminished from 4.67 in 1911 to 3.14 in 1961. This reflected a reduction in the number of children, as the percentage of the population under the age of fifteen dropped from over 35 percent in 1911 to under 25 percent in 1961. The average number of households per occupied dwelling also dropped from 1.43 in 1921 to 1.13 in 1961. The number of occupied houses diminished from 49,280 in 1931 to 39,066 in 1951, before rebounding to 44,097 in 1961. University of Portsmouth, "West Ham MB/CB through Time," A Vision of Britain through Time, http://www.visionofbritain.org.uk/unit/10025904.

13 John Marriott provides a very good overview of industrial decline in West Ham. See Marriott, "West Ham: Stabilization and Decline."

14 Powell, "West Ham: Industries," 79–89.

15 "House of Commons Hansard Debates for 6 July 2005 (Pt 33)," col. 404, http://www. publications.parliament.uk/pa/cm200506/cmhansrd/vo050706/debtext/50706-33.htm.

16 Leo Hickman, "Journey along the River Lee," *The Guardian* (Guardian Media Group), October 9, 2009, https://www.theguardian.com/environment/2009/oct/09/river-lee -polluted-source; Grant Kingsnorth, "Waterways Charity Calls for Solutions to River Lea Pollution," *Hackney Citizen,* January 17, 2013, https://www.hackneycitizen.co.uk/2013/ 01/17/waterways-charity-thames-21-river-lea-pollution/.

17 Anne Power, "Many Direct Impacts of the Olympics Are Already Positive, Not Least That the Follow-Through Is Actually Happening," *British Politics and Policy,* London School of Economics, July 26, 2013, http://blogs.lse.ac.uk/politicsandpolicy/the-olympic-legacy/.

18 Iain Sinclair writes extensively on London's confused relationship with the Lea Valley. Iain Sinclair, *London Orbital: A Walk around the M25* (London: Penguin, 2002); Iain Sinclair, "The Olympics Scam," *London Review of Books* 30, no. 12 (June 19, 2008): 17–23; Iain Sinclair, *Ghost Milk: Calling Time on the Grand Project* (London: Penguin, 2012).

19 "London 2012: A Valley Reborn," Wayback Machine, Internet Archive, 2006, http://web. archive.org/web/20060618043116/www.london2012.org/en/ourvision/greengames/ a+valley+reborn.htm.

20 "Buried Olympic Gold: Prehistoric Axe and Skeletons Found at 2012 Site in UK's Largest Archaeological Dig," *Daily Mail,* March 5, 2009, http://www.dailymail.co.uk/sciencetech/ article-1159700/Prehistoric-axe-skeletons-Olympic-site-UKs-largest-archaeological-dig. html; Nadia Durrani, "London 2012: Archaeology and the Olympics," *Archaeology* 65, no. 4 (July-August 2013).

21 William Morris, *News from Nowhere* (Boston: Roberts Brothers, 1890), 76–77.

22 "London 2012: A Valley Reborn."

23 London Borough of Newham, "Newham's Population Has Risen"; Duncan Smith, "London's Population High: Top Metropolis Facts," *BBC News,* February 2, 2015, http:// www.bbc.com/news/uk-england-london-31056626.

24 A legacy of the Olympic Park, the Queen Elizabeth Olympic Park remains a major sporting venue, along with playgrounds and walking paths. The level of the ground was raised significantly, and the back rivers flow through small canyons. They remain embanked, so the promise of renaturalized rivers has not been realized, but reed beds have become es-tablished in their waters and will enhance their ecological health. "Reedbeds Could Help Revive Polluted River Lea," *Thames21,* June 18, 2013, http://www.thames21.org.uk/2013/ 06/reedbeds-could-help-revive-polluted-river-lea/.

25 Sinclair, *Ghost Milk.*

26 "London 2012 Legacy: The Battle Begins on a Newham Estate," *The Guardian,* June 13, 2012, https://www.theguardian.com/sport/2012/jun/13/london-2012-legacy-battle-newham; "Olympics 2012 Have Changed the Lower Lea Valley beyond Recognition," *The Guardian,* July 24, 2012, https://www.theguardian.com/uk/2012/jul/24/olympics-changed-lower-lea -valley.

27 "London's Poverty Profile," LPP 2013 Newham press release.

28 Lizzie Presser, "What's Behind the Huge Fall in Deprivation in East London? And No, It's Not Gentrification," *The Guardian,* January 12, 2016, https://www.theguardian.com/

society/2016/jan/12/what-behind-deprivation-east-london-newham-unemployment; Power, "Many Direct Impacts."

Appendix

1 Ian Gregory and Paul S. Ell, *Historical GIS* (Cambridge: Cambridge University Press, 2007); Anne Kelly Knowles and Amy Hillier, *Placing History: How Maps, Spatial Data, and GIS Are Changing Historical Scholarship* (Redlands, CA: ESRI Press, 2008); Anne Kelly Knowles, ed., *Past Time, Past Place: GIS for History* (Redlands, CA: ESRI Press, 2002); Jennifer Bonnell and Marcel Fortin, eds., *Historical GIS Research in Canada* (Calgary: University of Calgary Press, 2014).
2 "Ordnance Survey Maps, London, Five Feet to the Mile, 1893–1896," National Library of Scotland, http://maps.nls.uk/os/london-1890s/.
3 "Seamless Layer of All the Ordnance Survey Maps, London, Five Feet to the Mile, 1893–1895 as a Mosaic on a Google Maps Base," http://maps.nls.uk/os/london-1890s.
4 Georeferencing involves assigning geographic co-ordinates to the scanned images so they can be loaded as a mosaic and layered with other digital features (points, lines, and polygons). Digimap, "Welcome to the Digimap Collections," http://digimap.edina.ac.uk/.
5 Digimap provides a clearing house of geospatial data, including historical Ordnance Survey maps. Ibid. The First Revision maps are also now publicly available from the David Rumsey Historical Map Collection, "The Collection," http://www.davidrumsey.com/. These digitized versions of historical maps are georeferenced with real world co-ordinates. This makes it possible to stack numerous historical maps along with modern spatial data as layers in an HGIS database.
6 For a constructive discussion regarding the limits of cartography, see Rob Kitchin and Martin Dodge, "Rethinking Maps," *Progress in Human Geography* 31, no. 3 (June 1, 2007): 331–44.
7 British History Online, http://www.british-history.ac.uk/; Andrew Tweedie, Grace's Guide to British Industrial History, http://www.gracesguide.co.uk/Main_Page.

Bibliography

ARCHIVAL SOURCES

British National Archives
Lee Conservancy Board Records, RAIL 845.

London Metropolitan Archives (LMA)
East London Waterworks Company Corporate Records, ACC/2558/EL.
Lee Conservancy Board Engineer Office Records, ACC/2423.
Rivers Committee Minutes, London County Council, 1894–1904, LCC/MIN/10.

London School of Economics Archive
Outer London Inquiry Collection, 1905–08.

Newham Archives and Local Studies Library
Borough of West Ham, Council Minutes, 1898–1910.
County Borough of West Ham, Charles Sanders, *Annual Report of the Medical Officer of Health*, 1895–1901, 1903–14, 1920–21, 1923, 1925. [Most years' reports are also available online through the Wellcome Library: http://wellcomelibrary.org/moh/browse/?place =West+Ham]
County Borough of West Ham Distress Committee, Annual Reports, 1905–14.
Havering Level Commission of Sewers Rate Surveys, 1851, 1870, 1881.
Kelly's Directories, 1887–89, 1893.
Lee Conservancy Catchment Board, Flood Relief Papers, 1930–38.
Public Health Committee, Minutes, 1898–1910.
West Ham Local Board, Minutes, 1875.
West Ham Sewers, Minutes, 1890–1903.

NEWSPAPERS

Borough of West Ham and South Essex Mail (formerly *Borough of West Ham and South Essex Herald*) [microfilm and originals]

Borough of West Ham and Stratford Express [microfilm]

Borough of West Ham, East Ham and Stratford Express [microfilm]

County Borough of West Ham Guardian [microfilm and originals]

Daily News [The 19th Century British Library Newspapers collection, (electronic resource)]

Lloyds Illustrated Weekly [The 19th Century British Library Newspapers collection, (electronic resource)]

Pall Mall Gazette [The 19th Century British Library Newspapers collection, (electronic resource)]

Penny Illustrated Paper [The 19th Century British Library Newspapers collection, (electronic resource)]

South Essex Mail and West Ham Herald [microfilm and originals]

The Times [*The Times* digital archive, 1785–1985 (electronic resource)]

West Ham Herald [microfilm and originals]

OTHER SOURCES

Ackroyd, Peter. *Thames: The Biography.* New York: Nan A. Talese, 2008.

Andorn, J. (pseud.), and A.W. Barnett. *Industrial Explorings in and around London.* London: J. Clarke, 1895.

Armstrong, Christopher, and H.V. Nelles. *Monopoly's Moment: The Organization and Regulation of Canadian Utilities, 1830–1930.* Philadelphia: Temple University Press, 1986.

Ball, Michael, and David T. Sunderland. *An Economic History of London, 1800–1914.* London: Routledge, 2002.

Bannington, B.G. "Health, Rates and House Rents." *Public Health* 22 (1909): 370–77. http://dx.doi.org/10.1016/S0033-3506(08)80308-3.

Belich, James. *Replenishing the Earth: The Settler Revolution and the Rise of the Angloworld, 1783–1939.* Oxford: Oxford University Press, 2009. http://dx.doi.org/10.1093/acprof:oso/9780199297276.001.0001.

Benidickson, Jamie. *The Culture of Flushing: A Social and Legal History of Sewage.* Vancouver: UBC Press, 2007.

Bonnell, Jennifer, and Marcel Fortin, eds. *Historical GIS Research in Canada.* Calgary: University of Calgary Press, 2014.

Boyer, George R. "The Evolution of Unemployment Relief in Great Britain." *Journal of Interdisciplinary History* 34, no. 3 (2004): 393–433. http://dx.doi.org/10.1162/002219504771997908.

Bray, R.A. Review of *West Ham: A Study in Social and Industrial Problems, Being the Report of the Outer London Inquiry Committee,* by Edward G. Howarth and Mona Wilson. *Economic Journal* (Oxford) 18, no. 69 (March 1908): 60–64. http://dx.doi.org/10.2307/2221209.

Breeze, Lawrence E. *The British Experience with River Pollution, 1865–1876.* New York: P. Lang, 1993.

Brodie, Marc. *The Politics of the Poor: The East End of London, 1885–1914*. Oxford: Clarendon Press, 2004. http://dx.doi.org/10.1093/acprof:oso/9780199270552.001.0001.

Broich, John. *London: Water and the Making of the Modern City*. Pittsburgh: University of Pittsburgh Press, 2013.

Brown, Kenneth D. "Conflict in Early British Welfare Policy: The Case of the Unemployed Workmen's Bill of 1905." *Journal of Modern History* 43, no. 4 (December 1971): 615–29. http://dx.doi.org/10.1086/240684.

–. "The Labour Party and the Unemployment Question, 1906–1910." *Historical Journal* (Cambridge) 14, no. 3 (September 1971): 599–616. http://dx.doi.org/10.1017/S0018246X00007573.

Castonguay, Stéphane, and Matthew Evenden, eds. *Urban Rivers: Remaking Rivers, Cities, and Space in Europe and North America*. Pittsburgh: University of Pittsburgh Press, 2012.

Childs, M. "Labour Grows Up: The Electoral System, Political Generations, and British Politics 1890–1929." *Twentieth Century British History* 6, no. 2 (1995): 123–44. http://dx.doi.org/10.1093/tcbh/6.2.123.

Cooper, Timothy. "The Politics of the Working-Class Suburb: Walthamstow, 1870–1914." In *Urban Politics and Space in the Nineteenth and Twentieth Centuries: Regional Perspectives*, ed. Barry M. Doyle, 160–72. Newcastle upon Tyne: Cambridge Scholars, 2007.

Copping, Arthur, and A.G. Gardiner. *Pictures of Poverty. Being Studies of Distress in West Ham with an Account of the Origin and Administration of "The Daily News" Relief Fund*. London: Daily News, 1905.

Craig, Fred W.S. *British Parliamentary Election Results, 1885–1918*. London: Parliamentary Research Services, 1989.

Cronon, William. "Modes of Prophecy and Production: Placing Nature in History." *Journal of American History* 76, no. 4 (March 1990): 1122–31. http://dx.doi.org/10.2307/2936590.

Crosby, Alan G. "Urban History in Lancashire and Cheshire." *Northern History* 42, no. 1 (March 2005): 75–89. http://dx.doi.org/10.1179/174587005X38921.

Crouch, Archer Philip. *Silvertown and Neighbourhood (Including East and West Ham)*. London: T. Burleigh, 1900.

Daunton, Martin. "Introduction." In *The Cambridge Urban History of Britain*, ed. Martin Daunton, 3:1–58. Cambridge: Cambridge University Press, 2001. http://dx.doi.org/10.1017/CHOL9780521417075.002.

–. "The Material Politics of Natural Monopoly: Consuming Gas in Victorian Britain." In *The Politics of Consumption*, ed. M.J. Daunton and M. Hilton, 69–88. Oxford: Berg, 2001.

Davis, J., and D. Tanner. "The Borough Franchise after 1867." *Historical Research* (Oxford) 69, no. 170 (1996): 306–27. http://dx.doi.org/10.1111/j.1468-2281.1996.tb01860.x.

Davis, John. "London Government 1850–1920: The Metropolitan Board of Works and the London County Council." *London Journal* 26, no. 1 (May 1, 2001): 47–56. http://dx.doi.org/10.1179/ldn.2001.26.1.47.

–. *Reforming London: The London Government Problem, 1855–1900*. Oxford: Oxford University Press, 1988.

Dennis, Richard. "Modern London." In *The Cambridge Urban History of Britain*, ed. Martin Daunton, 3:95–132. Cambridge: Cambridge University Press, 2001. http://dx.doi.org/10.1017/CHOL9780521417075.004.

Dickens, Alfred. *Report to the General Board of Health on a Preliminary Inquiry into the Sewerage, Drainage, and Supply of Water, and the Sanitary Condition of the Inhabitants of the Parish of West Ham, in the County.* London: Eyre and Spottiswoode for H.M.S.O., 1855.

Dobson, Mary. *Contours of Death and Disease in Early Modern England.* Cambridge: Cambridge University Press, 2003.

—. "Malaria in England: A Geographical and Historical Perspective." *Parassitologia* 36, nos. 1–2 (1994): 35–60.

Draper, Nick. "Across the Bridges: Representations of Victorian South London." *London Journal* 29, no. 1 (2004): 25–43. http://dx.doi.org/10.1179/ldn.2004.29.1.25.

Durrani, Nadia. "London 2012: Archaeology and the Olympics." *Archaeology* 65, no. 4 (July–August 2013). http://archive.archaeology.org/1207/features/london_2012_olympic _park.html.

Dyhouse, Carol. "Working-Class Mothers and Infant Mortality in England, 1895–1914." *Journal of Social History* 12, no. 2 (Winter 1978): 248–67. http://dx.doi.org/10.1353/ jsh/12.2.248.

Dyos, Harold James. *Urbanity and Suburbanity: An Inaugural Lecture Delivered in the City of Leicester, May 1973.* Leicester: Leicester University Press, 1973.

—. *Victorian Suburb: A Study of the Growth of Camberwell.* Leicester: Leicester University Press, 1961.

E.H.S. "Obituary: Charles Sanders, M.B. M.R.C.S. Late Medical Officer of Health, West Ham." *British Medical Journal* 1, no. 4017 (January 1, 1938): 49–50.

Emsley, Clive, Tim Hitchcock, and Robert Shoemaker. "Bibliography: London and Its Hinterlands." *Old Bailey Proceedings Online,* Version 7.0, December 2016. https://www. oldbaileyonline.org/static/LondonBibliography.jsp.

Environmental Agency. "Case Study – Water Quality in the Lower Lee Catchment." *Environment Agency,* 2010. http://web.archive.org/web/20130526162051/http://www. environment-agency.gov.uk/research/library/publications/116038.aspx.

—. "Fact Sheet – Newham Borough: Environmental Summary, 2009." Accessed May 19, 2010. http://www.environment-agency.gov.uk/static/documents/Research/NEWHAM_ factsheet.pdf.

Everard, Stirling. *The History of the Gas Light and Coke Company, 1812–1949.* London: Benn, 1949.

Fink, Leon. "The Forward March of Labour Started? Building a Politicized Class Culture in West Ham, 1898–1900." In *Protest and Survival: Essays for E.P. Thompson,* ed. John Rule and Robert Malcolmson, 279–321. New York: Merlin Press, 1993.

Galloway, James A. "Storms, Economics and Environmental Change in an English Coastal Wetland: The Thames Estuary c. 1250–1550." In *Landscapes or Seascapes? The History of the Coastal Environment in the North Sea Area Reconsidered,* ed. E. Thoen, G.J. Borger, A.M.J. de Kraker, T. Soens, D. Tys, L. Vervaet, and H.J.T. Weerts, 379–96. Turnhout, Belgium: Brepols, 2013. http://dx.doi.org/10.1484/M.CORN.1.101561.

Goddard, Nicholas. "'A Mine of Wealth'? The Victorians and the Agricultural Value of Sewage." *Journal of Historical Geography* 22, no. 3 (July 1996): 274–90. http://dx.doi. org/10.1006/jhge.1996.0017.

—. "Sanitate Crescamus: Water Supply, Sewage Disposal and Environmental Values in a Victorian Suburb." In *Resources of the City: Contributions to an Environmental History of Modern Europe,* ed. Dieter Schott, Bill Luckin, and Geneviève Massard-Guilbaud, 132–48. Aldershot, UK: Ashgate, 2005.

Goddard, Nicholas, and John Sheail. "Victorian Sanitary Reform: Where Were the Innovators?" In *Environmental Problems in European Cities in the 19th and 20th Centuries*, ed. Christoph Bernhardt, 87–103. New York/Munich: Waxmann Verlag GmbH, 2004.

Gray, W.F., and H.C.G. Matthew. "Bruce, Alexander Hugh, Sixth Lord Balfour of Burleigh (1849–1921)." In *Oxford Dictionary of National Biography*, online ed. Oxford: Oxford University Press, 2008. http://dx.doi.org/10.1093/ref:odnb/32129.

Gregory, Ian, and Paul S. Ell. *Historical GIS*. Cambridge: Cambridge University Press, 2007. http://dx.doi.org/10.1017/CBO9780511493645.

Hamlin, Christopher. *Public Health and Social Justice in the Age of Chadwick*. Cambridge: Cambridge University Press, 1998.

–. *A Science of Impurity: Water Analysis in Nineteenth Century Britain*. Berkeley: University of California Press, 1990.

Hammond, J.L. "The Industrial Revolution and Discontent." *New Statesman* (London), March 21, 1925.

Hanley, James G. "The Metropolitan Commissioners of Sewers and the Law, 1812–1847." *Urban History* 33, no. 3 (December 2006): 350–68. http://dx.doi.org/10.1017/S0963926 806004020.

–. "Public Health, London's Levels and the Politics of Taxation, 1840–1860." *Social History of Medicine* 20, no. 1 (April 1, 2007): 21–38. http://dx.doi.org/10.1093/shm/hkl084.

Hardy, Anne. *The Epidemic Streets: Infectious Disease and the Rise of Preventive Medicine, 1856–1900*. Oxford: Clarendon Press, 1993.

–. *Health and Medicine in Britain since 1860*. Houndmills, UK: Palgrave, 2001.

Harris, José. *Private Lives, Public Spirit*. Oxford: Oxford University Press, 1993.

–. *Unemployment and Politics: A Study in English Social Policy, 1886–1914*. Oxford: Clarendon Press, 1972.

Harvey, David. *The Urban Experience*. Baltimore, MD: Johns Hopkins University Press, 1989.

Haywood, R. "Railways, Urban Reform and Town Planning in London: 1900–1947." *Planning Perspectives* 12, no. 1 (1997): 37–69. http://dx.doi.org/10.1080/026654397364771.

Hillier, Joseph. "The Rise of Constant Water in Nineteenth-Century London." *London Journal* 36, no. 1 (March 2011): 37–53. http://dx.doi.org/10.1179/174963211X12924714058689.

Hobson, John Atkinson. *The Problem of the Unemployed: An Enquiry and Economic Policy*. London: Methuen, 1896.

Howarth, Edward Goldie, and Mona Wilson. *West Ham: A Study in Social and Industrial Problems: Being the Report of the Outer London Inquiry Committee*. London: J.M. Dent, 1907.

Howell, David. *British Workers and the Independent Labour Party, 1888–1906*. Manchester: Manchester University Press, 1984.

Hurley, Andrew. "Creating Ecological Wastelands: 'Oil Pollution in New York City, 1870–1900." *Journal of Urban History* 20, no. 3 (May 1994): 340–65.

Isenberg, Andrew C., ed. *The Nature of Cities*. Rochester, NY: University of Rochester Press, 2006.

Johnson, Frederic. *Weldon's Guide to the River Lea, from London to Hertford*. London: Weldon, 1880.

Kitchin, Rob, and Martin Dodge. "Rethinking Maps." *Progress in Human Geography* 31, no. 3 (June 1, 2007): 331–44. http://dx.doi.org/10.1177/0309132507077082.

Knowles, Anne Kelly, ed. *Past Time, Past Place: GIS for History*. Redlands, CA: ESRI Press, 2002.

Knowles, Anne Kelly, and Amy Hillier. *Placing History: How Maps, Spatial Data, and GIS Are Changing Historical Scholarship*. Redlands, CA: ESRI Press, 2008.

"The Lee Valley: Sewage Farms." *British Medical Journal* 1, no. 2051 (April 21, 1900): 987–88. http://dx.doi.org/10.1136/bmj.1.2051.987.

Lewis, Jim. *Water and Waste: Four Hundred Years of Health Improvements in the Lea Valley*. London: Libri, 2009.

Local Government Board, P.M. Crosthwaite. "Rivers Lee and Stort Flooding." London, 1920. Identifier: 001111178, British Library.

London Borough of Newham. "Newham's Population Has Risen." https://www.newham.gov.uk/Pages/News/Newhamspopulationhasrisen.aspx.

"London's Poverty Profile." LPP 2013 Newham Press Release. http://www.londonspovertyprofile.org.uk/press/lpp-2013-newham-press-release/.

Luckin, Bill. "At the Margin: Continuing Crisis in British Environmental History?" *Endeavour* 28, no. 3 (September 2004): 97–100. http://dx.doi.org/10.1016/j.endeavour.2004.06.003.

–. *Death and Survival in Urban Britain: Disease, Pollution and Environment, 1850–1950*. London: I.B. Tauris, 2015.

–. "Perspectives on the Mortality Decline in London, 1860–1920." *London Journal* 22, no. 2 (November 1, 1997): 123–41. http://dx.doi.org/10.1179/ldn.1997.22.2.123.

–. *Pollution and Control: A Social History of the Thames in the Nineteenth Century*. Boston: A. Hilger, 1986.

Mackay, Charles. *The Thames and Its Tributaries*. London: R. Bentley, 1840.

MacLeod, Roy M., ed. *Government and Expertise: Specialists, Administrators, and Professionals, 1860–1919*. Cambridge: Cambridge University Press, 1988.

Malden, H.E. "Parishes: Bermondsey." In *A History of the County of Surrey*, 4:17–24. London: Victoria County History, 1912. http://www.british-history.ac.uk/vch/surrey/vol4/pp17-24.

Marriott, John. *The Culture of Labourism: The East End between the Wars*. Edinburgh: Edinburgh University Press, 1991.

–. "'London over the Border': A Study of West Ham during Rapid Growth, 1870–1910." PhD diss., University of Cambridge, 1983.

–. "Smokestack: The Industrial History of the Thames Gateway." In *London's Turning: Thames Gateway – Prospects and Legacy*, ed. Philip Cohen and Michael J. Rustin, 17–30. London: Ashgate, 2008.

–. "West Ham: London's Industrial Centre and Gateway to the World I: Industrialization, 1840–1910." *London Journal* 13, no. 2 (1987): 121–42. http://dx.doi.org/10.1179/ldn.1987.13.2.121.

–. "West Ham: London's Industrial Centre and Gateway to the World II: Stabilization and Decline 1910–1939." *London Journal* 14, no. 1 (1989): 43–58. http://dx.doi.org/10.1179/ldn.1989.14.1.43.

McDougall, Donald. *Fifty Years a Borough, 1886–1936: The Story of West Ham*. West Ham: Curwen Press, 1936.

McEvoy, Arthur F. "Working Environments: An Ecological Approach to Industrial Health and Safety." *Technology and Culture* 36, no. 2 (April 1995): S145–73. http://dx.doi.org/10.2307/3106693.

McKeown, Thomas, and R.G. Record. "Reasons for the Decline of Mortality in England and Wales during the Nineteenth Century." *Population Studies* 16, no. 2 (November 1962): 94–122. http://dx.doi.org/10.1080/00324728.1962.10414870.

McKibbin, Ross. "Why Was There No Marxism in Great Britain?" *English Historical Review* 99, no. 391 (April 1984): 297–331. http://dx.doi.org/10.1093/ehr/XCIX.CCCXCI.297.

Metropolitan Borough of Poplar, and Fredk. Wm. Alexander. *Annual Report for the Year 1907, on the Sanitary Condition and Vital Statistics of the Metropolitan Borough of Poplar.* Poplar, 1907. London's Pulse: Medical Officer of Health Reports, 1848–1972. Wellcome Library. http://wellcomelibrary.org/moh/report/b18245821#?asi=0&ai=0&z=-0.7836% 2C0%2C2.5672%2C1.6913.

Miller, Geoffrey Christie, Gerard Collier, and Edward Goldie Howarth. *Report of a Temporary Colony at Garden City for Unemployed Workmen Mainly from West Ham during February, March and April 1905.* London: P.S. King and Son, 1905.

Mitman, Gregg. "In Search of Health: Landscape and Disease in American Environmental History." *Environmental History* 10, no. 2 (2005): 184–210. http://dx.doi.org/10.1093/ envhis/10.2.184.

Mooney, Graham. "Did London Pass the 'Sanitary Test'? Seasonal Infant Mortality in London, 1870–1914." *Journal of Historical Geography* 20, no. 2 (April 1994): 158–74. http://dx.doi.org/10.1006/jhge.1994.1013.

Mooney, Graham, Bill Luckin, and Andrea Tanner. "Patient Pathways: Solving the Problem of Institutional Mortality in London during the Later Nineteenth Century." *Social History of Medicine* 12, no. 2 (August 1, 1999): 227–69. http://dx.doi.org/10.1093/shm/ 12.2.227.

Morgan, Nigel. "Infant Mortality, Flies and Horses in Later-Nineteenth-Century Towns: A Case Study of Preston." *Continuity and Change* 17, no. 1 (2002): 97–132. http://dx. doi.org/10.1017/S0268416002004083.

[Morley, Henry.] "Londoners over the Border." *Household Words,* September 12, 1857. Dickens Journals Online. http://www.djo.org.uk/household-words/volume-xvi/page -241.html.

Morris, William. *News from Nowhere.* Boston: Roberts Brothers, 1890.

Mort, Frank, and Miles Ogborn. "Transforming Metropolitan London, 1750–1960." *Journal of British Studies* 43, no. 1 (January 1, 2004): 1–14. http://dx.doi.org/10.1086/378372.

Mosley, Stephen. *The Chimney of the World: A History of Smoke Pollution in Victorian and Edwardian Manchester.* Cambridge: White Horse Press, 2001.

–. "Common Ground: Integrating Social and Environmental History." *Journal of Social History* 39, no. 3 (2006): 915–33. http://dx.doi.org/10.1353/jsh.2006.0007.

Ordnance Survey London Town Plans. *Sheet 53: Bow, Bromley and West Ham 1914* (facsimile of original 25-inch to the mile Ordnance Survey maps with reduced scale of approximately 14 inches to the mile). Leadgate, UK: Alan Godfrey Maps, 1992.

Ordnance Survey London Town Plans. *Sheet 66: Canning Town and Custom House 1914* (facsimile of original 25-inch to the mile Ordnance Survey maps with reduced scale of approximately 14 inches to the mile). Leadgate, UK: Alan Godfrey Maps, 1994.

Osterhammel, Jürgen. *The Transformation of the World: A Global History of the Nineteenth Century.* Trans. Patrick Camiller. Princeton: Princeton University Press, 2014.

Otter, Christopher. "Cleansing and Clarifying: Technology and Perception in Nineteenth-Century London." *Journal of British Studies* 43, no. 1 (January 1, 2004): 40–64. http:// dx.doi.org/10.1086/378374.

–. *The Victorian Eye: A Political History of Light and Vision in Britain, 1800–1910.* Chicago: University of Chicago Press, 2008. http://dx.doi.org/10.7208/chicago/9780226640785.001.0001.

Parker, D.E., T.P. Legg, and C.K. Folland. "A New Daily Central England Temperature Series, 1792–1991." *International Journal of Climatology* 12, no. 4 (1992): 317–42. http://dx.doi.org/10.1002/joc.3370120402.

Parks, W.A. "The Development of the Heavy Chemical Industry of West Ham and District." Master's thesis, University of London, 1949.

Pomeranz, Kenneth. *The Great Divergence: China, Europe, and the Making of the Modern World Economy.* Rev. ed. Princeton, NJ: Princeton University Press, 2001.

Porter, D. "'Enemies of the Race': Biologism, Environmentalism, and Public Health in Edwardian England." *Victorian Studies* 34, no. 2 (1991): 159–78.

Porter, Dale H. *The Thames Embankment: Environment, Technology, and Society in Victorian London.* Akron, OH: University of Akron Press, 1998.

Powell, W.R., ed. "Metropolitan Essex since 1850: Population Growth and the Built-Up Area." In *A History of the County of Essex,* 5:2–9. Victoria County History. British History Online, Institute of Historical Research, University of London, 1973. http://www.british-history.ac.uk/vch/essex/vol5/pp2-9.

–. "West Ham: Agriculture." In *A History of the County of Essex,* 6:74–76. Victoria County History. British History Online, Institute of Historical Research, University of London, 1973. http://www.british-history.ac.uk/vch/essex/vol6/pp74-76.

–. "West Ham: Ancient Mills." In *A History of the County of Essex,* 6:89–93. Victoria County History. British History Online, Institute of Historical Research, University of London, 1973. http://www.british-history.ac.uk/vch/essex/vol6/pp89-93.

–. "West Ham: Industries." In *A History of the County of Essex,* 6:76–89. Victoria County History. British History Online, Institute of Historical Research, University of London, 1973. http://www.british-history.ac.uk/vch/essex/vol6/pp76-89.

–. "West Ham: Introduction." In *A History of the County of Essex,* 6:43–50. Victoria County History. British History Online, Institute of Historical Research, University of London, 1973. http://www.british-history.ac.uk/vch/essex/vol6/pp43-50.

–. "West Ham: Local Government and Public Services." In *A History of the County of Essex,* 6:96–112. Victoria County History. British History Online, Institute of Historical Research, University of London, 1973. http://www.british-history.ac.uk/vch/essex/vol6/pp96-112.

–. "West Ham: Markets and Fairs, Marshes and Forest." In *A History of the County of Essex,* 6:93–96. Victoria County History. British History Online, Institute of Historical Research, University of London, 1973. http://www.british-history.ac.uk/vch/essex/vol6/pp93-96.

–. "West Ham: Rivers, Bridges, Wharfs and Docks." In *A History of the County of Essex,* 6:57–61. Victoria County History. British History Online, Institute of Historical Research, University of London, 1973. http://www.british-history.ac.uk/vch/essex/vol6/pp57-61.

–. "West Ham: Worthies, Entertainments, Sports and Pastimes." In *A History of the County of Essex,* 6:64–67. Victoria County History. British History Online, Institute of Historical Research, University of London, 1973. http://www.british-history.ac.uk/vch/essex/vol6/pp64-67.

Raw, Louise. *Striking a Light: The Bryant and May Matchwomen and Their Place in History.* New York: Bloomsbury Academic, 2011.

Rees, Henry. "A Growth Map for Northeast London during the Railway Age." *Geographical Review* 35, no. 3 (July 1945): 458–65. http://dx.doi.org/10.2307/211332.

Rosen, Christine, and Joel Tarr. "The Importance of an Urban Perspective in Environmental History." *Journal of Urban History* 20, no. 3 (May 1, 1994): 299–310. http://dx.doi.org/10.1177/009614429402000301.

Ross, Ellen. *Love and Toil: Motherhood in Outcast London, 1870–1918.* New York: Oxford University Press, 1993.

Sanders, Charles. "Sanitary Advantages of Social Amenities. An Address Delivered before the Metropolitan Counties Branch." *British Medical Journal* 2, no. 3287 (December 29, 1923): 1246–49. http://dx.doi.org/10.1136/bmj.2.3287.1246.

Savage, Michael, and Andrew Miles. *The Remaking of the British Working Class, 1840–1940.* London: Routledge, 1994. http://dx.doi.org/10.4324/9780203416624.

Shaw-Lefevre, George. "The London Water Supply." *Nineteenth Century,* December 1898.

Sheail, John. "New Towns, Sewerage and the Allocation of Financial Responsibility: The Post-war UK Experience." *Town Planning Review* 66, no. 4 (October 1, 1995): 371–87. http://dx.doi.org/10.3828/tpr.66.4.n541571u7364j737.

Sinclair, Iain. *Ghost Milk: Calling Time on the Grand Project.* London: Penguin, 2012.

–. *London Orbital: A Walk around the M25.* London: Penguin, 2002.

–. "The Olympics Scam." *London Review of Books* 30, no. 12 (June 19, 2008): 17–23.

Snook, D.L., and P.G. Whitehead. "Water Quality and Ecology of the River Lee: Mass Balance and a Review of Temporal and Spatial Data." *Hydrology and Earth System Sciences Discussions* 8, no. 4 (2004): 636–50. http://dx.doi.org/10.5194/hess-8-636-2004.

Soloway, Richard. "Counting the Degenerates: The Statistics of Race Deterioration in Edwardian England." *Journal of Contemporary History* 17, no. 1 (January 1982): 137–64. http://dx.doi.org/10.1177/002200948201700107.

Stedman Jones, Gareth. *Outcast London: A Study in the Relationship between Classes in Victorian Society.* Harmondsworth, UK: Penguin, 1976.

–. "Working-Class Culture and Working-Class Politics in London, 1870–1900: Notes on the Remaking of a Working Class." In *Languages of Class: Studies in English Working Class History,* 179–238. Cambridge: Cambridge University Press, 1983.

Szreter, Simon. *Health and Wealth: Studies in History and Policy.* Rochester, NY: University of Rochester Press, 2005.

Szreter, Simon, and Anne Hardy. "Urban Fertility and Mortality Patterns." In *The Cambridge Urban History of Britain,* ed. Martin Daunton, 3:629–72. Cambridge: Cambridge University Press, 2001. http://dx.doi.org/10.1017/CHOL9780521417075.021.

Terrett, J.J. *"Municipal Socialism" in West Ham: A Reply to "The Times," and Others.* London: Twentieth Century Press, 1902.

Thane, Pat. "Labour and Local Politics: Radicalism, Democracy and Social Reform, 1880–1914." In *Currents of Radicalism,* ed. Eugenio F. Biagini and Alastair J. Reid, 244–70. Cambridge: Cambridge University Press, 1991. http://dx.doi.org/10.1017/CBO9780511522482.012.

Thompson, Paul Richard. *Socialists, Liberals and Labour.* London: Routledge and Kegan Paul, 1967.

Thorne, James. *Rambles by Rivers.* London: Charles Knight, 1844.

Thorsheim, Peter. "The Corpse in the Garden: Burial, Health, and the Environment in Nineteenth-Century London." *Environmental History* 16, no. 1 (January 2011): 38-68. https://doi.org/10.1093/envhis/emq146.

–. "Green Space and Class in Imperial London." In *The Nature of Cities,* ed. Andrew C. Isenberg, 24–37. Rochester, NY: University of Rochester Press, 2006.

–. *Inventing Pollution: Coal, Smoke, and Culture in Britain since 1800.* Athens: Ohio University Press, 2006.

Times. *Municipal Socialism: A Series of Articles Reprinted from the Times.* London: G.E. Wright, Times Office, 1902.

Trentmann, Frank, and Vanessa Taylor. "From Users to Consumers: Water Politics in Nineteenth-Century London." In *The Making of the Consumer,* ed. Frank Trentmann, 53–79. Oxford: Berg, 2006.

–. "Liquid Politics: Water and the Politics of Everyday Life in the Modern City." *Past and Present* 211, no. 1 (May 2011): 199–241. http://dx.doi.org/10.1093/pastj/gtq068.

Tully, John. *Silvertown: The Lost Story of a Strike That Shook London and Helped Launch the Modern Labor Movement.* New York: Monthly Review Press, 2014.

United Kingdom, House of Commons. "East London Waterworks Company. Copy of Report by Captain Tyler to the Board of Trade on the Quantity and Quality of the Water Supplied by the East London Waterworks Company, and of the Memorial from Certain Inhabitant Householders of the East of London upon Which the Inquiry Was Made." *Nineteenth Century House of Commons Sessional Papers,* 1867. Proquest U.K. Parliamentary Papers (1867-043632).

United Kingdom, House of Commons. "First report of Her Majesty's Commissioners Appointed to Inquire into the Subject of the Water Supply within the Limits of the Metropolitan Water Companies." *Nineteenth Century House of Commons Sessional Papers,* 1899. Proquest U.K. Parliamentary Papers (1899-077054).

United Kingdom, House of Commons. "Report from the Select Committee on Rivers Pollution (River Lee); Together with the Proceedings of the Committee, Minutes of Evidence, and Appendix." *Nineteenth Century House of Commons Sessional Papers,* 1886. Proquest U.K. Parliamentary Papers (1886-062337).

United Kingdom, House of Commons. "Royal Commission on Metropolitan Water Supply. Report of the Royal Commission Appointed to Inquire into the Water Supply of the Metropolis." *Nineteenth Century House of Commons Sessional Papers,* 1893-94. Proquest U.K. Parliamentary Papers (1893-070339).

United Kingdom, House of Commons. "Second Report of the Commissioners Appointed to Inquire into the Best Means of Preventing the Pollution of Rivers (River Lee) Vol. 1. Report and Map." *Nineteenth Century House of Commons Sessional Papers,* 1867. Proquest U.K. Parliamentary Papers (1867-043182).

Venn, John, and John Archibald Venn, eds. *Alumni Cantabrigienses: A Biographical List of All Known Students, Graduates and Holders of Office at the University of Cambridge, from the Earliest Times to 1900,* vol. 2, part 1. Cambridge: University of Cambridge Press, 1940.

Walkowitz, Judith R. *City of Dreadful Delight.* Chicago: University of Chicago Press, 1992. http://dx.doi.org/10.7208/chicago/9780226081014.001.0001.

Weightman, Gavin. *London's Thames: The River That Shaped a City and Its History.* New York: St. Martins Press, 2005.

Wheeler, Alwyne C. *The Tidal Thames: The History of a River and Its Fishes.* Boston: Routledge and Kegan Paul, 1979.

White, Jerry. *London in the Nineteenth Century.* London: Jonathan Cape, 2007.

White, Richard. "From Wilderness to Hybrid Landscapes: The Cultural Turn in Environmental History." *Historian* 66, no. 3 (2004): 557–65. http://dx.doi.org/10.1111/j.1540-6563. 2004.00089.x.

Williams, Naomi, and Graham Mooney. "Infant Mortality in an 'Age of Great Cities': London and the English Provincial Cities Compared, c. 1840–1910." *Continuity and Change* 9, no. 2 (August 1994): 185–212. http://dx.doi.org/10.1017/S0268416000002265.

Williams, Raymond. *Marxism and Literature*. Oxford: Oxford University Press, 1977.

Winter, James. *Secure from Rash Assault*. Berkeley: University of California Press, 2002.

Wohl, Anthony S. *Endangered Lives: Public Health in Victorian Britain*. London: Dent and Sons, 1983.

Worboys, Michael. *Spreading Germs: Disease Theories and Medical Practice in Britain, 1865–1900*. Cambridge: Cambridge University Press, 2000.

Wrigley, E.A. *Energy and the English Industrial Revolution*. Cambridge: Cambridge University Press, 2010. http://dx.doi.org/10.1017/CBO9780511779619.

Wroe-Brown, Robin, Ian Betts, Lyn Blackmore, Damian Goodburn, Bob Spain, Geoff Egan, Jackie Keily, and Jacqui Pearce. "Saynes Mill: Excavation of a Tide Mill on the River Lea, London." *Post-medieval Archaeology* 48, no. 2 (November 1, 2014): 357–87. http://dx.doi.org/10.1179/0079423614Z.00000000061.

Map Credits

MAIN SOURCE MATERIAL

OpenData Ordnance Survey VectorMap District Data

Contains OS data © Crown copyright and database right (2014).

Ordnance Survey London Town Plans First Revision

Ordnance Survey London Town Plans. 1st Revisions [TIFF geospatial data], Scale Five
Feet to the Mile, London and Its Environs, Surveyed 1893–1895, Landmark Information
Group, UK. Using EDINA Historic Digimap Service, http://edina.ac.uk/digimap,
downloaded 2013.

Ordnance Survey London Town Plans First Series

Ordnance Survey London Town Plans. 1st Edition [TIFF geospatial data], Scale Five Feet
to the Mile, London and Its Environs, Surveyed 1862–1875, Landmark Information
Group, UK. Using EDINA Historic Digimap Service, http://edina.ac.uk/digimap,
downloaded 2013.

Vision of Britain

This work is based on data provided through www.VisionofBritain.org.uk and uses historical
material that is copyright of the Great Britain Historical GIS Project and the University
of Portsmouth.

LAYERS USED ON NUMEROUS MAPS

Industry Database before 1860

Limited to West Ham, these data were created using archival maps cross-referenced with
secondary sources that discuss early industry in West Ham:

Crouch, Archer Philip. *Silvertown and Neighbourhood (Including East and West Ham)*. London: T. Burleigh, 1900.

Dickens, Alfred. [Map of West Ham]. In *Report to the General Board of Health on a Preliminary Inquiry into the Sewerage, Drainage, and Supply of Water, and the Sanitary Condition of the Inhabitants of the Parish of West Ham, in the County*. London: Eyre and Spottiswoode for H.M.S.O., 1855.

"Map of the River Lee Navigation from the River Thames at Limehouse to Lee Bridge Also of the River Lee with Its Tributary Streams from the River Thames at Bow Creek to Lee Bridge in Four Parts." 1852. ACC/2423/X/. London Metropolitan Archive.

Marriott, John. "West Ham: London's Industrial Centre and Gateway to the World I: Industrialization, 1840–1910." *London Journal* 13, no. 2 (1987): 121–42. http://dx.doi.org/10.1179/ldn.1987.13.2.121.

"Navigation and Proposed Improvements: Parliamentary Plans." Lee Conservancy Board Engineer's Office Plans, Lee Conservancy Board Engineer Office Records, 1849. ACC/2423/X/007. London Metropolitan Archive.

Parks, W.A. "The Development of the Heavy Chemical Industry of West Ham and District." Master's thesis, University of London, 1949.

Powell, W.R., ed. "West Ham: Industries." In *A History of the County of Essex*, 6:76–89. Victoria County History. British History Online, Institute of Historical Research, University of London, 1973. http://www.british-history.ac.uk/vch/essex/vol6/pp76-89.

Industry after 1860

Includes all of Greater London and is based on the First Series and First Revision of the Ordnance Survey London Town Plans. Each factory is coded to indicate whether it is on both or just one of the series of Ordnance Survey London Town Plans.

The River Thames, Canals, and Tributaries, Excluding the River Lea

Revised Open Ordnance Survey VectorMap District data with limited corrections based on the Ordnance Survey London Town Plans. There are small differences between the layer for the first series and the first revision. The canals in particular were edited to better match the historical waterways. VectorMap data included in these layers:

– TQ Tidal Water
– TQ Surface Water Area

Lower River Lea

GIS data for these waterways were created by digitizing the Ordnance Survey London Town Plans; there are minor differences between the 1867–70 layer and the 1893–95 layer. The earlier maps use the 1867–70 version.

Docks

Based on the First Series and First Revision of the Ordnance Survey London Town Plans. Each dock is coded to indicate whether it is on both or just one of the series of Ordnance Survey London Town Plans.

Roads and Railways

Limited to West Ham, with a few major roads and the railways extending slightly beyond the suburb's limits. GIS data for these roads and railways were created by digitizing the Ordnance Survey London Town Plans; there are differences between the 1867–70 layer and the 1893–95 layer. The roads and railways found on earlier maps use the 1867–70 version, but are adapted based on secondary sources and early maps that suggest which roads and railways existed before the 1860s.

Dickens, Alfred. [Map of West Ham]. In *Report to the General Board of Health on a Preliminary Inquiry into the Sewerage, Drainage, and Supply of Water, and the Sanitary Condition of the Inhabitants of the Parish of West Ham, in the County*. London: Eyre and Spottiswoode for H.M.S.O., 1855.

Mudge, William. "Ordnance Survey, Sheet 1." First Series (England and Wales, 1805). A Vision of Britain through Time. http://visionofbritain.org.uk/maps/sheet/first_edition/sheet1.

Powell, W.R., ed. "West Ham: Transport and Postal Services." In *A History of the County of Essex*, 6:61–63. Victoria County History. British History Online, Institute of Historical Research, University of London, 1973. http://www.british-history.ac.uk/vch/essex/vol6/pp61-63.

Contour Lines

Open Ordnance Survey Terrain 50 data.

London County Council Boundary

Merged Great Britain Historical GIS Project Local Government 1891 Registration Districts data.

West Ham Boundary

Edited Great Britain Historical GIS Project Local Government 1911 data.

Flood Zone

Created based on a map in "Fact Sheet – Newham Borough: Environmental Summary." Environmental Agency, 2009. Accessed May 19, 2010. http://www.environment-agency.gov.uk/static/documents/Research/NEWHAM_factsheet.pdf.

MAPS THAT INCLUDE ADDITIONAL LAYERS
OR REPRODUCTIONS OF HISTORICAL MAPS

Map 2 Lower Lea Valley and East London, Ordnance Survey, First Series, 1805

Ordnance Survey. 1st edition [JPEG image], scale one inch to the mile, Essex, Published 1805, Vision of Britain Maps, http://visionofbritain.org.uk/maps/sheet/first_edition/sheet1. The scanned Ordnance Survey map was provided by the Great Britain Historic GIS Project at the University of Portsmouth and is licensed under a Creative Commons Attribution 4.0 International License.

Inset map cartography by Eric Leinberger.

Map 4 The Environs of London, 1856

Colton, G.W. "The Environs of London, 1856." In *Colton's Atlas of the World, Illustrating Physical and Political Geography*. New York: J.H. Colton, 1856. David Rumsey Historical Map Collection. http://www.davidrumsey.com/luna/servlet/s/5yok92.

Map 10 Greater London population distribution, 1801, and Map 11 Greater London population distribution, 1851

Boundaries
Great Britain Historical GIS Project Registration Districts, 1851.

Population
Data collected from the Vision of Britain website, using the unique identification numbers exported from the GIS boundary layer. See the Hackney Poor Law Union/Regional District Total Population page for an example of the individual source webpage. A Vision of Britain through Time. http://www.visionofbritain.org.uk/unit/10167681/cube/ TOT_POP.

Map 12 Greater London population distribution, 1911

Boundaries
Great Britain Historical GIS Project Registration Districts, 1911.

Population
Same as Maps 10 and 11.

Map 13 Lea Valley population distribution, 1911

Boundaries
Great Britain Historical GIS Project Local Government Districts, 1911.

Population
Same as Maps 10 and 11.

Map 14 West Ham, 1867–70

Sewer Buildings and Northern Outfall
Created using the same methods and sources as the industry and docks layers.

Map 15 West Ham, 1893–95

Open Space, Gardens, and Parks Labels
Identified using the First Revision series of Ordnance Survey London Town Plans.

Map 16 The twelve wards of West Ham, 1901

Wards
Howarth, Edward Goldie, and Mona Wilson. *West Ham: A Study in Social and Industrial Problems: Being the Report of the Outer London Inquiry Committee*. London: J.M. Dent, 1907.

Population Statistics
County Borough of West Ham, Charles Sanders. *Annual Report of the Medical Officer of Health for 1901*. Newham Archives and Local Studies Library.

Map 17 Infant mortality rates, London and West Ham, 1880–84

Boundaries
Great Britain Historical GIS Project, Regional Districts, 1881.

Data
London: Data downloaded by extracting unique identifiers for each registration district in London and then scraping the Vision of Britain website, using an algorithm written in Mathematica. The algorithm downloaded the total births and infant deaths, calculated the infant mortality rate, and created a spreadsheet with all of the results. Finally, the five-year averages were calculated using Excel before the table was imported into ArcGIS. See the Hackney Poor Law Union/Regional District Life and Death page for an example of the individual source webpage. A Vision of Britain through Time. http://www.vision ofbritain.org.uk/unit/10167681/theme/VITAL.
West Ham: Table of vital statistics for West Ham from 1877 to 1925.
County Borough of West Ham, Charles Sanders. *Annual Report of the Medical Officer of Health for 1925*. Newham Archives and Local Studies Library.

Map 18 Infant mortality rates, London and West Ham, 1896–1900

Boundaries
Great Britain Historical GIS Project, Regional Districts, 1881.

Data
Same as Map 17.

Map 19 Deaths per thousand in eight health areas, 1897–99

Health Areas and Statistics
County Borough of West Ham, Charles Sanders. *Annual Report of the Medical Officer of Health* (1897, 1898, 1899). Newham Archives and Local Studies Library.

Map 20 Infant mortality rates by ward, 1901–14

Infant Mortality Statistics
County Borough of West Ham, Charles Sanders. *Annual Report of the Medical Officer of Health* (1901, 1904, 1911, 1914). Newham Archives and Local Studies Library.

Ward
Same ward layer from Map 16.

Map 21 Infant mortality rates, London and West Ham, 1911

Boundaries
Great Britain Historical GIS Project, Local Government Districts, 1911.

Data
Similar to Map 17, but using local government districts from 1911.

Index

NATURE|HISTORY|SOCIETY
GENERAL EDITOR: GRAEME WYNN

Printed and bound in Canada by Friesens
Set in Garamond by Artegraphica Design Co. Ltd.
Copy editor: Deborah Kerr
Indexer: Sergey Lobachev